QUESTION TIME

VOLUME 2

QUESTION TIME

VOLUME 2

A collection of often-asked

questions and answers from the

Saints' Herald

Well indexed for ready use

Reorganized CHURCH OF JESUS CHRIST

of Latter Day Saints

HERALD HOUSE

1967

Library of Congress Catalog
Card Number: 55-12245

Printed in the United States of America

Preface

After having served the church under appointment for nearly thirty years in all the states of Australia and in New Zealand, Elder Charles A. Davies came to America in 1959 under appointment to labor in Far West Stake. His tenure there was short as in March of that year Church Historian Evan A. Fry died and in May Brother Davies was appointed to fill the vacancy. He served in this capacity until the summer of 1965 when serious illness brought about a decision to return to his homeland where he died November 26, 1965.

During Brother Davies' term in the office of Church Historian, he wrote the answers to "Question Time" in the *Saints' Herald*, these appearing in print from the June 14, 1960, issue to that of November 1, 1965. From material supplied by Brother Davies for this period the editors at Herald House have selected the contents of this present book.

In a sense, Charles A. Davies wrote his own preface for the book when he answered a question concerning his "Question Time" column thus:

"This column was never intended as a channel of official statement or pronouncement nor is it a place to direct questions concerning a particular administrative situation with which the questioner may be involved.

"Answers given here are in the spirit of helpfulness aimed at enabling members to come to better understanding of the gospel and the church.

"A deliberate attempt is made to avoid dogmatic statements. In matters of doctrine, the church itself has been reluctant to formulate a creed of such nature that truth would be circumscribed in so many words. Rather it has been content with the affirmation that the gospel is to be found in the Three Standard Books—the Bible, Book of Mormon, and Doctrine and Covenants.

"Where historical facts are involved, great care is taken to make sure of correct documentation, and you can be sure that this is done with integrity. Where a question is asked that involves a matter already ruled upon by General Conference or by an authority or council entitled to so do, then the answer rests upon such action and may be so regarded. Here again meticulous care is given to documentation.

"Where procedure of a general nature is concerned, care is taken to seek the knowledge of those most intimately concerned with current administration and procedures. At no time is a question on a matter at issue in a branch or other administrative area of the church properly addressed to 'Question Time.' These questions are easily recognized and are excluded. They should be answered by the administrative officer responsible. Only questions considered of wider interest are dealt with."

This is the second volume of *Question Time*. The first one was published in 1955, and many complimentary comments and requests for additional collections have led to the preparation of this volume. Herald House is pleased to present this new collection from "Question Time."

Contents

God, Christ, Holy Spirit

1. Worship Object Questioned

QUESTION

How can I know that my worship of God is not simply the worship of an object of my own thinking?

ANSWER

Probably everyone worships a God that is somewhat a product of his own thoughts. I once asked the members of a class to frankly describe the God they worship. The result was to present as many concepts of God as there were members of the class.

This is why it is most difficult to define God; and the most enlightened efforts fall short of the full concept. Doctrine and Covenants 85:11, 12 tells of ways that we can sense the reality of God. One example is given in the phenomena of the heavens. "Behold, all these are kingdoms, and any man who hath seen any or the least of these, hath seen God moving in his majesty and power."

This section presents the thought that though God's reality is sensed through his created work, the orderly system of the universe, he cannot be fully comprehended. In paragraph 12 e the statement is made that the time will come when, quickened in him, we shall comprehend him.

This indicates to me that the worship of God in truth depends greatly upon one's power of spiritual perception. As this is encouraged to grow and develop it will expand. The very nature of this experience demands a seeking heart and mind. The apostle Paul preached to the people of Athens, who had erected an altar to the unknown God, telling them of the spiritual nature of the true God. He explained that He was not to be found in man-made edifices, but that all colors and classes of men could find him by seeking after him, "if haply they might feel after him, and find him, though he be not far from every one of us" (Acts 17:27).

We therefore do not know God in a sufficient degree to worship him except by an intelligent response to his seeking power. As we examine this intellectual perception in the light of those who have recorded their experiences with Divinity, we come to a realization that there is a common basis of understanding which is more than a figment of imagination, and that one is in the company of the great souls of history when one senses God's presence.

Now this surely requires a step in faith, not wholly without reason but blended with the gift of intellect. Experience then enlarges our understanding of God and testifies by his Spirit that we are his children (Romans 8:16).

So we conclude that the real knowledge of God is not external. It will be a growing concept from childhood and qualified by our experience until we know him in fullness. So do not be suspicious of the only channel of perception, your mind. In worship and study frankly share with other seekers, and out of your experience you will bear a testimony of his reality.

2. One God

QUESTION

Does the church take the official position that God, Jesus Christ, and the Holy Ghost are one God? Should there not be an official statement on this?

ANSWER

You have asked one of the questions that has concerned many councils from the early centuries of the Christian church. The historical church has been divided—men have been excommunicated and even martyred over this question—only to leave it without a final solution. The difficulty lies in the capacity for human comprehension of Divinity. The more one learns of the universe the more it becomes evident that there are many degrees of understanding and many aspects of truth that cannot be expressed in terms of black and white. Nor can one always have the simple answer of "Yes" or "No" to his questions about the Creator.

I like to make a distinction between "belief" and "dogma." The history of dogma shows that when men have tried to confine the great concepts of divinity within the limitations of human words, and then have proceeded to make them ultimate pronouncements, something tragic has occurred in the spiritual life of adherents of the faith.

The dogmatic pronouncements of the Catholic Church resulted in a situation where obedience rather than faith was the rule. This is why the statement of a creed has never been made by the Restoration church. Even the statement of Joseph Smith taken from the Wentworth letter and now known as the "Epitome of Faith" was not prepared with a preciseness of definition that makes impossible a rephrasing or restatement of the truths involved.

President Joseph Smith III, when asked the question you propound, said, "The consensus of opinion among the elders is . . ." I need not amplify to show why. It is obvious.

The church has never "pronounced" on this point to my knowledge. I think there is very little variation of opinion on the belief that the Father, Son, and Holy Spirit are one God (Doctrine and Covenants 17:5), but to say this does not explain *how* they are one. Upon this there are differences. Some see great difficulty in unifying them as one person because of the basic Christian belief in the Incarnation. This in turn raises questions of the *modus operandi,* and some fantastic theories have been presented as to how the Lord took upon himself a body. When the last word has been said it remains a great mystery, of undoubted theological interest, but most likely unsolvable in this life.

President Israel A. Smith wrote an article on "The Godhead Dogma and the 'Iron Bedstead'" (*Saints' Herald,* February 1, 1954) because there was "a desire on the part of some members to secure from the First Presidency *ex cathedra* opinions as to controverted matters, apparently with the idea of getting the church committed on immaterial questions."

President Israel Smith then gave quotations from both Joseph Smith, Jr., and Joseph Smith III. These statements obviously indicated a belief in a Trinity with unity of purpose as compared with a single

11

being in both roles of Father and Son accordingly as he was Christ on earth or God in heaven.

Then the late president of the church went on to say, "We must admit that the question of the Godhead is a difficult one. However, there is *no* doctrine of salvation involved. I am sure nobody is going to be disciplined by Divinity or denied salvation for resolving it wrongly. It is one among possibly hundreds of theological questions wherein one will not become a heretic however wrong he may be." This applies to a number of contentious points of belief.

We are promised in Doctrine and Covenants (85:12 e) that the time will come when we will comprehend even God. Then words will be unnecessary. The discernment of spiritual things is beyond the power of words to utter. These things we know: that there is unity of purpose in the Godhead, that the man Jesus Christ exemplified that purpose, and that the Holy Spirit is vouchsafed as the guide in our movement toward divine fulfillment.

The mistake made by the Roman See has been to make belief into dogma. This involves an obligation to accept certain tenets even against one's own reasoning. This is a fallacious approach, and is why the church has never defined many beliefs in final terms. Correct understanding is helpful only when beliefs are held freely and acted upon in the same spirit.

3. Plurality of Gods

QUESTION

I have recently read a booklet entitled "The King Follett Discourse" by Joseph Smith the Prophet. It was published in Salt Lake City with notes and references by B. H. Roberts of the Utah Mormon church. It contains the doctrine of plural Gods. What is the position of the Reorganized Church on this document and subject of plurality of Gods?

ANSWER

In the RLDS *Church History* (Volume 2, pages 735, 736) the following is given by the authors, Joseph Smith III and Heman C. Smith:

"It was at this conference that Joseph Smith preached the funeral sermon of King Follett. A synopsis of this sermon was published in the *Times and Seasons* in August 1844. We do not feel justified in presenting this synopsis as containing the teachings

12

of Joseph Smith, for several reasons. First: The sermon was said to be a very long one, while this extract covers less than five pages of the *Times and Seasons,* and can leisurely be read in about twenty-five minutes. One cannot get the true sense of a discourse from so meager an extract. Second: It was not found in print until after Joseph's death, and hence was not subjected to his inspection as published. Third: Its style and diction, as well as its doctrinal teachings, differ so widely from the productions of Joseph Smith as found elsewhere that it suggests suspicion as to its genuineness. Fourth: We have no evidence that a *verbatim* report was made when delivered, and hence it must have been written from memory, or at best from notes. So without indorsing or condemning we decline to present it as historically correct."

The newspaper, the *Nauvoo Neighbor* of March 20, 1844 (Volume 1, No. 47), contains the following obituary:

"DIED--In this city, on the 9th of March inst., Elder King Follett, whose death was occasioned by the breaking of a rope and the falling of a tub of rock upon the deceased while men above were in the act of lowering it."

The funeral sermon involved was not preached until April 6. The report of the sermon did not appear until August, 1844, when it was published in the *Times and Seasons.* In commenting on this time delay, the Utah historian Roberts says in the brochure to which you refer:

"It must be remembered that the report of the prophet's speech made by the brethren was not a stenographic report, but one made in longhand and afterwards perfected as nearly as possible by consultation and mutual correcting and developing others' notes. It may therefore be concluded that there are some imperfections."

Note that publication was not until four months after the sermon and two months after Joseph Smith's death. It was not a stenographic report and, according to Roberts, was "perfected" by "consultation and mutual correcting" and "developing." Roberts admits "some imperfections."

The sermon was to have lasted two hours, and the report in *Times and Seasons* can be read in twenty to twenty-five minutes. Because the alleged copy of the sermon contains teachings which do not harmonize with scripture given by Joseph Smith and approved by the church we cannot accept the document as being a correct report on what was said.

Plurality of Gods, being unscriptural, is definitely not a doctrine of this church.

4. Reorganized Church and Plurality of Gods

Did the Reorganized Church ever publish a book of texts which contained a section entitled "Plurality of Gods," thus indicating a belief in plurality of Gods?

ANSWER

A book entitled *Synopsis of the Faith and Doctrines of the Church of Jesus Christ of Latter Day Saints* was published by the Reorganization at Plano, Illinois, in 1865. This consisted of a compilation of texts from the Three Standard Books of the church.

Among other classified lists the work contains a chapter captioned "Godhead." There are subheadings to this chapter, among which is one "Plurality of Gods." No comment is made by way of explanation of the meaning of the texts or endorsement given to any of the references listed for study. The whole chapter contains twenty-two pages on God, and the subsection on "Plurality of Gods" takes five pages.

One should always read a preface of a book because, unless this is done, one may get a totally incorrect view of what the author is trying to say. In this case it is most helpful to quote from the preface of the book. I quote exactly:

"It is not designed to prevent, but to facilitate the study of the scriptures. Passages which are often used to support conflicting religious tenets are also inserted in this work that they and their contexts may be easily found, so that our readers may be able to show the fallacy of incorrect applications."

It is quite evident in the light of this statement that the work was published to make easier reference to all texts on a given subject. Plurality of Gods was a subject of importance to be settled in 1865, as Utah officials were vigorously presenting the doctrine.

In the early years of the Reorganization there was urgent need to separate truth from the errors of apostasy, and this task the early officials and members faced with a refreshing frankness in their discussions and publications. This subject like others needed airing and so all texts were given, as the preface says, whether used for conflicting points of view or not.

The Reorganization before long rejected outright this doctrine and presented in evidence before courts that this was one of the apostasies from the true doctrines officially accepted in the Doctrine and Covenants.

That there was considerable study to be done to cleanse the theology which had begun to deviate and ended in apostasy cannot be gainsaid. However, to take such a study as evidence of belief in this doctrine does not show sound reasoning. Some have done this. The church as a body has never endorsed plurality of Gods. This doctrine is an aberrancy which will be obvious to anyone studying the list of texts given in the book about which you inquire.

5. Place of Jesus' Birth

QUESTION

Was Jesus born in Bethlehem or Jerusalem?

ANSWER

The New Testament writers are not unanimous as to the birthplace of Jesus. Mark, the oldest gospel, gives his birthplace as Nazareth (Mark 6:1). Some have taken this to mean the area where he spent his early years but not necessarily his birthplace.

I mention it not by way of supporting the idea of Nazareth as the birthplace but to indicate that even the New Testament is not as specific as is popularly supposed. Matthew and Luke accept Nazareth as Jesus' native place, while specifically naming Bethlehem as the town of his birth. Bethlehem is in Judea (Matthew 2:1). Luke adds the words "the city of David" (Luke 2:4).

According to Matthew, Joseph and Mary dwelt in Bethehem prior to the birth of Jesus. According to Luke, they came there for the census. Here we find a contradiction in historic data. The theme of the Matthew document is that Jesus was born according to the Old Testament prophecies which name Bethlehem as the place, but the oldest gospel, Mark, appears to know nothing of this detail. Incidentally, Nazareth is first mentioned in the New Testament and is not noted by either Josephus or the Talmud. It was not marked on maps until many years after the gospel narratives first appeared in text.

The Book of Mormon states that Jesus was born in Jerusalem. Alma 5:19 states: "And behold he shall be born of Mary at Jerusalem, which is in the land of our forefathers." Throughout the Book of Mormon the reference "land of Jerusalem" is found. This is a fairly broad description. Those who would take the position that there is an error in the Nephite text because of the more comprehensive description "at Jerusalem" or "land of Jerusalem" have not considered that the same difficulty occurs with the Old World scriptures.

15

6. Only Begotten Son

QUESTION

Please explain "only begotten son" found in the text, "For God so loved the world, that he gave his Only Begotten Son. . . ." (John 3:16).

ANSWER

This particular phrase is one of interest because it is not found in the earliest manuscripts of the Johannine Gospel. The word "begotten" does not appear in John 3:16 in any version earlier than the Latin Vulgate, which was the work of Jerome. Jerome's version was in Latin and was from translations which earlier had been taken from the Greek.

Reference to the earliest Greek manuscript indicates that the word begotten is not in John 3:16. The word translated "only begotten" by Jerome simply meant "single kind" or "one of a kind" in the sense of being unique. Quite a different word was used in Greek for "begotten."

The sources from which Jerome took his version used the Latin equivalent of "only one" which is "unicus." However, when he was revising the scripture text in the fifth century after Christ he changed "unicus" to "unigenitus" which means "only begotten." His right to do this is not supported on the grounds of correct translation.

It is therefore apparent that Jerome felt under obligation to make the text read according to the dogma of the church and to support the accepted theological explanation of the Christological concept which had become universal after the council of Nicea, A.D. 325.

It is of significance that the word "unicus" was not varied by Jerome where this theological dogma was not involved, as in Luke 7:12 where the text is "the only son of his mother."

The first Greek-into-English translations by William Tyndale did not correct Jerome's error, but later in 1526 and 1534 editions John 3:16 was corrected by Tyndale to harmonize with the Greek and translated simply "only son."

The King James Version reverted to "only begotten son" in 1611. This was probably influenced by the Catholic tradition which accepted Jerome's Vulgate. The modern Revised Standard Version simply translates this text "only son."

Probably in the light of all the factors involved the basic meaning of both renderings ("only son" and "only begotten") is that Christ

16

is the only full and perfect representation of God—the only perfect image of the divine nature. Other theological interpretations are secondary.

Those who come into proper relationship with the heavenly Father are referred to in scripture as sons and daughters begotten of God (see I Corinthians 4:15; Philemon 10; I Peter 1:3; I John 5:1, 18). However, it remains a fact that Christ, the Son, is the only true image of the Father portraying in perfection the godly nature. To me this is the basic meaning.

7. Two Terms about Christ

QUESTION

Why are the two different terms used in scripture with reference to Jesus Christ, that is, "Son of God" and "Son of Man"?

ANSWER

There is no doubt that the scripture represents Jesus as holding the conviction that he was the "Son of God" in the Messianic sense. In the Old Testament at times "Son of God" is used in a less specific sense, but that Jesus was believed to be God's Son in a very direct way is unquestionable from the New Testament evidence. At the same time he appeared not to be anxious to be too previous in proclaiming the fact of his Messiahship. This was probably due to the political situation of the time. In fact, eventually the charge was made that he was guilty of the treason of claiming kingship. At his trial he was challenged with, "Art thou a king?"

At the same time while directly representing Divinity on earth, he was anxious to identify himself with mankind and therefore often made use of the description "Son of Man." This indicates his kinship with his brethren and in the Hebrew sense conveys the concept of affinity with humankind. He was God dwelling in flesh and therefore the link between man as he is and man as he may be, a Son of God. Both terms have something more than literal meanings and indicate his nature more than a particular familiar relationship. Again it is the underlying spiritual meaning we must look for rather than a categorical definition according to human understanding. I always find the statement of Abinadi (Mosiah 8:28-31) helpful in meditation upon the dual role of Jesus as God and man at the same time.

8. Other Children of Joseph and Mary

QUESTION

What are the scriptural references proving Joseph and Mary had children after the birth of Jesus, if any?

ANSWER

The following is from Matthew 13:55: "Is not his mother called Mary? and his brethren, James, and Joses, and Simon, and Judas?"

Also Mark 6:3 reads: "Is not this the carpenter, the son of Mary, the brother of James, and Joses, and of Juda, and Simon? and are not his sisters here with us?"

Some critics have held that these references use these terms of affinity in a lax sense indicating near relations but not as close as the terms "brother" and "sister" imply.

However, the belief that Jesus had brothers and sisters is based upon these texts and also upon the statement of Paul in Galatians 1:19: "But other of the apostles saw I none, save James the Lord's brother."

9. Inspired Version Footnote

QUESTION

The Authorized and Inspired Versions of the scriptures differ in Hebrews 5:7, 8 in that the word "Son" is capitalized in the former but not in the latter. In the Inspired Version these two verses are in parenthesis and there is a footnote I.V.M.S. Could you elaborate on this?

ANSWER

It should always be borne in mind that the Inspired Version of the scriptures is a correction rather than a translation. The word "translation" is used loosely in many of the historical references and by Joseph Smith, Jr., himself. However, the method used was to read the Authorized Version and mark corrections in the edition used or where changes were extensive rewrite it on manuscript paper. In addition to corrections in the published text of the Authorized Version, revelation was received concerning parts that had become lost through the passage of time. This is mostly evident in the early chapters of the Old Testament.

We have in our possession both the Authorized Version Bible used and the manuscript prepared by Joseph Smith. The manuscript makes note of references where alteration was required, or simply records that the chapter is correct. Printing was done by reference to both.

Now in Hebrews 5:7, 8 the exact wording is left as in the Authorized Version but a note was made in the manuscript as follows:

"Note—the 7th and 8th verses of this chapter are parenthesis alluding to Melchisedec and not to Christ."

This chapter was not written into the manuscript copy, and the only reference under the heading is the note given above. The change made in the Inspired Version published in 1867—"son" without capitalizing the "S"—was evidently an editorial committee action to bring the text into proper literary form necessitated by the footnote. As the correction by Joseph Smith indicated that "son" alluded to Melchisedec it did not require treatment as a proper noun.

To realize that the Inspired Version contains revelation in restoration of lost passages, correction of others, and an interpretive change as in the verses under consideration is to be able to use this version more intelligently.

10. Lineage of Jesus

QUESTION

The first chapter of Matthew gives the lineage of Jesus ending with Joseph. Presuming that the lineage descends from father to son, why is this lineage concerned with Joseph when he is not the actual father of Jesus?

ANSWER

Two genealogies of Jesus are given in the Gospels, one in Matthew 1 and the other in Luke 3. Both are through Joseph. Any differences in these two listings are not important.

According to Jewish law, descent must follow through the male line to have the rights of lineage. Hence the Jews were very concerned with their genealogies.

The Jews believed in the Messianic prophecy that the deliverer was to be of the royal line of David. The compilers of the Gospel narratives were aware of this prophetic hope and, being fully convinced of the Messiahship of Jesus, they introduced their records with orthodox Jewish approach—that is, by seeking to show that Jesus was of the kingly line.

19

Because of the Jewish acceptance of the male lineage it was necessary to do this through Joseph who was the "legal" father in the eyes of the Jews. Jesus was born into the family of Joseph, and through him the line was reckoned. Luke speaks of Joseph, saying, "being, as was supposed of the world, the son of Joseph."

The genealogies as given in both Matthew and Luke are not presented as inspired documents but as documents gleaned from available records. Many of the prized records of the Jews were destroyed when invaders carried the people into exile. On their return many endeavored to reconstruct their genealogies with varying degrees of success (see Ezra 2:62; Nehemiah 7:64).

From these sources the Gospel narratives took their data. Some have thought that Matthew's genealogy is of Mary, but most authorities do not now accept this theory because of Jewish insistence on the male lineage. Matthew would not use such an approach as that to establish Christ's messiahship.

11. Foreknowledge of Christ's Name

QUESTION

In the Inspired Version, the name Jesus Christ appears four times in Genesis 6, 7, and 8. The name apparently does not appear in other versions. Do we believe that Moses actually used the name in his original writings and that the Israelites had foreknowledge of the name, even before the annunciation?

ANSWER

When you ask what we believe about such a question, I feel that I can only say what I personally believe. Undoubtedly there would be many who would simply say they do accept the literal fact because it is in the Inspired Version. This is not a column for argumentation; therefore, perhaps with some temerity I may indicate that I do not feel this is a reasonable deduction. Actually, I think what we have here is a classic example of proleptical writing--that is, the use of later knowledge in writing up an earlier historical event. Joseph Smith, penning the revelation which he affirmed supplied some of the missing truths which the Book of Mormon states were taken from the scriptures over the centuries and having afterknowledge of the Messiah's coming and saving work, used the name by which the Savior has been known ever since his coming into the world.

20

We have the same problem in the Book of Mormon. I know of no tradition of the name Jesus Christ in any form surviving among the ancients of the Americas. I do know that efforts have been made by students of the subject to connect Quetzalcoatl, Wiracocha, and other mythical heroes with the Messiah tradition. I do not know of any prophecy in the Old Testament which directly names him either, nor do I think this necessary to show.

It may help in thinking this problem through to remember that the name Jesus is the Greek form of the Hebrew Joshua, and, therefore, this may well have been the name annunciated to Mary. The oldest texts we have of the Christian scriptures are Greek. The texts from which they came are lost and, therefore earlier usage is not available. The word Joshua means "the Lord, the Savior."

12. Christ's Birthday

QUESTION

If we believe that Jesus was born in April, why do we celebrate Christmas (December 25) as his birthday?

ANSWER

Tradition regards December 25 as the birth date of Christ. We, as a church, are committed to the time enunciated in the Book of Mormon. However, this does not necessitate the changing of the date of our celebration of Christmas. The keeping of a date is not the main point; rather the meaning behind the celebration is the important factor. A day with the importance of Christmas should not be allowed to lose its significance, but we have no commandment on the celebration of this and similar days. Our responsibility is to keep the celebration, whatever the date, significant. The question of a particular day or date is a stumbling block to many who would seek to prove that Christians keep the wrong day when they keep the first day of the week as the Lord's day. Paul counseled those who were concerned about deciding which was the correct day to keep as a holy day. He wrote: "One man esteemeth one day above another; another esteemeth every day alike. Let every man be fully persuaded in his own mind" (Romans 14:5).

I would say this reasoning applies to the celebration of Christmas on December 25, as no principle is involved. I see no reason why we should be out of step with the community.

21

13. Priesthood Teachings

QUESTION

If we still believe as Joseph Smith III stated in "Church History" regarding the birth of Christ, what is the attitude of the church toward those of the priesthood who teach otherwise?

ANSWER

Joseph Smith III said, "The scriptural statement is the accepted faith of the church, and he who teaches to the contrary does not express the voice of the church." This he further indicated does not interfere with a person's inherent right to hold particular views which may at times differ from those of others, but those representing the church should be conscientious in the use of their standing as ministers.

This church has wisely avoided issuing precise statements of belief which demand conformation, realizing that our concepts of the Divine Mind and plan are ever growing and expanding. But when this has been said there are some basics which all reasonable minds realize are essential if the unity of the body and effective witness are to be maintained.

Joseph Smith III also pointed out that men of the ministry are obligated to "teach the things which are given in the scriptures, according to the church covenants and commandments." On other occasions, when asked for a specific statement of belief, the same leader said, "The consensus of opinion of the elders is . . ." This is, wisely, a guarded statement and leaves room for some opinion as to the meaning of some matters.

I, for one, would resent any attempt to have my thinking or beliefs cast into a mold, but while affirming my right to free and uncoerced belief I respect the instruction given as to ministerial obligation and would not use the prestige of priesthood or of the power of the pulpit to promulgate ideas not acceptable to the "consensus of opinion of the elders."

There is no doubt that the scriptures as translated in the Authorized Version, and as restated in the Inspired Version and the Book of Mormon, record as fact the "virgin birth" of our Lord.

14. Immaculate Conception

QUESTION

Does the church believe in the Immaculate Conception? This question arises often in class and in private conversation. I understand that

Joseph Smith III stated it was a doctrine of the church ("Church History," Volume 3, pages 584-586). Do we still hold to that view?

ANSWER

It is necessary to be clear as to what we mean by the term "immaculate conception." The word "immaculate" is not a scriptural term. We must depend upon Webster for a concise meaning. In the dictionary it is defined as, "perfectly clean, without spot or stain, unsoiled, pure, innocent, without sin."

Webster also gives a definition of "Immaculate Conception:"

"Immaculate Conception, in the Roman Catholic Church, the doctrine that the Virgin Mary, though conceived naturally, was from the moment of conception free from any stain of original sin: sometimes confused with virgin birth."

Because of the fact that the doctrine of the Immaculate Conception is a tenet of the Roman Catholic Church about the virgin Mary, a misunderstanding is occasioned if we use this term. Also it is "sometimes confused with virgin birth" (Webster).

As the scriptures nowhere use the word "immaculate" it would appear more correct to avoid the word when referring to the birth of Jesus Christ, especially in the light of Roman Catholic theology in this connection.

In the quote from church history to which you refer Joseph Smith III did use the words, "immaculate conception of Christ." I would be of the opinion that he meant "the virgin birth of Christ," as it is certain he did not intend to subscribe to the Roman Catholic tenet. If one says, "I believe in the virgin Mary," it in actuality conveys more than to say "I believe Christ was born of a virgin." Roman Catholic doctrine goes much further and has woven impossible theories around the person of Mary and her family.

It is good to define our words occasionally, and you have stimulated an excellent inquiry.

15. Statement of Brigham Young

QUESTION

Brigham Young said that Jesus Christ was not begotten of the Holy Ghost ("Journal of Discourses," Vol. 1, pages 50, 51). Is there scripture anywhere to support this?

23

Brigham Young said many things he could not back up with scripture, but, believing he was a living oracle, he seemed to feel this unnecessary. There is no scripture to endorse his statement but there is to the contrary. Matthew states that Mary was "with child of the Holy Ghost" and "that which is conceived in her is of the Holy Ghost" (Matthew 1:18, 20, A. V.). The Utah doctrine of Adam God worship substituted Adam for the power of the Holy Spirit. Matthew's record does not attest to this, and we cannot even see upon what premise Young would base his error.

The sermon from which you quote has many marked errors. From it we quote further: "When our father Adam came into the garden of Eden, he came into it with a celestial body and brought Eve, one of his wives, with him." Young went on to say that Christ was begotten in the same way "as Cain, Abel and the rest of the sons and daughters of Adam and Eve." Then, as if realizing this was a heretical trend, he said, "but were I to tell you the whole truth, blasphemy would be nothing to it in the estimation of the superstitious and over-righteous of mankind."

16. Christ's Baptism

QUESTION

Why did Christ wait until he was thirty years of age before being baptized?

ANSWER

The age of Jewish accountability was thirty years. Jesus followed the law and did not go out of his way to flout the traditions of his people. He stated that he did not come to destroy the law but to fulfill it. No doubt he desired to be recognized as a fully competent adult when he commenced his epoch-marking ministry. To have this standing he had to wait till he was thirty years of age.

Jesus chose to make the occasion of his baptism a significant testimony of principle. He also had completed all of his filial responsibilities to his parents at that age and was free to fulfill his mission thereafter (see Matthew 3:23-25, I. V.).

Social and legal acceptance are involved. Had his baptism occurred during his minority, his mission may have lacked the elements of testimony, proclamation of his mission, and ability to immediately gather his chosen helpers for his program.

24

There is no commandment that one may not be baptized after eight years of age, but there is a rule which indicates that baptism should not be performed before this age, by which time the parents in the church are admonished to see that their children are instructed sufficiently to choose. Many children at eight years are not yet competent to make the decision but require more maturity. This is not in any way a reason for not training children toward the decision for baptism before adult years. They must be given the basic knowledge upon which to make their decision.

17. Christ in Hell

QUESTION

Is there only one place in the Bible that says Christ preached to the spirits in hell?

ANSWER

There are two statements which support this belief. They are found in I Peter. One is in I Peter 3:18-20 and the other in I Peter 4:6. The Inspired Version rendering is slightly different from that of the Authorized Version. I suggest you compare them for clarity.

18. Christ's Mission

QUESTION

Please explain Matthew 15:21-27. Does this lesson teach Christ's world mission, or is it emphasizing a mission to a select few?

ANSWER

I am of the opinion that the story emphasizes the larger view. The fact is that Jesus healed the woman who by lineage was not of Israelite blood. Commentators have had different views about this passage. Matthew 15:22 and Mark 7:26 differ in the record. Matthew calls the woman a Canaanite. Mark says she was a Greek. They are both agreed that she was a Gentile. The fact that the woman is differently described indicates this is not a strictly verbatim record. Jesus had departed into the borders of Tyre and Sidon (non-Israelitish territory) for a rest. He was not there primarily for ministry. However, Jesus often performed his ministry in hours chosen for him rather than by him. Christ recognized that the spearhead of his work was with Israel (Matt. 15:24); he also demonstrated that it was not nationality but faith that was efficacious in one's receiving the grace of God (Matt. 15:28).

Jesus was not prepared to open foreign missions at that time because his initial effort was through the house of Israel. He adroitly uses the situation to teach a lesson. The use of the Jewish saying concerning giving the children's food to the dogs is to bring a lesson home to the disciples who were at that time Jews. They were to await the brave actions of Peter and Paul before Gentiles could be accepted into the fold of the church, but we could not suggest that the love of all mankind was not in the heart of the Lord. Peter later was to crystallize the previously unrealized truth in the words, "I perceive that God is no respecter of persons; but in every nation he that feareth him, and worketh righteousness, is accepted with him" (Acts 10:34, 35).

A consideration of practical importance is evident here. Jesus could not spread his ministry into all the areas of need which were so demanding in the Orient of his time. His work must be strategically focused and to the best advantage. At the same time he embraced all in his love, and when opportunity presented itself he did not deny his gracious power.

19. Christ in America

QUESTION

Paul made the following statement found in Colossians 1:23:

"If ye continue in the faith grounded and settled, and be not moved away from the hope of the gospel, which ye have heard, and which was preached to every creature which is under heaven; whereof I Paul am made a minister . . ."

Does this provide proof of Christ's ministering to the people in America at that time?

ANSWER

The basic meaning of this verse is concerned with Paul's testimony of the sureness of the gospel witness and an admonition to the saints of Colossae to withstand the influences of apostasy. Paul tells them that that which they have received is true.

The apostle has already appealed to the universal nature of the

26

witness of the fruitfulness of the gospel in all the world as well as to the saints of Colossae (see verse 6).

It must be remembered that the phrase "in all the world" does not mean in the text what it necessarily means when used today as a result of almost complete exploration of the globe. Luke mentions the reason for the pilgrimage of Joseph and Mary to Bethlehem as a decree being made by Caesar Augustus that "all the world should be taxed." This is obviously a more limited area than would be implied by the expression if used today.

Therefore I would not give an affirmative answer to your question. Though the preaching of the gospel was in the new world at that time I would not concur with the thought that Paul had this in mind. Rather is he emphasizing that the gospel experience was universal and not confined to any one group or race. Paul was the apostle of the universal gospel as opposed to a selected group or nation. To hold otherwise would imply that the gospel was preached to all ancient peoples from Australia to the Arctic circle, of which there is no evidence in support.

20. The Comforter

QUESTION

A question has been raised as to the definition of the Comforter. Are the words "the Comforter" and "Holy Spirit" synonymous? If they are not, will you please explain the difference.

ANSWER

The "Comforter" is the "Holy Spirit." In John 14:16, 17 we find this statement by Jesus, "And I will pray the Father, and he shall give you another Comforter, that he may abide with you forever; even the Spirit of truth."

More definitely John 14:26 states, "But the Comforter, which is the Holy Ghost, whom the father will send in my name, he shall teach you all things, and bring all things to your remembrance, whatsoever I have said unto you."

Used as it is here the word "Comforter" is distinctly identical with "Holy Spirit." The Greek root from which it is taken is *Paraklesis,* which holds the concept of coming to one's assistance or help. Often the word is used to convey consolation, encouragement; to refresh or to cheer. Though there may be variations in the application of the word "Comforter," it is without doubt used in the scriptures quoted as an alternative and descriptive name for the Holy Spirit.

27

The use of the word "Comforter" by the translators is an endeavor to catch up some of the function of the Holy Spirit. Perhaps one could say that there are qualities of the Spirit other than those conveyed in the English word "Comforter." It is certainly truth, power, and light, but it is basically the helper, encourager, leader, and guide.

21. Tongues and Interpretation

QUESTION

Are there scriptural references to the effect that a man speaking in tongues should not himself interpret what is given through him? I have studied I Corinthians 14:5, 13, 27-29, and there appears to be a contradiction.

ANSWER

There appears to be no text forbidding one giving the interpretation of a manifestation of this kind. I do not feel there is any real basis for seeing a contradiction in I Corinthians 14. The text is the same in both the Inspired Version and the Authorized Version. Verse 5 gives the following:

"For greater is he that prophesieth than he that speaketh with tongues, except he interpret, that the church may receive edifying."

Note how the same text reads in the New English Bible:

"The prophet is worth more than the man of ecstatic speech—unless indeed he can explain its meaning, and so help to build up the community."

It will be noted that the main emphasis of these scriptures is that the exercise of spiritual gifts is justifiable only when as a result the church, or the community of believers, is strengthened and edified. Any conflict between verse 5 and the other verses you cite is more apparent than real. Verse 13 states: "Wherefore let him that speaketh in another tongue pray that he may interpret."

Verses 27-29 read as follows:

"If any man speak in another tongue, let it be by two, or at the most by three, and that by course; and let one interpret. But if there be no interpreter, let him keep silence in the church; and let him speak to himself, and to God. Let the prophets speak two or three, and let the other judge."

It is difficult to interpret any of these verses as prohibiting a person from interpreting what he has uttered through the gift of tongues. Verses 27-29 appear to me to be an urgent appeal by Paul to the Corinthian saints to use wisdom and order in their use of this gift. He simply suggests:

1. that no more than three in any one service exercise the gift of tongues
2. that each speak in his turn
3. that one person serve as interpreter of that which was uttered

This last point implies that when those speaking in unknown tongues are unable to interpret for themselves, there surely ought to be, for the sake of edification, someone present to interpret by the Spirit. Otherwise the use of the gift of tongues in public worship is not justified.

Some translators have rendered the beginning of verse 28 as follows: "Unless he is an interpreter . . . ," to allay the complaint of some that Paul was arbitrarily trying to quench the Spirit. (For, after all, how except by previous arrangement could anyone know in advance whether another would have the gift of interpretation?)

22. Tongues

QUESTION

What does the apostle Paul mean when in I Corinthians 12:10 he says, when speaking of spiritual gifts, "To another 'divers' kinds of tongues"?

ANSWER

The word "divers" as in the New Testament text simply meant several, sundry, various, more than one, not definite in number. Thus God had blessed some members of the church with the linguistic ability to speak in a number of languages. Many of these, I have no doubt, were the result of study and preparation, as with missionaries today when they are sent to lands where different languages are spoken. The scriptural prototype is found in Acts 2 where it is stated that every man heard the gospel "in his own tongue." On that occasion the recorder definitely stated it to be the power of the Holy Spirit transcending human limitations.

It appears that due to the culture in which Paul did most of his work, this phenomenon got out of hand, and so in I Corinthians 14 he admonishes the exercise of restraint and intelligence in the use of this "gift." My experience has been that it is particularly desirable that Paul's counsel be studied and applied. His counsel involved the functioning of the gift of discernment as a primary necessity and prerequisite.

This phenomenon of the gift of "divers tongues" has not been limited to the Restoration but appears after the Reformation in many sects through the years, especially since the eighteenth century. "Tongues" were featured in the early Restoration, particularly. Brigham Young and others spoke "in tongues" at the Kirtland Temple dedication, and many have exercised this gift. People have borne testimony of hearing this expression of language in the Reorganization and of their assurance that it was of divine origin.

Not having personally witnessed this phenomenon in a situation which to me was relevant or meaningful, I have approached this answer as a student of the scripture. There is no doubt about the scriptural basis for this gift and its operation as stated in paragraph one of this answer.

23. Sevenfold Gifts or Ninefold

QUESTION

In the "Hymnal" these words appear: "who dost thy sevenfold gifts impart" (Hymn No. 218), and "The sevenfold gift of grace is thine" (Hymn No. 227). I Corinthians 12:8-10 gives nine gifts of the Spirit, and Galatians 5:22 gives nine fruits of the Spirit. Can you account for the discrepancy?

ANSWER

I cannot find either the expression "sevenfold gifts" or "sevenfold gift of grace" listed in any concordance of scripture. However, there are several texts in the Old Testament particularly which contain the expression "sevenfold."

Very often numbers are used without any particular intention to be precise—three, four, seven, forty, seventy, etc. Three holds the significance of completeness—beginning, middle, and end. Seven is used in this way also.

It has been traditionally taught and based upon I Corinthians 12 that there are nine spiritual gifts. This was a convenient teaching approach and suited catechistic approach. Actually there are, in my

27. Negro Origin

QUESTION

Is there any scripture which states that God cursed the Negro and that is why he has a black skin? This was stated to be so in a recent class discussion.

ANSWER

I know of no text that can be rightly used to sustain the statement that God cursed the ancestors of the Negro race. The false idea stems from a misinterpretation of Genesis 9:29, 30, I.V.

"And Noah awoke from his wine, and knew what his youngest son had done unto him, and he said, Cursed be Canaan; a servant of servants shall he be unto his brethren.

"And he said, Blessed be the Lord God of Shem; and Canaan shall be his servant, and a veil of darkness shall cover him, that he shall be known among all men."

If this text is read closely it will be quickly recognized that these are the reported words of Noah and not God. The curse, for which Noah apparently had no authorization, was upon Canaan who was the youngest son of Ham. It was not Canaan but Ham who offended his father. Noah, after getting drunk, had been found in a state of nudity by Ham, and when Noah realized his shameful situation he uttered the revengeful curse upon Canaan.

It would appear that the cause of the problem lay primarily with Noah. As the text reads there is no indication of more than the repeating of the incident by Ham to Noah's discomfiture. At any rate it was not God who was said to have uttered the curse.

28. Church View on Origin of Man

QUESTION

What is the position of the church regarding the origin of man? Is the church receptive to modern ideas of anthropologists and their findings, particularly fossil discoveries?

ANSWER

I am always puzzled in framing a reply to a question which asks what the church believes about certain scientific theories. One reason is that there are no specifics involved in what science believes in the sense that science is a form of seeking light and therefore not so much an affirmation as a process of discovery. Anthropological scientists may make certain postulations from the available data of research. This data is increasing daily and has required continuous revision of postulations.

The church has made no official pronouncement on matters involved in your question, nor would I feel that it would be competent to do so. I am not aware of any scripture which lays down by what *modus operandi* man came into being or that there is any statement of scripture which determines the point in time when the first man made his appearance. The dates given in the various versions of the Bible are editorial additions based upon chronologies by such men as Ussher and definitely not part of the text.

On matters of science I believe a minister is not called to pronounce. For instance, I do not feel called upon as a minister to pronounce on the correctness or incorrectness of evolution. One is neither faithful nor unfaithful according to whether he accepts this theory. The question belongs to an area of scientific exploration and to me, at least, is not a question of religion.

There are those whom I respect highly who take different positions on the anthropological deductions of modern scientists, and the ministry of both is unaffected thereby. It is important that the church hold high its affirmation of God as the Author of our being, and this is required of its ministers. I personally see no conflict between true scientific research and religion. Science is continually revising its estimates of time and origin, and no doubt we are just on the brink of discovery in what we call the space age. The scripture ventures to say only, "In the beginning."

Whatever knowledge of man's past is gained in the years ahead one thing stands sure: God is Alpha and Omega, from all eternity to all eternity, and in him we live and move and have our being. This is the gospel message as found in scripture, and as it is expressed by God in the person of Jesus Christ, that man might become at one with the Divine.

With this rock as our foundation man is safe as an explorer into the ageless rock fossils or into the infinite reaches made possible by scientists in this day of the space capsule.

29. Skeletons Discovered before Adam and Eve

QUESTION

Have skeletons been discovered dating before Adam and Eve? Were they the first man and woman on earth?

ANSWER

I will answer your second question first; this will make the first

36

opinion, no grounds for limiting the "gifts" to nine. If we read on to I Corinthians 12:31, we can readily see that a number of abilities, callings, and functions are all listed as gifts of the Spirit. There are diversities of gifts. The central thought of this chapter is not limited to the first eleven verses. The central thought is that there are many members, each with a gift or function to perform, and the Holy Spirit motivates them all. I like the thought that apostleship is a gift as well as a calling, and so while not in any way minimizing the "nine," we can see a more comprehensive meaning in the full text. One should not stop at verse 11 but continue with the elucidation which begins at verse 12.

The expression "sevenfold" used in the hymns seems to be used by the poets to express the fullness of God's giving and, therefore, of his grace.

Numerical consistency is not found throughout scripture, and where apparent contradiction arises, one must take the inherent rather than the mathematical meaning.

24. Spirit of Christ in Other Denominations

QUESTION

Is it the belief of our church that the Spirit of Christ does not prevail or is not present in any other church or denomination?

ANSWER

No, this is not our belief. However, this is not intended to be so liberal a statement that you may conclude that church membership is not of vital concern.

The scriptures promise the Holy Spirit as an abiding comforter only to those who comply with the commandments which initiate them into the "Church of Jesus Christ." This is by repentance and baptism of water and through the laying on of hands.

There are degrees of availability of the divine Spirit, and God leads men to more and more complete understanding and compliance with his laws and will.

The narrow conception of exclusiveness has at times been traced to a misinterpretation of Doctrine and Covenants, Section 1:5 e, which states that this church is the "only true and living church upon the face of the whole earth, with which I the Lord am well pleased, speaking unto the church collectively and not individually."

In other words it is the only church properly organized and commissioned to do the work for which Christ established his church on earth. We have no corner on divine grace; only inasmuch as we are obedient are we acceptable as his people and entitled to the Holy Spirit. Elbert A. Smith, at a Lamoni, Iowa, Communion service, gave this message: "I have many forces at work in the world, saith the Lord. I have many spiritual forces at work that you know not of. . . ." (*Saints' Herald*, November 14, 1917, Volume 64, No. 46, page 1081).

Nature and Life of Man

25. Soul of Man

QUESTION

An elder drew my attention to the statement in Doctrine and Covenants 85 that says the spirit and the body is the soul of man. This seems to contradict texts in the Book of Mormon, such as "the souls and the bodies . . . shall all be reunited" (Alma 19:53). Please explain this for me.

ANSWER

There is no real contradiction here. Other verses on the same page in the Book of Mormon refer to the "spirit and the body." The words "spirit" and "soul" are used interchangeably if somewhat loosely. If one is being specific with a view to theological definition, one should use the word "spirit" to indicate that real personality or entity which is housed in the "body" and without which joyous expression is not complete. The usage as quoted from Doctrine and Covenants is not unique as it is found in Genesis, "and man became a living soul." This obviously indicates the whole person as distinguished from body alone. A third word, "mind," is also used somewhat loosely, but mostly to indicate that activity of the spirit in the body involving thought and consciousness. When resurrected, and thus reunited, the body and the spirit will be united, and the souls of the righteous will live in eternity according to their fitness to enjoy that life.

26. Spirit and Soul

QUESTION

In Doctrine and Covenants 85:4 there is a statement to the effect that the body and spirit make up the soul. "A Commentary on the Doctrine and Covenants" says that this means exactly what it says. If this is so, then why in the Bible does Matthew 10:25 (Inspired Version) and I Thessalonians 5:23 speak of both body and soul as being separate and not as the body being a part of the soul? Also why does Alma 19:40 through 19:50 use the terms spirit and soul interchangeably?

ANSWER

I agree with the Commentary that Doctrine and Covenants 85:4 is an interpretive statement of fact. This section is more definitive than other references to the soul, spirit, and body and does not necessarily exclude the use of the word "soul" for spirit. Language is simply a means of communication by sounds and symbols which have a common meaning within a group. When I have had contact with those responsible for translating our Restoration scriptures into other tongues I have been frequently reminded of the difficulty of getting an exact word which has identical meaning with the English.

Preachers, writers, and teachers are always challenged to make their meaning clear by words suitably chosen, and one is most clear when using words within the cognition of the hearer. The words you refer to have been and are used interchangeably and will continue to be.

In Restoration theology, because of Section 85, the word "soul" therefore carries the specific connotation of "body and spirit," but because of usage the employment of "soul" for "spirit" is permissible and may be necessary to be understood outside of theological classwork.

With reference to Alma 19 all I can offer by way of explanation is to say that either Alma did not have the more definitive concept given in Doctrine and Covenants 85 or words were chosen within the understanding of those concerned as listeners. This may also apply to the translator (Joseph Smith) in 1829.

On the question of I Thessalonians 5:23 it is not correct to assume that all theological details were revised in the Inspired Version. Because the word "spirit" appears in this text along with soul and body does not make the text out of harmony with the Doctrine and Covenants.

Certainly the writer used the three words to good effect to convey the idea of the need for the transformation of the whole man. The idea of the soul being the total person is found also in Genesis 2:8 (Inspired Version).

27. Negro Origin

QUESTION

Is there any scripture which states that God cursed the Negro and that is why he has a black skin? This was stated to be so in a recent class discussion.

ANSWER

I know of no text that can be rightly used to sustain the statement that God cursed the ancestors of the Negro race. The false idea stems from a misinterpretation of Genesis 9:29, 30, I.V.

"And Noah awoke from his wine, and knew what his youngest son had done unto him, and he said, Cursed be Canaan; a servant of servants shall he be unto his brethren.

"And he said, Blessed be the Lord God of Shem; and Canaan shall be his servant, and a veil of darkness shall cover him, that he shall be known among all men."

If this text is read closely it will be quickly recognized that these are the reported words of Noah and not God. The curse, for which Noah apparently had no authorization, was upon Canaan who was the youngest son of Ham. It was not Canaan but Ham who offended his father. Noah, after getting drunk, had been found in a state of nudity by Ham, and when Noah realized his shameful situation he uttered the revengeful curse upon Canaan.

It would appear that the cause of the problem lay primarily with Noah. As the text reads there is no indication of more than the repeating of the incident by Ham to Noah's discomfiture. At any rate it was not God who was said to have uttered the curse.

28. Church View on Origin of Man

QUESTION

What is the position of the church regarding the origin of man? Is the church receptive to modern ideas of anthropologists and their findings, particularly fossil discoveries?

ANSWER

I am always puzzled in framing a reply to a question which asks what the church believes about certain scientific theories. One reason is that there are no specifics involved in what science believes in the sense that science is a form of seeking light and therefore not so much an affirmation as a process of discovery. Anthropological scientists may make certain postulations from the available data of research. This data is increasing daily and has required continuous revision of postulations.

The church has made no official pronouncement on matters involved in your question, nor would I feel that it would be competent to do so. I am not aware of any scripture which lays down by what *modus operandi* man came into being or that there is any statement of scripture which determines the point in time when the first man made his appearance. The dates given in the various versions of the Bible are editorial additions based upon chronologies by such men as Ussher and definitely not part of the text.

On matters of science I believe a minister is not called to pronounce. For instance, I do not feel called upon as a minister to pronounce on the correctness or incorrectness of evolution. One is neither faithful nor unfaithful according to whether he accepts this theory. The question belongs to an area of scientific exploration and to me, at least, is not a question of religion.

There are those whom I respect highly who take different positions on the anthropological deductions of modern scientists, and the ministry of both is unaffected thereby. It is important that the church hold high its affirmation of God as the Author of our being, and this is required of its ministers. I personally see no conflict between true scientific research and religion. Science is continually revising its estimates of time and origin, and no doubt we are just on the brink of discovery in what we call the space age. The scripture ventures to say only, "In the beginning."

Whatever knowledge of man's past is gained in the years ahead one thing stands sure: God is Alpha and Omega, from all eternity to all eternity, and in him we live and move and have our being. This is the gospel message as found in scripture, and as it is expressed by God in the person of Jesus Christ, that man might become at one with the Divine.

With this rock as our foundation man is safe as an explorer into the ageless rock fossils or into the infinite reaches made possible by scientists in this day of the space capsule.

29. Skeletons Discovered before Adam and Eve

QUESTION

Have skeletons been discovered dating before Adam and Eve? Were they the first man and woman on earth?

ANSWER

I will answer your second question first; this will make the first simpler. It matters not by what names the first humans were called. It is obvious that there were first people from which the human race has stemmed.

To date the appearance of man on earth is a difficult problem scientifically or historically. Various fossil remains of manlike skeletons have been unearthed, and the dating reaches far back into antiquity—into prehistory.

In Hebrew the simple meaning of "Adam" is "man." Historically there is no definite, provable date for his advent. When Doctrine and Covenants 22:21c defines the meaning of Adam as "many" it injects the concept of the whole human race.

Because humans need to limit their perception to specifics we will continue to talk about Adam as the first human being, but unconsciously we imply the whole of humankind as represented.

30. Belief in Evolution

QUESTION

What does the church believe concerning the Darwinian theory of evolution? I am disturbed by conflicting views expressed by church members. I have always understood that scripture contradicts the idea of evolution.

ANSWER

The solution to your problem may lie in a more correct interpretation of the relation of science and religion.

The purpose of scripture is to reveal the fact of God and his purposes for mankind. The basis of the whole scriptural record is found in the first few words of the Authorized Version, "In the beginning God created the heavens and the earth." The method by which this was done is not explained. The text goes on to tell what man is made of and that later he was a living soul. That he is physically of the same material as the earth is demonstrable.

The process by which this was brought about is left for science to show. As a minister of God I do not feel called upon to affirm or deny the theory of evolution. I do feel it a matter of religious faith to affirm that God is the creator, and therefore I cannot accept the idea of chance. It is not correct to equate evolution with atheism, and this error may be at the root of your concern.

Many faithful Christians hold the view that creation was brought about by God in an orderly process until he achieved his purpose in man's being. They would not necessarily want to label their concepts as Darwinian, but they do feel that they can see the nature and methods of God revealed in his handiwork. Few informed people today subscribe to the view that to accept the theory of evolution is to exclude divine action. This is an issue which was characteristic of a former period when atheists sought to use the evolutionary theory to discredit religious faith. Scientists are not unanimous upon details.

This is not a religious issue but a scientific one, and the church therefore has made no pronouncement other than to affirm belief in God the creator.

31. Where Is Paradise

QUESTION

Where and what is paradise?

ANSWER

Frankly, I do not know where. I think of paradise as a condition rather than a specific place. In our present stage of comprehension, it is difficult to think of "being" without "location." Wherever it is, "place" is secondary to "condition." Paradise has been defined as an intermediary state of rest before the resurrection. This is distinguished as being for the faithful as contrasted with "the prison house" for the disobedient.

Much time and thought energy have been spent in an endeavor to specify places and time in the life beyond. There is no blueprint which satisfies me personally as having fully explained the detail. I am satisfied with a basic assurance of immortality according to my fitness to occupy, although often I yearn like all others for "paradise" as a place of release from the strains of mortal existence. I am not so sure that we have not overstressed the rest from labor. This universe is ongoing, and to stop is to stagnate if not to disintegrate. Doctrine and Covenants 76 is quite an expansive eschatological document and could be read with profit in connection with your question.

32. People to Heaven

QUESTION

Do you believe that members of our church are the only people going to heaven?

38

I do not. I do not think our members as a whole believe it either. I take your use of the word "heaven" to mean God's presence. One will find his place in the hereafter exactly as he is fitted for it. It is not a situation where those who have performed certain prescribed rituals and given assent to certain doctrines qualify for the highest reward in the future life.

Fitness to occupy is the controlling factor. There is only one reason for correctness of belief or of organization, and that is its effectiveness in the quality of soul achieved. This takes into account mercy as well as justice, for "all have sinned and come short of the glory of God"—that is, the standard of perfection as seen in Jesus Christ.

Many people have faith in ordinances, etc., and fail to seek quality of life. Ultimately all people who are to be adjudged fit for the presence of God must have been obedient to the divine way. Thus affiliation with an organization, the church, is not the criterion of judgment. That the obedient are members of God's church is a corollary.

33. Proof of Immortality

QUESTION

Is there any proof of immortality, or is it merely a question of faith?

ANSWER

In a rationalistic age when men expect every belief to be completely attested by the processes of intellect, it is difficult to say there is proof. However, the Christian faith postulates immortality upon certain premises which we claim lead us to assurance. Faith is an assurance based on hope and evidence of things unseen. It is impossible to check the premises or the conclusion upon wholly intellectual grounds.

Millions, because of their acceptance of the phenomenal life and teachings of Jesus of Nazareth, testify that they have come to a state where they can say they know. You might say this relates to the second phase of your question and that I am saying it is solely a matter of faith. It is not wholly that, for one is hardly in a position to deny the result of a religious experience that comes because of the application of a reasonable postulation unless one has moved to apply the principles involved. Alma 16 outlines this process toward knowledge of the eternal in a most helpful way.

It is difficult to reconcile all the phenomena which various people claim are evidences of immortality or existence beyond this life, but it is not intelligent to rely solely on the ability of the mind to formulate proof. Emotion is as real as thought, even if considered less reliable or definable as a witness, but belief in afterlife is certainly comforting. There is an instinctive desire for life continuance, but to say that man has created the concept of immortality to satisfy this is not sufficient. The person who lives as seeing the invisible certainly lives with and not against his instincts.

The conviction of a majority of the great ones of the ages has been that there is life beyond although there has been great variation of opinion on the nature of the beyond. To me this is a secondary consideration, but to believe in divinity and concomitant immortality is to change one's whole attitude and desires. Belief in immortality kindles a light in human existence which makes life meaningful.

This is where I believe the principle of the resurrection to be so important and in particular the resurrection of Jesus. If Christ was resurrected as historically attested, here we have grounds for belief, and faith and hope are possible in contrast with the awful bleakness which such a day as ours would bring. This is why I have cast my lot with the company of faith rather than with people who demand the removal of the last possible doubt. One of the results of recognizing my finiteness is the logical conclusion that there is a life beyond of infinity. (Otherwise there is no meaning to the frustrating sense of limitation about this mortal life, the truth which no thinking person can logically deny.)

34. Knowing Loved Ones

QUESTION

Will we know our loved ones in heaven or paradise?

ANSWER

There is every reason to believe we shall be aware of our friends and loved ones in the hereafter. We shall know each other in a more complete way (see Genesis 7:71, Inspired Version; I Corinthians 13:12).

35. Consciousness in Departed

QUESTION

Is there any scriptural support for the idea that our departed loved ones look back upon this earth with a consciousness of what is now happening to us?

40

That there is consciousness after death and before the resurrection is undoubtedly supported by scripture. Though in the form of a parable, this is brought out in Luke 16:24-36, I.V., where a conversation is represented as being carried on by the rich man who had died and had gone to hell. He asks that Lazarus be sent from paradise to warn his brethren on earth of their impending problems. This is generally accepted as one statement which indicates consciousness of previous experience and therefore memory of past associations.

There is no reference I can offer which indicates that our loved ones are aware of our doings. The statements often made concerning our loved ones "looking down" arise out of speculation and emotional attitude which have no factual evidence in support.

One might reason in the case of those whose spirits rest in paradise that to be conscious of the problems and activities of those left behind would not be "rest" in the sense of "peace." However, I hesitate to enter into speculation when there is no specific scripture available.

36. No Consciousness in Death

QUESTION

John 3:13 states that no man has ascended into heaven but Christ who came from heaven and who is now there. Is this evidence, as a friend contends, that all others who are gone before are without consciousness in death?

ANSWER

Certainly not. Ecclesiastes 12:7 expresses the concept that at death the body returns to the earth from which it came and the spirit returns to God who gave it. The interpretation which your question implies is that there is no other condition of existence than being in heaven (interpreted by your friend as the grave). Paul clearly qualifies the common belief of the simple alternative of two conditions by his wonderful teaching in I Corinthians 15. He uses the analogy of the differing glories of light in the physical heavens and likens the world beyond to this. Though it may be said that this does not apply until after a resurrection has taken place, I use it here to deny the simple alternatives of heaven or hell.

For the spirit to return into the care of God does not necessarily mean "into his immediate presence." The scriptures indicate that at death men go to paradise or the prison house depending on how they have prepared their lives here. You may find a more direct answer in the words of Jesus on the cross. He said to the thief who pleaded for remembrance in His kingdom, "Today thou shalt be with me in paradise" (Luke 23:43). Here is one other at least who was not to sleep in oblivion in the grave but was that day with Jesus in paradise. If one were to argue that paradise is not a third alternative but is synonymous with heaven, the point of spiritual existence after death is still made. Most Latter Day Saints accept the concept that paradise is an intermediate state.

37. Scriptural Public Funeral Service

QUESTION

Is there any record of a public funeral service in the scriptures? If not, is the custom which imposes such a trying ordeal on the bereaved a heathen practice?

ANSWER

There is no actual record of a funeral service in the Old or New Testaments nor in the Book of Mormon to my knowledge. Burial customs vary considerably, but special rituals seem to have been associated with the disposal of the dead since earliest times.

Usually these rites and ceremonies reflect the religious beliefs of the group. All peoples have some procedures even when minimal, some crude and others more refined. Respect for the body is usually found, although primitives have some undesirable customs.

Customs vary considerably according to religion, and even in the same religion according to geographical location. It seems proper to give respectful attention to the physical tabernacle of our loved ones. The ritual and degree of public participation is a matter of personal preference, but whatever is done should reflect our faith and belief in immortality. A funeral service provides opportunity for deep thought on the eternal, and the death of a respected loved one may mean an opportunity for family and community to emphasize the eternal qualities. It definitely should not be a morbid thing.

Good stewardship requires a restrained expenditure, and this is a matter of personal conscience and judgment. In some societies this has not always been in correct focus.

No, a funeral service of a faithful Saint should not be a distressing thing but a time of looking up and beyond with the eyes of faith and an occasion for the sensing of the divine purpose. I have found this so both as a mourner and as a minister.

There is no requirement of public funeral services. If one for some reason or other feels unable to participate, there is no reason why private burial or cremation of one's loved one should not be asked for and arranged. Nevertheless, one should not brush lightly aside the desire of one's fellows to pay tribute to the lasting values which come into focus whenever one of God's children dies.

If the minister and the bereaved plan together for a service of gospel hope, the ministry of comfort is experienced, and thus the sense of earthly loss is minimized.

Prophets and Divine Revelation

38. Reconcile Fullness with Continuous

QUESTION

How can the statement that the scriptures contain the fullness of the gospel be reconciled with a belief in continuous revelation? If the fullness is revealed, what more is there to be expected through revelation?

ANSWER

Man is always limited in the expression of truth by the inadequacy of words themselves as well as by his own lack of facility in using them.

Perhaps the key to the apparent conflict you remark on is in defining "gospel" in a basic way. Then, again, some insight as to the function of revelation should be enlightening. The gospel was revealed in the person of Jesus Christ. The basic meaning of the word gospel is "the good news," the good news being the revelation of God's saving grace extended to man. All other expressions through prophetic channels are incidental and minor in comparison with the fullness of the gospel revealed in the person of Jesus Christ. Unfortunately we as Latter Day Saints, along with other groups, have often limited our understanding of the gospel to a set of doctrines, expressed catechistically.

An example of this is the trite reply given to the question "What is the gospel?" Hebrews 6:1, 2 is used as a convenient package answer. We should be well aware that these principles are secondary to the one great revelation in Jesus Christ. Joseph Smith, after answering some twenty questions in the *Elders' Journal* on what Latter Day Saints believe, stated that belief in Christ, living, dying, and being resurrected, was the foundation of faith, and that "all else is an appendage to this." Therefore, Christ the Savior is central.

Now as to further revelation, this is not precluded by what has just been said. All men and peoples are entitled to divine guidance in seeking to understand the ways of God and his designs and purposes for mankind. Individuals and the church have available the channel of revelation for guidance in relevant matters. This applies to procedures and principles of giving effective expression to the Christian faith and order, both for the now and in the eschatological sense. Comprehension of Deity is still limited by Doctrine and Covenants 85:11 e, which states that revelation will be progressive until the day when we shall be able to comprehend God.

The good news is that God offers salvation to man, and revelation is concerned with the unfolding of all truth which man must ultimately comprehend to be prepared for divine companionship.

39. Fulfillment of Prophecy in Matthew and Mark

QUESTION

Matthew 16:28 and Mark 9:1 state that some who were there at that time should not taste of death till they had seen the kingdom of God come with power. Is there any evidence that this was fulfilled? What is the RLDS explanation?

ANSWER

There are three or four texts which need to be considered in relationship to this problem. Matthew and Mark use similar words, as follows:

"Verily, I say unto you, There be some standing here, which shall not taste of death, till they see the Son of man coming in his kingdom."—Matthew 16:28.

"Verily I say unto you, That there be some of them that stand here, which shall not taste of death, till they have seen the kingdom of God come with power."—Mark 9:1.

In apparent explanation of these words we have a reference in John 21:20-24.

45

"Jesus saith unto him, If I will that he tarry till I come, what is that to thee. . . .

"Then went this saying abroad among the brethren, that that disciple should not die: yet Jesus said not unto him, He shall not die; but, If I will that he tarry till I come, what is that to thee?"

In this last text, it appears the writer is concerned that what Jesus said be clear. He takes the stand that the previous statements of what was said were inaccurate. This writer asserts that Jesus made no such promise.

If this were all the scripture we have, we must agree that the Johannine explanation is acceptable. However, Doctrine and Covenants 7 was given by revelation in answer to the inquiry of Joseph Smith, Jr., and Oliver Cowdery concerning John 21. This indicates that John (at least) did tarry on earth.

Many students who do not take the Doctrine and Covenants into account believe John 21 disposes of the problem, but the RLDS interpretation must involve Doctrine and Covenants 7:1.

In connection with this, Revelation 10:11, "Thou must prophesy again before many peoples, and nations, and tongues, and kings" is of interest.

See *A Commentary on the Doctrine and Covenants* (page 50) by F. H. Edwards.

40. Dreams and Visions

QUESTION

What is the meaning of Acts 2:17 and Joel 2:28-32: "Old men shall dream dreams and young men shall see visions"? Is age a factor in these experiences, and if so where do we draw the line?

ANSWER

I think you are concerned with an over literal application. This is fine poetry and must be understood in this way. The whole passage is a gem of literary expression. The prophet is obviously suggesting the imagery of which the mind is capable to convey the expectancy of the universal outpouring of God's Spirit and the manifestation of his power.

The approaches of age and youth differ. God speaks to each through his own channel. Youth is a period of optimism and vision.

46

Age is a period of recollection, reflection, and hopefulness for coming generations.

The enlightenment of the Holy Spirit is expressed through the subconscious as we sleep and dream, and youth literally envisions possibilities of attainment by the same spirit. Yet there is no disposition to limit either of these aspects of spiritual insight to either age or youth.

This answer in no way contradicts the traditional acceptance of the dream and vision as spiritual phenomena. I suggest you see also the poetic expression involved.

41. Pentecostal Outpouring in Acts

QUESTION

How do we account for the statement in Acts 2:17 that says the Pentecostal outpouring was the event prophesied by Joel as occurring in the "last days"? How could that be true when history shows that almost 2,000 years have passed since then?

ANSWER

Probably the prophet Joel could have been recorded quite properly as saying "In days to come" instead of "in the last days." I am sure Peter would want the emphasis placed upon the experience more than the timing, although it would appear that he and other early Christians believed they were nearer the end of the world than they were. He was concerned with the fact that there was being witnessed a great endowment of power. He was deeply concerned with the fact of the Holy Spirit working in the minds and hearts of the assembled multitude and not only in the spectacular, although amazing phenomena—both visual and audible—occurred. Strong men's hearts were melted to a realization of their sin; the barriers of race and tongue were transcended as everyone heard the gospel in his own tongue.

The term "last days" or "latter days" occurs a number of times in scripture. As you commented, history proves the last days not to have been in the first century after Christ. Through spiritual insight the prophets saw the developments of the future, both of apostasy and triumph, and it was this that was important. Actual timing is not so important.

As often emphasized in answers in this column we miss the point

47

if we pin the scripture to proof by dates. That some of the Bible writers did so is no defense of this tendency. Their knowledge of time was not complete. However, their testimony of the divine manifestation was not in error. This was their experience and they sought to explain it, but more than that they sought to share the power because of what it had done in their lives. Peter was such a person.

If Joel's words as expressed in English are to be accepted as literal, and if Peter believed he was living in the last days, then Peter was in error on this point. If my alternative is accepted and the experience is considered as the more important, and the text implies "in days to come," there is no conflict.

It is of interest to note that Joseph Smith stated in his history in *Times and Seasons* (Vol. 3, p. 753) that on the evening of September 21, 1823, an angelic visitor quoted to him Joel 2:28 to the end of the chapter, and said these things were not then fulfilled but would soon be.

The experience of the Holy Spirit is not limited to time and place. Outpourings of the Spirit are claimed throughout the Restoration period. Errors, however, have been made in these days in timing. Joseph Smith and his early followers undoubtedly expected the final days to be nearer than history shows they were, but the further endowment of the Holy Spirit is to be looked for not only in "later times" but in the very daily life which involves us. Then men's hearts will melt and barriers of race, tongue, and division shall be broken down. Note that the outpouring is to be upon "all flesh." This is comprehensive and must eventually be ecumenical.

42. Gift of Aaron

QUESTION

What was the "gift of Aaron" mentioned in Doctrine and Covenants 8?

ANSWER

Section 8 of the Doctrine and Covenants differs somewhat from the earliest published version which was to be Chapter 7 in the Book of Commandments, the printing of which was interrupted in July, 1833. Some changes made were simply corrections of error in manuscripts, but the revision of this chapter is too extensive to be so regarded. The earlier printing makes the statement that Oliver

Cowdery had "a gift of working with the rod, behold it has told you things." It is also referred to as a "rod of nature."

Both the Smith and Cowdery families had lived in communities where divining by means of a rod was practiced (see *Joseph Smith and His Progenitors*, page 103-4, footnotes 1 and 2, 1912 edition). Undoubtedly there was some uncertainty and, therefore, speculation concerning the power by which this article worked. The witch-hazel stick was used to find water, minerals, and in some cases, treasure. Joseph Smith evidently concerned himself with the question, as he states in the Book of Commandments: "Behold there is no other power save God, that can cause this rod of nature to work in your hands. . . ."

Cowdery wanted to translate. He failed. He was told that henceforth his gift was to assist Joseph Smith as Aaron did Moses (see Doctrine and Covenants 9). The gift of Aaron was epitomized by the rod of Aaron, as was Joseph Smith's calling to translate by the Urim and Thummim.

I believe a study of the Book of Commandments (1833) in comparison with the Doctrine and Covenants (1835) at this point indicates a development of Joseph Smith's understanding between 1830 and the publication of 1835. When his concept changed, he revised the text to conform. He inserted the words Urim and Thummim where they were not previously used, and also modified the section involved in your question. This is an illustration of the fact that if one insists on the literal accuracy of verbal inspiration, there is insurmountable difficulty. To take into account the growing understanding of the prophetic agent and his ability to express truth dissolves many such textual problems.

43. Canon of Scripture Closed?

QUESTION

What does one answer to explain our expectation of divine revelation today when Revelation 22:18, 19 is quoted to support the idea that the canon of scripture was closed?

ANSWER

The verses referred to state:

"For I testify unto every man that heareth the words of the prophecy of this book, If any man shall add unto these things, God shall add unto him the plagues that are written in this book; and if any man shall take away from the words of the book of this prophecy, God shall take away his part out of the book of life, and out of the holy city, and from the things which are written in this book."

When these words were written there was no Bible as we now have it. The various books of the present canon were not selected and collated until much later (after A.D. 200). Therefore the writer of Revelation could not have been referring to the New Testament as a whole but only to his own writings.

This is not the only place where such restrictions are found in the scriptures. In the Old Testament are similar statements. For instance Deuteronomy 4:2 states, "Ye shall not add unto the word which I command you, neither shall ye diminish aught from it, that ye may keep the commandments of the Lord your God which I command you."

If this is interpreted in a strict sense then there should be no new scriptures after that writing. This is obviously not intended. In the broad sense the instruction is against tampering with the divine law.

44. Any Revelations Rejected

QUESTION

Could you tell me if at any time any of the revelations presented to the church have been rejected by the people or more specifically by any of the quorums?

ANSWER

No revelation presented to the church by its leader has ever been rejected. On one occasion, however, a document was presented as a revelation but rejected as such by two of the quorums. The Quorum of Twelve unanimously declined "to accept the communication . . . presented to the General Conference, October 2, as a revelation from God." This report is found in *General Conference Minutes,* page 3232 for the year 1922. The seventy took similar action by a vote of 41 to 25. A minority report of twelve seventies supported the document as revelation (see *General Conference Minutes* for 1922, page 3233).

The document was approved as revelation by the high priests, order of bishops, evangelists, elders (115 to 48), and Aaronic priesthood

(46 to 41). It was presented to the General Conference as a whole on October 11, where action was taken to refer back to a joint council of Presidency, Twelve, and Seventy for "consideration and adjustment."

The council met and Elbert A. Smith, for the First Presidency, reported on October 12 that no progress had been made. President Smith asked the assembly to fix a time to decide the matter. The time set was for 4:00 P.M. on that day. The voting resulted in acceptance of the document as revelation by 656 to 452. Of the yeas 451 were delegates and 205 ex officiis. Of the nays, 310 were delegates and 142 ex officiis. This document is now Doctrine and Covenants 134, dated October 2, 1922.

There have been other documents presented as revelation but not formally brought before the church for action at the time. Revelations are not included in the Doctrine and Covenants without Conference action.

45. Prophecy about War between States

QUESTION

Would you inform me as to the origin of the prophecy attributed to Joseph Smith concerning the war between the States? Where can this document be found, and what are the facts concerning it?

ANSWER

The document referred to was first printed in *The Pearl of Great Price* which was published in Liverpool, England, in the year 1851 by F. D. Richards. It was attributed to Joseph Smith, Jr., and appears to be sufficiently authenticated. Why it was not included in the Doctrine and Covenants if the published form is a correct copy is not known, except that one may assume the committee did not think the matter contained therein had relevance to the purpose for which the book was being compiled—that is, an arrangement of "Covenants and Articles" for the conduct and guidance of the church.

It merits serious attention as a prophecy because it was given on December 25, 1832, and was in print in 1851 some years before the outbreak of the Civil War, which fulfilled the provisions stated in the document. The substance appeared in an anti-Mormon book entitled *Mormonism* (page 174) written in 1857 by Elder Hyde.

There is an earlier reference, which though meager indicates the existence of the basic prophecy (see *Evening and Morning Star*,

Volume 1, Number 8, page 122, January, 1833). Under the editorial caption, "Signs of the Times," among other portents is listed "The dissolution of South Carolina from the Union." We have every reason to believe the prophecy is based upon a prediction made by the prophet Joseph Smith. History is evidence of its fulfillment. It can be found in Utah publications and in RLDS *Church History,* Volume 1, pages 262, 263.

The prophecy was printed at one time at the end of the Reorganized Church Doctrine and Covenants. It was never given a section number, and I have not discovered by what authority it was inserted and then removed. It never did receive approval in the accepted manner as provided in church procedure.

46. Washington's Vision

QUESTION

Was Washington's vision as related to Wesley Bradshaw by Anthony Sherman published in the "Saints' Herald" or any church publication? If so, when?

ANSWER

Washington's vision was printed in the *Saints' Herald,* Vol. 21, p. 718; Vol. 50, p. 102; Vol. 78, p. 1,068; Vol. 83, p. 941. In Volume 83, p. 941, the following editorial comment is made:

"A request has come from some of our readers for the reprinting of 'Washington's Vision,' which last appeared in this publication November 11, 1931. It was reprinted from the *National Tribune,* of Washington, with the following introduction: 'For many years copies of Washington's vision at Valley Forge as related by one Wesley Bradshaw, told to him by Anthony Sherman, have been in existence. The earliest publication was in 1859.'

"The Editors of the *Herald* can make no affirmation of the authenticity of this article. George Washington died in 1799. Sixty years is a long time for anything of this character to be left unpublished. Apparently nothing in Washington's handwriting can be cited to vouch for its genuineness. We present it simply because a number of our readers have manifested their interest. If any of them know of anything to prove it, we should be glad to hear of it.—THE EDITORS."

Question Time, Vol. 89, p. 309, March 7, 1942, dealt with the question of authenticity and the writer concluded as follows:

"At most we have an alleged story told eighty-one years after being heard by the sole narrator, and then an attempt to repeat it with precise accuracy by another person after a further lapse of twenty-one years or more."

This answer was by Bishop A. B. Phillips who frankly stated there was little evidence to support its authenticity and much to indicate its falsity.

47. Contradiction of Visions

QUESTION

Could you explain the strange contradiction of the vision and revelation given to Joseph Smith, Jr., and Sidney Rigdon found in Doctrine and Covenants, Section 76, specifically verse 6 a-f, with that of a vision given to Joseph Smith, Sr., patriarch of the church, found in "Church History," 1836-1844, Volume 2, page 16. Which are we to believe?

ANSWER

The vision mentioned in *Church History*, Volume 2, page 16, was not had by Joseph Smith, Sr., but by his son Joseph Smith, Jr., on January 21, 1836. Section 76 was approved by the general assembly of the church which met in Kirtland, August 17, 1835, and thus becomes the standard of reference on the question you have raised.

The vision at the time of the ordination of Patriarch Joseph Smith, Sr., is recorded as a matter of history and, insofar as it harmonizes with approved revelation, may be accepted as illuminatory thereto. On a basis of principle where expressions of a prophetic nature are given, no matter through whom they come, they are to be adjudged by that which has been approved according to the law. Only when thus approved are these expressions binding.

Documents coming before the church from the President of the High Priesthood are always considered in the light of previously accepted revelation and discussed by the quorums and the body in that setting. The statements of Joseph the Martyr should also be considered in relation to this principle.

53

48. Collation of Revelations

Has there been any collation of all the revelations presented to the church, etc., other than the Doctrine and Covenants? These, I understand, are selections only. Assuming there is value in other messages in communications through men like Elbert A. Smith, where can I find a complete catalog?

ANSWER

There has been no work done of the nature you suggest. It is true that the original collection in the Doctrine and Covenants is a selection of items considered to be relevant to the purpose of the book.

There is undoubtedly much counsel and wisdom in other documents presented to the Saints from time to time, especially in the case of the presiding patriarchs and other responsible officers in their respective jurisdictions. Nevertheless, local manifestations are of such a nature that the printing and circulating of them has been disapproved. As has been often said it does not affect the truth or value of a matter to print it or not to print it, but because of the strong influence of the printed word local messages are likely to be taken out of context and many unwarranted generalizations made.

Therefore, only those revelations that have received the due consideration of the quorums and World Conference are included in the official publication of the Doctrine and Covenants. By revelation and acceptance they then become binding upon us as the law. With possible exception these communications should be through the president of the church.

No revelation other than through the prophet has as yet found place in the Doctrine and Covenants, although there are other documents such as Sections 111, 112, and 123 which stand upon their merits as actions of the General Conference—and in the case of Section 123, upon the authority of the council presenting it.

On occasion spiritual communications have been printed in the *Saints' Herald*. Where this is done it is by approval of members of the First Presidency and obviously considered by them as of general import and value but not necessarily as governing law or binding procedure. Examples of this are found in Elbert A. Smith's message to the Conference at Lamoni, Iowa (*Saints' Herald*, Vol. 64, No. 46, page 1081, November 14, 1917), and in his message to the Conference of 1946 concerning the call of President Israel A. Smith (*Saints'*

Herald, Vol. 93, No. 17, p. 742, April 27, 1946). Another example would be that of the words of Presiding Patriarch Roy A. Cheville given before the 1959 Conference of High Priests at Kirtland (*Saints' Herald,* Vol. 106, No. 43, October 26, 1959).

The Utah church has researched early records and has included a number of documents from other sources that were not selected originally for inclusion in the Doctrine and Covenants. These did not have Conference approval, and the Reorganization has not included them.

To find a complete coverage of revelations, one would have to search through the earliest publications of the church to the present. This has never been done and presented as a complete work.

49. Revelation to Build at Far West

QUESTION

"*A Commentary on the Doctrine and Covenants,*" page 352, states, "On April 26, 1838, the First Presidency, Presiding Bishopric, and High Council were commanded by revelation to build the city and temple of Far West." Where is this revelation found?

ANSWER

The first publication of this document, to my knowledge, was in the *Millennial Star,* Volume XVI, No. 10, March 11, 1854. The paper was published at that time by S. W. Richards in Liverpool, England. The *Millennial Star* was by then under the control of the Salt Lake City church. A feature "The History of Joseph Smith" which was commenced in the *Times and Seasons* in Nauvoo by Joseph Smith, Jr., himself, was carried on after the martyrdom by Editor John Taylor, although the history had only covered at the time of Joseph's death up to December, 1831. It was later continued in the *Millennial Star.* It was in this feature that the document on the Far West house of the Lord first appeared. Exactly how much of this record had the approval or scrutiny of Joseph Smith it is impossible to say, as the last issue in his lifetime containing this serial was *Times and Seasons,* Volume 5, No. 9, May 1, 1844. He died June 27 of that year.

The Utah church made a number of alterations in the Doctrine and Covenants published by it in 1876. At this time the statement on marriage which enjoined monogamy was removed and a substitute document on polygamy inserted. Several other documents also were added at this time, among them the one mentioned in your inquiry. It is Section 115 in the Utah edition. It has never appeared in any Reorganized Church edition.

The Utah leaders took with them from Nauvoo many documents of the original church, and this source is no doubt the only basis by which it could be documented. Unlike the polygamy document there appears to be no point other than to present a more complete account of what did occur.

We do know that work was commenced on the building, although it did not proceed beyond the initial stages because the Saints were expelled from Missouri during the fall and winter of 1838-1839. On the basis of these facts the *Commentary* quite legitimately includes the statement as fact.

50. Local Manifestations

QUESTION

If a manifestation of the Spirit is given to a particular group such as a local congregation or a reunion gathering, should it be given out as applying to any others than those immediately concerned?

One member of our class raised the question of the letters of Paul saying that these were of a local character, written to specific groups, and that if considered in the light of the first part of this question they did not apply to others than those to whom they were addressed.

ANSWER

The administrative rule is that manifestations of a local character be not printed and circulated as documents to govern the church either locally or generally.

Doctrine and Covenants 125:14 b states:

"And these affairs [of branches and districts] are not to be conducted by manifestations of the Spirit unless these directions and manifestations come through the regularly authorized officers of branch or district."

It is then to be presumed that spiritual guidance is available in each area in harmony with this principle. This limits the applicability of any given counsel to the situation and locality concerned. However, what is true in principle is true everywhere.

Guidance is normally through those chosen to supervise in the regularly approved way, and God does not appear to guide the wider areas of administration by those officers of lesser areas of jurisdiction. Therefore, matters of guidance and counsel, when intended for the whole church, normally come through the prophet. To become part of our doctrine and have the standing of a covenant these communications must be accepted and approved by the church in World Conference. The word "covenants" means that there is two-way action—by God and his people.

You will note, however, that there are many items in the Doctrine and Covenants which appear to be of only personal or local significance. You will find upon further study that they involve a principle of wider application. All of these, however, should receive World Conference approval and where not so approved would be open to question as to their binding power upon us as a church.

The writings of Paul are a parallel to scriptures in modern times. One must read them in the light of the principles involved for the very reason that they were often locally addressed letters and not general epistles. Paul does not claim inspiration for all his utterances. If we did not take this more liberal view of the text, women today would be offending by cutting their hair. Paul gave counsel of a local nature and it has been preserved. It should be thus interpreted where this is so. Where his instructions are concerned with basic principles and are of divine insight and not his own opinion, they apply as scripture.

51. Spiritual Confirmation

QUESTION

Is any spiritual confirmation required by the presiding elder in a service in which a spiritual gift such as prophecy is manifested through another elder or a member of the congregation? If a gift is received, but is not confirmed to the presiding officer, what should he do about it—if anything?

ANSWER

One cannot give hard and fast rules for the conducting of meetings or prescribe procedures which will meet every situation that may arise. The spirit of wisdom must guide on any specific occasion. We have been counseled that the elders should lead the meetings of the church as they are led by the Spirit, and this would cover your question in a general way.

Now concerning professed manifestions of the Spirit, it would not be my opinion that a presiding officer should be expected to pronounce as to the divinity of such phenomena on any or all occasions. The manifestation may be of such a nature that no comment is required. Usually the hallmark of divinity is clear when God speaks to his people, and this the Saints joyously sense. They do not need to have such inspiration overly labeled. It has been suggested that a good pictorial representation of a horse does not need labeling. If it does, the picture is of doubtful value as a method of communication.

There are, of course, occasions when a branch president needs to give some statement of his discernment for the protection of those who may be misled. This requires considerable care and tact as impulsive action either to endorse or negate can lead to deep trouble in the hearts of God's people. Often the presiding officer need make no comment, letting the matter rest on its own merits. Deuteronomy 18:22 states as follows:

"When a prophet speaketh in the name of the Lord, if the thing follow not, nor come to pass, that is the thing which the Lord hath not spoken, but the prophet hath spoken it presumptuously; thou shalt not be afraid of him."

Should the need for protection of those who may be misled be evidenced, then the instruction given in Doctrine and Covenants 50:7 which is printed here in part should guide.

"Wherefore, it shall come to pass, that if you behold a spirit manifested that you can not understand, and you receive not that spirit, ye shall ask of the Father, in the name of Jesus, and if he give not unto you that spirit, that you may know that it is not of God; and it shall be given unto you power over that spirit, and you shall proclaim against that spirit with a loud voice, that it is not of God; not with railing accusation, that ye be not overcome; neither with boasting, nor rejoicing, lest you be seized therewith."— Doctrine and Covenants 50:7 a, b, c.

If the presiding officer has not confirmation and the matter does not appear to be contentious he may need to do nothing. If a well-meaning but misguided person persists to a degree which is detrimental to the genuine expression of the gifts, he should receive personal counsel—if possible, privately.

It may be helpful to state that the branches are not to be directed by manifestations of the Spirit unless those so speaking are in proper official relationship. This is clearly stated in the law.

"And these affairs are not to be conducted by manifestations of the Spirit unless these directions and manifestations come through the regularly authorized officers of branch or district. If my people will respect the officers whom I have called and set in the church, I will respect these officers; and if they do not, they can not expect the riches of gifts and the blessings of direction."—Doctrine and Covenants 125:14 b, c.

The Bible

52. Church Stand on Spiritual Writing

QUESTION

What is the church stand on automatic spiritual writing? I am perplexed with experiences I have had under self-hypnosis, and I do not wish to follow a wrong lead.

ANSWER

Such matters as you are concerned with are certainly not within the framework of the gospel of Christ. Much discussion has occurred as to the sources of such occult manifestations. A general concensus of Christian opinion would indicate that they are not of God and, of whatever origin, should be left alone.

Your term, self-hypnosis, indicates some kind of trance situation. At no time should one place himself and his faculties under the control of so-called spiritual mediums or endeavor to induce such a state by his own manipulation. God will not lead one into these dark areas of experience.

Medical hypnosis is another matter and not covered in my disapproval. On legitimate medical practice I do not presume to speak. I gather you are not concerned with hypnosis as such.

In short I would advise you to leave spiritualistic mediums and associated phenomena alone and concentrate on fulfilling the requirements of Christian life as found in the scriptures.

53. Inspired Version, a Clarification

QUESTION

In what light is the Inspired Version a translation?

ANSWER

The confusion occasioned by the use of the word translation in connection with the version of the Bible prepared by Joseph Smith arises because of a free use of the word.

Joseph Smith himself used the word translation freely, although in one sense the process so described in the work on this document is permissible. One of the meanings of "to translate" given by Webster is "To change the form, expression or mode of expression of, so as to interpret or make tangible, real or apparent, or the like."

In short, this means a process of clarification by use of other words. These scriptures were always referred to as the New Translation in the writings of the early church.

When published from the original manuscript handed to the Reorganization by Joseph's widow, the title page read, "The Holy Scriptures, Translated and Corrected by the Spirit of Revelation."

Later editions, in consequence of a more accurate usage of the word translation, describe the work as "An Inspired Revision of the Authorized Version" (see present edition title page).

This improvement in terminology is evident when we realize that a considerable amount of material not appearing in any other edition of the Authorized Version was added by revelation. The word translation cannot be applied to these passages. It is definitely established that no other language version was used in the process of revision.

Thus we use the term Inspired Version rather than Inspired Translation.

54. Inspired Version Deviations

QUESTION

Why does the Inspired Version deviate from the standard versification in certain places, notably in Genesis and Matthew?

ANSWER

The numbering of the verses is different in the Inspired Version because of the quantity of additional material inserted into the text. A few examples will suffice. In Genesis 1 there are 31 verses in the

King James Version (A.V.) and 33 in the Inspired Version (I.V.). The difference in numbering is explained by the fact that verses 1 and 2 in the Inspired Version are not in the King James at all; consequently verse 1 in the King James Version becomes verse 3 in the Inspired Version.

Three such additions occur in the Inspired Version, Chapter 2 between verses 1 and 9. Verses 5, 6, and 9 are absent from the King James Version. Careful comparison will indicate that these additions are more extensive as one proceeds further in reading Genesis. The same number of chapters are in both works, although the same material is not necessarily in the same numbered chapter (these additions necessitate some new division of chapters). These comments apply to your question regarding New Testament changes which are not as extensive as in the Old Testament.

The additional material contained in the Inspired Version was stated by Joseph Smith to be of a revelatory nature. Some of that in Genesis is also in the Doctrine and Covenants (see Doctrine and Covenants 36). I suggest you compare this with Genesis 7:1-78, I.V.

An interesting comment made by Joseph Smith in this connection is found in the periodical *Times and Seasons*.

> "It may be well to observe here that the Lord greatly encouraged and strengthened the faith of his little flock, which had embraced the fulness of the everlasting gospel, as revealed to them in the Book of Mormon, by giving some more extended information upon the scriptures, a translation of which had already commenced.
>
> "Much conjecture and conversation frequently occurred among the saints, concerning the books mentioned and referred to in various places in the Old and New Testaments, which were now nowhere to be found. The common remark was, they were lost books; but it seems the apostolic churches had some of these writings, as Jude mentions or quotes the prophecy of Enoch, the seventh from Adam. To the joy of the flock, which in all, from Colesville to Canadaigua, New York, numbered about seventy members, did the Lord reveal the following doings of olden times, from the prophecy of Enoch."—*Times and Seasons*, Vol. IV, No. 22, page 336, October 1, 1843.

55. Present New Testament

When was the present New Testament formally decided?

There was no formal decision by any ecumenical council as to what constituted the books of the New Testament. The canon became recognized by usage. The Latin Vulgate of Jerome is the basis upon which the present canon became the acceptable version. The twenty-seven books of this work thus became "authoritative" by usage and common consent. This consent was informal, although local councils made pronouncements which were not, however, binding on the catholic body. The present collections of documents were developed over centuries.

56. Utah Church and Book of Moses

QUESTION

How did the Utah church obtain what is called the Book of Moses, which was published in the "Pearl of Great Price"? This is almost identical with the relevant Inspired Version passages.

ANSWER

There were earlier publications of this material available to the compiler of the *Pearl of Great Price*, 1851, Liverpool, England. As early as August, 1832, there appeared in the *Evening and Morning Star* extracts from the prophecy of Enoch. This was reprinted in March, 1835, in Kirtland (reprint page 45), and it again appeared in *Times and Seasons*, November 1, 1840. A still later reference is *Times and Seasons*, October 1, 1843.

It has been claimed by some members of the Utah church that J. M. Bernhisel, onetime clerk in Joseph Smith's office, took a copy of the work that had been done for the publication of what was then called the New Translation of the Scriptures (now known as the Inspired Version), and that this is in their possession. This purported copy has never been exhibited for our inspection. I would question the claim because research done in my department indicates that the Utah church continued to reprint the text of the *Pearl of Great Price* exactly as in 1851 until 1878, when that work was made to conform to the renditions of the Inspired Version text as published by the Reorganization in 1867. This suggests to me that Utah was dependent on the early publications mentioned for the *Pearl of Great Price*.

After the Reorganization published the text of the Holy Scriptures, the Utah publishers of the *Pearl of Great Price* (knowing that its source was manuscripts in Emma Smith's possession) corrected their text to harmonize with the more complete data. If there is a more credible explanation, we would be most happy to have it as our interest is only in the facts. If the copy referred to is still in existence, a comparison with the manuscripts in our possession would be most enlightening.

The original *Pearl of Great Price* was a work of fifty-six pages containing the following:

Extracts from the Prophecy of Enoch
The words of God which he spoke unto Moses, etc.
The Book of Abraham
Corrected version of Matthew 24, and the "Key to the Revelations of St. John"
A prophecy claimed to be given by Joseph Smith, December 25, 1832, now known as the "Civil War Prophecy"
Extracts from the Doctrine and Covenants and *Articles of Faith,* and also a poem entitled "Truth" by one "Jacques" in 1845.

A number of changes were made in subsequent editions including the addition of the famous document on plural marriage as espoused by the Salt Lake church. This document now appears in the Utah Doctrine and Covenants as Section 132. The *Pearl of Great Price* is a standard work of the Utah church.

57. Bible Used by Joseph Smith

QUESTION

Exactly what kind of Bible was used by Joseph Smith in translation work? If the Bible used by Joseph is still in existence, where may it be found?

ANSWER

The Bible used by Joseph Smith in his preparation of the Inspired Version was an edition of the Authorized (King James) Version printed in 1828 by H. & E. Phinney in Cooperstown, New York. It is now in the keeping of the Church Historian at Independence, Missouri. It is a stereotype edition and contains the books of the Old and New

Testament, and in addition, the Apocrypha, Canne's Marginal notes and references, an index with names and weights and measures, tables, coins, etc.

The flyleaf is inscribed by Joseph Smith in his handwriting in the following words:

"The Book of the Jews and the property of Joseph Smith, Junior, and Oliver Cowdery, bought October the 8th, 1829, at Egbert and Grandin's Book Store, Palmyra, Wayne County, New York."

At the bottom of this page is the price in the same handwriting: "Price $3.75." One line of handwriting below this is illegible.

The historical files show this Bible was in the possession of Joseph Smith's son and daughter-in-law, Alexander and Elizabeth Smith, who gave it to their daughter, Vida. Vida Smith (Yates) presented it to President I. A. Smith on July 9, 1942, who executed legal transfer to the church at Independence, Missouri, May 12, 1944.

It is important to note that the Inspired Version is not a translation as is indicated when it is wrongly called "The Inspired Translation." It is a corrected version, no other language than English being directly involved. Joseph Smith appears to have read from the Authorized Version, dictating corrections of such errors as seemed important under the inspiration he received. Where the text was deemed sufficiently correct or clear no notes other than to so state in the manuscript notes were made. At times whole chapters were transcribed. When a correction was necessary, sometimes a word in the printed text was underlined or a line drawn through it and a note made in the manuscript of the correct rendering. This work was finished on July 2, 1833. It was not printed in its entirety until 1867, after Emma Smith Bidamon gave the manuscript to the Reorganization. This manuscript is also in the possession of the church.

58. Wording of Lord's Prayer

QUESTION

Why does the prayer given by Christ in the Third Book of Nephi 5:105 say "lead us not into temptation"? Should it not be the same as that in the Inspired Version of the Bible, which emphasizes that God does not lead us into temptation?

65

In a broad sense both are correct. At the time Joseph Smith dictated the words of the Lord's Prayer for the manuscript of the Book of Mormon, he was obviously unaware of the problem of any question about the suitability of the word "lead." Some have offered the explanation that when it became obvious to the scribe that the Lord's Prayer was to follow, he made the error of writing from memory and, therefore, included the King James Version rendering.

The New English Bible (1961) gives the passage in question: "And do not bring us to the test, but save us from the evil one." Most of the orthodox translations hold to "lead us not," including the Revised Standard Version. So we must look for some explanation not involving accidental copying.

Joseph Smith revised the Book of Mormon manuscript in 1837 and did not change the wording as he did in his correction of the text of Matthew 6:13.

The way the correction was made becomes important here. From a study of the manuscript material it is certain the method was not automatic. The many and various changes in the manuscript copy of the Inspired Version itself indicate that a process of study, reference to other texts, consideration, and prayer were involved. This is clearly indicated in Doctrine and Covenants 9 where Oliver Cowdery is told how inspirational translation operates. The emphasis is upon study and a seeking of assurance that one has arrived at the truth.

The texts under consideration would be those that caught the interest and attention of the reviser. It is apparent that the version presented by Joseph Smith dealt with only a fragment of the whole Bible. The word that caught the attention in Matthew 6:13 was "lead."* Since he was aware to some degree of the whole Bible, the statement in James 1:13, "Let no man say when he is tempted, I am tempted of God, . . . neither tempteth he any man," came naturally to bear on the question. Had Joseph Smith been correcting the text with later knowledge coming with his greater experience and study, he might have concerned himself with the word "temptation" and the alternative meanings in the Greek text. It is obvious that he chose not to alter the Book of Mormon in this particular incident of the Lord's Prayer.

A more recent consideration has actually concerned itself with the variations in meaning of the Greek word translated "temptation," an alternative for which is the word "trial." The first part of James 1:1-12 seems to hold this concept of trial or testing. Some scholars think that there should be a new chapter beginning with James 1:13

because from then on the word temptation is involved with "desire," which the writer says is at the root of human weakness. The remainder of the chapter is focused around this aspect of temptation and this contrasting with the first twelve verses.

We are not sure that the literal words of this prayer have been preserved, coming as it has through many editorial hands. The first recorder, who we are sure did not take down the prayer in shorthand, was probably influenced by the Jewish idea that God planted two impulses in man—one for good and the other evil. This may be the reason for James's attempt to clear up this point of Jewish theology in his fine exposition.

I have not told you how the word "lead" came to be retained in one and not in the other, for no one really knows, but the translator of the Book of Mormon was not accidental in leaving it there, since he had given thought to it during the revision of the New Testament. If I have avoided a definite answer I have done so in order that you may consider factors of wider implication than usual on this question. Joseph Smith, by substituting "suffer us not to be led" for "lead us not," was endeavoring to harmonize it with the second half of James 1 and moving further away from the older concept that God actually caused men to sin.

59. New English Bible

QUESTION

What is the opinion of the church on the New English Bible?

ANSWER

It is always a matter of interest to have questions phrased as to what "the church" believes. The institution is often personified in such a way as to oversimplify its identity. When asked what the church believed on a given point, the late Joseph Smith III was often cautious and, as has been mentioned in other answers, used phrases like "the consensus of opinion of the elders is." This no doubt was deliberate.

Nevertheless it may be quite permissible to say "The church believes in baptism by immersion." A fine answer as to what the church believes is, I feel, "Our creed is all truth." This, while not being weakly noncommittal, is not too dogmatic and leaves room for the acceptance of those ideas which can be brought within the classification of truth. Throughout the history of the church dogmatic pronouncements have led to difficulty and tend to close the door to new light.

Our democratic phase of church organization makes it possible for the church to discuss some things and come to a majority opinion. The aim, of course, is "common consent" which would be really one hundred percent unanimity. Experience has taught that even here some conclusions arrived at have had to be modified in the light of new revelation, and so there are some areas where as a people we are not over hasty to pronounce. Men argued once—and from scripture too—that the world is flat. In the light of the revelations of this space age, this is demonstrably false. The *True Latter Day Saints' Herald* gave many inches of space to that viewpoint in the last century but of course was not bound by the view of its contributor. Had a vote been taken then one wonders what the decision may have been.

The restored church used the Authorized Version for nearly forty years before the Inspired Version was in print. The Reorganized Church is on record as accepting the Inspired Version but has not discarded other translations as valueless. The body has not expressed itself on any of the modern translations, but "the consensus of opinion" seems to be that many modern versions help to make clear the original intent of the earliest manuscripts by using modern words. Words, like fashions, change and need to be intelligently revised. I for one find the New English Bible helpful among others. I do not speak for the church because in this, as in many matters, the church has not spoken. I believe "she" will continue to be cautious in her pronouncements. In the meantime we must continue to study all good books to show ourselves approved and unashamed workmen.

60. Apocrypha

QUESTION

What is the Apocrypha?

ANSWER

The apocryphal books are a group of writings originating in the two centuries before Christ and the first century after Christ. They appeared in the Greek Septuagint version of the Old Testament but were not accepted by the Council of Jamnia in A.D. 90 when the Hebrew scriptural canon was finally decided. However, they were included in St. Jerome's *Latin Vulgate* and consequently are included in Roman Catholic Bibles based on Jerome's *Vulgate*. They originally appeared in most English Bibles between the Old and New Testament. They seem to have been regarded highly by the early Christian Church.

Jerome had taken the view that these books were without authority of belief. When the Reformers were giving serious consideration to the scriptural canon, the statement of Jerome, the fact that certain Roman Catholic doctrines were derived therefrom, and the fact that the canon of Hebrew scriptures excluded the apocryphal books influenced Luther and others to reject them. Thus today they do not appear in most Bibles other than Roman Catholic and when they do are listed as apocryphal which literally means "outside books." The Westminster Confession (1647) states in article 3:

> "The books commonly called Apocrypha, not being of Divine inspiration, are not part of the Canon of Scripture."

Doctrine and Covenants 88 states in effect that these books, though containing some truth, are not sufficiently valid to be considered worthy of inclusion in scripture.

The books commonly listed as apocryphal are I and II Esdras, Tobit, Judith, Additions to Esther, Wisdom of Solomon, Ecclesiasticus, Baruch, Letter of Jeremiah, Prayer of Azariah, Song of the Three Young Men, Susanna, Bel and the Dragon, Prayer of Manasseh, and I and II Maccabees.

61. Forbidden Fruit

QUESTION

What was the forbidden fruit which Eve ate and gave to Adam?

ANSWER

Questions of this kind are rather pointless, but I recognize that many people are quite concerned. It is immaterial to the text. The lesson is the important consideration that we should look for in any scripture.

Personally I doubt if any literal fruit was involved, although somewhere along the path of the ages the idea has crystallized in some minds that it was an apple. Where this guess came from would be difficult to determine.

The lesson to be learned is that disobedience to the divine law brings condemnation from God, and this is graphically portrayed in the text of Genesis 3.

I know some feel that a literal tree was involved; others allegorize the meaning and read into the story an act of physical moral lapse. Neither interpretation in my opinion is sound in the light of God's commandments to our early parents. To me the early chapters of Genesis breathe a message of God in contact with mankind and his guiding principles toward eternal life.

Undue concern with detail so often prevents a proper appreciation of the deep truths of scripture. For instance, in our consideration of the Book of Mormon sometimes we have lost the beauty of its message by limiting our presentation to the method of translation or to evidences of archaeological nature, rather than bearing witness to the truths contained therein. Another example of this is that countless hours have been spent discussing the gastronomical capabilities of the fish in the book of Jonah, while the main message of the love and concern of God has been overlooked.

When we get the principles of divine power and God's beneficent laws in focus, many details become of secondary importance. For this reason I am reluctant to be more specific.

62. Eve and the Serpent

QUESTION

Will you please explain the text of Genesis 3:15 where it is stated that Eve shall bruise the serpent's head and he shall bruise her heel?

ANSWER

I doubt if many people take literally the statement of Genesis which presents the snake as having a conversation with Eve. The Hebrews caught up many truths and presented them in their narrations in a form easily understood in their primitive experience as a people. There is indication of realization of deep meaning and of a capacity to penetrate beneath the apparent superficial phenomena in the Hebrew narration of the dealings of God with Adam and Eve as they grew in understanding of their stewardship of life. This consisted basically in their growing to recognize the constructive power inherent in the right to choose, to be tempted, and to succumb or to triumph.

The idea that the story of the serpent's temptation of Eve and her failure to choose rightly was simply an event in history from which all our troubles stem is not borne out in the text you inquire about. Rather it is a presentation of the fact that throughout the generations this problem of dealing with evil will have to be met.

The continuing tension resulting from the opposition between good and evil responses is illustrated in the text. Eve represents all her children, and the serpent the forces with which they too must contend.

There is something here, too, which many miss in their consideration and that is the note of hope and triumph in the statement that Eve's heel shall bruise the serpent's head. Ultimately, the record is saying, man will contend with and crush evil, and out of this tension will come final good.

We miss the point if we dwell unduly on problems such as whether snakes had legs, etc. We also have the embarrassing task of explaining why serpents do not really eat dust as the story suggests.

The Book of Mormon expresses the underlying truth of Genesis 3:14, 15 in II Nephi 1:81, 82:

"For it must needs be, that there is an opposition in all things.

"If not so, my first born in the wilderness, righteousness could not be brought to pass; neither wickedness; neither holiness nor misery; neither good nor bad."

Grace does not imply that one should not perform the good works required of God's children by the law, but when all is done we do and will actually receive far beyond our merits. We are "created unto good works" (Ephesians 2:10).

63. Witch or Murderer

QUESTION

Is there any basis in the original Hebrew text for the change made by Joseph Smith in Exodus 22:18 to "Thou shalt not suffer a murderer to live" instead of "a witch" as in the Authorized Version? Is the word "witch" different from "murderer" in Hebrew?

ANSWER

There is no doubt that the Inspired Version is the more enlightened rendering, but this passage must be viewed against the backdrop of ancient times when it was originally written. The change which Joseph Smith, Jr., made must also be seen in the setting of the culture of the nineteenth and twentieth centuries.

There is no similarity between the Hebrew word for witch, *mekash-shafah*, and the word for murderer, *rotsayah*. The former actually means "a female who practices sorcery" and the latter literally means "one who slays."

The verse under consideration comes from what is known as the Covenant Code. This is believed to be the earliest existing codification of the law in the Old Testament and was presented in that form after the occupation of Palestine but before the time of Saul. The text quoted was obviously not originally concerned with murder, because this was already dealt with in Exodus 21:12-20 in great detail, giving consideration to degrees of guilt and suitable penalties.

In the early Hebrew religious development witchcraft and wizardry were a threat to the national worship of the true God and therefore treasonable in nature, requiring the penalty of death by stoning (see Leviticus 20:27). This was the method of executing those guilty of offenses against the community. All were sinned against, therefore all should share in the execution by casting a stone.

The Hebrew word literally means "sorceress," one who practices the black arts of casting spells and such acts. Sorcerers were a menace to the national religious life and therefore were stoned.

Joseph Smith in his revision made the text meaningful for our times and did the most logical thing in substituting the word murderer for witch.

In a time (the 1800's) when people believed in plenary inspiration (every word of scripture inspired) such changes were essential if the book was not to contain unethical rules. To see this text and therefore the rule in perspective of the times is essential.

The work of Joseph Smith was not a translation in the usual sense. No other language than the English of the Authorized Version was used. Joseph Smith sought light and understanding as to truth and was inspired to do what others attempted by doctrinal reasoning. There is no need to find an error in the translation of the Authorized Version. The translators gave the correct rendering in this instance. What Joseph Smith did was remove a penalty which in an enlightened age was barbaric.

64. Book of Jonah

QUESTION

Is the book of Jonah actual history, or is it a parable? I have always accepted it as true, and I have been disturbed by the statement of one of our ministers that it is merely a story with great teaching value.

ANSWER

It is not a matter of basic faith whichever viewpoint you hold.

Of course if one believes the Bible is a document in which every word was dictated by God, there will be great difficulty in interpreting the book of Jonah. This is often the basis of concern by those who are perturbed about any interpretation other than the literal acceptance of the Bible as plenary inspiration.

The fact is that the Bible contains much more than God's direct speech. It contains history, poetry, allegory, prophecy, law, and revelation. There are the words of man as well as the words of God. At times it is stated clearly that what is written is the writer's opinion. There are times when the writer is confident that he is speaking for God and so states.

It is necessary to approach the study of scripture with several basic questions in mind before reaching a hasty conclusion. If it is known what the particular piece of writing purports to be, who wrote it and when, when it was included in the canon, why it was considered worthy of preservation, and so forth, this will form a foundation upon which to make an intelligent decision as to the meaning and value of scripture.

If one depends upon a work like the book of Jonah for evidence of the omnipotence of God, he evidences an immature approach. The power of God is not in question when we seek the deeper meaning of this book. It is a very fruitless discussion which centers around the size of the gastronomical cavity in the whale or upon the means by which Jonah got ashore. Many fruitless hours have been spent on these questions. Even if we choose to believe that the text is literal we still must guard against preoccupation with these details. They are not material to the basic interpretation or necessary to prove the power of God.

Most modern thinkers incline to the view that the book is allegorical in nature. Some still prefer to think of it as a marvelous story of the miraculous power of God. It is too late in history to check the record, but there is one thing certain: the principles taught in the story are eternal. The following truths are certainly taught, and they are very definitely important:

1. God loves all mankind of whatever nation or race.
2. One cannot escape the presence of God.
3. God requires us to play a courageous part in his work for mankind.
4. The basis of service must be bigger than a vindication of one's own ego.

The book of Jonah breathes the spirit of inspiration and is so basically authentic in its representation of the divine nature and intent for mankind that to argue about the details of its historicity is to miss the point.

Presiding Patriarch Roy A. Cheville makes this comment in his text, *The Bible in Everyday Living*, page 173:

"All this argument and misunderstanding is unfortunate. Rightly understood and properly used, the book of Jonah contains some of the loftiest teaching found anywhere in the Old Testament. Seen at its best, this treatise conveys an exalted and expanded concept of God. The common treatment of the book is similar to what would happen if we took the story of the Prodigal Son and spent our time worrying about the size and breed of the calf that was killed and the way in which husks from the hog lot could be digested in a human stomach."

Apostle Clifford Cole writing on the same theme in *The Prophets Speak* (page 180) said:

"It is a sad fact that those who have argued so vehemently about the historical accuracy of the book have completely missed the point of its message and ofttimes have displayed only the narrow egoism which the author sought to dispel."

These two writers have emphasized the allegorical approach to Jonah. This is the view of scholarship. It should not be a test of faith as to which view one holds. We must not miss the lesson by submerging it in a mass of detailed controversy.

65. Book of Jashar

QUESTION

I have been loaned a copy of a book entitled "Book of Jashar Referred to in Joshua and Second Samuel" published by J. H. Parry and Company. The date of publication has been erased. Is this an authentic work and really the book referred to in the Bible?

ANSWER

The *Book of Jashar* (sometimes Jasher) is referred to in two places in the Old Testament, Joshua 10:12, 13 and II Samuel 1:18. The Septuagint omits the reference to Jashar in Joshua 10. Nothing is known of an ancient text of this name beyond these meager references. A number of theories as to what was referred to have been advanced. It is thought by some that it was a collection of poems memorializing events of great significance to the Hebrews, as the quotes known are

74

of this nature. That is, of course, speculative. One rabbinical theory is that it was part of the Pentateuch.

Another scholar, Donaldson, attempted to develop a composition of all passages from the Old Testament which appeared to be drawn from this book. His work was entitled *Jasha: Fragmenta Archetypa Carminum Hebraicorum.* The work appeared in 1854 in London but did not gain scholarly recognition.

The meaning of the word Jashar is debatable. One concept is that it means "hero"; another, "song."

Since the fourteenth century, works purporting to be the original have appeared, one being based on the Pentateuch theory but depending for its origin on the compilation of a Spanish Jew in the thirteenth century. Forgeries have been produced as in many of the alleged discoveries of ancient texts. One in England was reprinted in 1827 with a false testimony of Wycliffe included. The latest of a number of these modern forgeries appeared in its fifth edition as late as 1953.

The book loaned to you is probably one of this type. The erasure of the date makes identification difficult. I would say that, notwithstanding the fact that it simulates lofty literary and theological sentiment, it is not authentic. This similarity to scripture is necessary to commend a false text, and this technique has often been resorted to in an endeavor to have books given credence. Its value? No more and no less than the good principles and concepts it possesses. This may be considerable but dependent purely upon the inherent truth of each. Even romances can contain wisdom.

66. Other Books after Revelation

QUESTION

Were there other books of the New Testament written after the book of Revelation?

ANSWER

The opinion that the historical situation which colored the expression of the book of Revelation was the persecution of the Christians by the Emperor Domitian has led students to state that this book was written about A.D. 95. The persecution resulted when Christians refused to worship the emperor of Rome.

Other New Testament books written in the latter part of the first century after Christ were the letters of John, Jude, and James, and the first epistle of Peter. It is believed that the second epistle of Peter was written later, which would place it in the second century. The reasoning usually advanced for this position is that the writer depended somewhat on the book of Jude and also that II Peter 3:15, 16 assumes that the Pauline epistles had already been accepted as scripture, which of course was not so in the first century. The dating of most of these books is approximate, and one cannot be explicit concerning dates.

This question is often asked because of concern with the text in Revelation 22:18, 19, which places strictures on tampering with the wording. Whether the book of Revelation is the last book, chronologically or not, does not affect a correct understanding of the text, as the restrictions referred to applied, no doubt, in the mind of the writer to his own book of prophecies. The entire canon of scripture as we know it was certainly not in existence in A.D. 95.

67. Author of Book of Acts

QUESTION

Who was the author of the Acts of the Apostles, Paul or Luke?

ANSWER

Scholars are almost unanimous on the point that Acts and Luke were written by the same author. This is based on the similarity of language and of interests chosen for emphasis. In fact, they are regarded by students as two parts of the same work. This is based upon Acts 1:1 where the author prefaces the book of Acts with, "The former treatise have I made, O Theophilus, of all that Jesus began both to do and teach," the former treatise being the book of Luke.

The book of Acts takes up where the Gospel of Luke leaves off, making a continuous narrative. These two works probably became separated because Luke has much in common with the other gospels, while Acts has a natural relation to the epistles of the period with which it is concerned.

I mention the apparent common authorship of these works because it is important in discovering who was the author.

The following three theories have been offered: (1) That Luke was the author of both the gospel bearing his name and the Acts. (2) That he was the author of the gospel and of an original sketch of the Acts, which has been altered by a subsequent editor. (3) That he is the author of only the "we sections" in Acts but not of the whole.

The most common answer to this question is that Luke was the author of both Luke and Acts, based upon tradition and an intensive historical study of the texts. That Luke was a companion of Paul and in a position to have personal access to most of the data is certain. The "we passages" indicate this (Acts 16:10-17; 20:5-15; 21:1-18; 27:1-29). Again the ecumenicity of the Acts and the knowledge of the author of church government and so forth indicates it was written with the perspective of some years later than Paul. The weight of evidence is toward Luke.

68. Luke

QUESTION

Is there any biblical record that Luke saw the Lord? What office did he hold, and where did he get his information?

ANSWER

There is no record of Luke's having seen Christ. We do not know what office he held in the church. We know that he was Paul's frequent companion and that he was a physician (Colossians 4:14). One tradition says he was a Jew of Antioch. Other students believe him to have been a Gentile. This is more generally the opinion. He was a man of letters and was the writer of the gospel which bears his name and of the Acts.

Luke obviously had access to other records such as Mark's account and had contact with eyewitnesses of many events. His introductory verses in his gospel are explanatory of his sources.

69. Prophecy by Caiaphas

QUESTION

In John 11:47-54 at a council of chief priests, Caiaphas is represented as having prophesied that Jesus would die for the nation and that he would gather in one all the children of God scattered abroad. Why should his enemy do this?

ANSWER

If you read the whole of John 11 you will note that the author not only records the events with which the chapter is concerned but makes his own explanatory comments in the light of his Christian experience. This is well illustrated in Chapter 12, verse 6. In this verse an explanation is given as to why Judas was concerned about the waste of money. This verse 6 was not part of the story.

If you examine verses 51 and 52 in this light it will be clear that these verses are of the same nature. Actually there was no spiritual insight in the prophecy of Caiaphas at all. What he was doing was a clever influencing of the council toward action to kill Jesus. He was propounding a principle that has been called the doctrine of selfish expediency. What he said was, "You do not seem to have understood that if this man lives we will all have the destruction of Rome on us and we will lose our own status as well as our nation."

The author explains that Caiaphas spoke officially, thus countenancing the persecution and ultimate crucifixion. Then the comment of the evangelist adds the Christian theological point in verse 52, "and not for that nation only, but that also he should gather together in one the children of God that were scattered abroad." This tendency to inject theological insight throughout is characteristic of John.

It has been said that the book of John combines history and interpretation, biography and theology so that the reader sees Jesus not only as a historical figure but in the light of enlarging Christian experience. Thus the text in question reports not only the words of Caiaphas but the theology of John.

70. Revelation 6 and 7

QUESTION

Can you give an interpretation of Revelation 6 and 7?

ANSWER

I cannot give much detail in this column when your question embraces two chapters. However, I can help by pointing to a few facts about the book of Revelation as a whole.

The book of Revelation is truly an apocalyptic work; that is, its theme is the triumph of God over evil and the illustration of the process of this final result for mankind. It is also an eschatological work, though the terms are not synonymous (eschatology being a study of final things). Because of this the book of Revelation is considered prophetic though the details of occurrences are not necessarily given.

It was written at a time when the Christians of Asia Minor were being persecuted for their unwillingness to bow to the Roman emperor as God, and many Christians suffered martyrdom as a result. This state of persecution began in the time of Domitian (A.D. 54-68). Some students hold, because of certain references therein, that the book was written later in the first century during the rule of Trajan (A.D. 98-117). A consensus would seem to place it in the last twenty years of the first century after Christ. Justyn Martyr ascribed this work to the apostle John. Some have questioned this, but the writer certainly calls himself John (Revelation 1:1, 4, 9; 22:8).

The Authorized Version (which the Inspired Version follows in the main) was based upon a text known as the Textus Receptus. This was not the most accurate of texts. It was translated by Erasmus from Latin back to the Greek from which it had been originally taken, and the Authorized Version scholars worked with this much translated version. The Revised Standard Version later had recourse to a group of older and probably, therefore, more accurate manuscripts. So it can be seen that to depend upon exactness of verbal translation in detail is unwise.

The book opens with chapters written to the seven churches of Asia. In Chapter 4 the saints are reminded of the power and might of God and its ultimate control. The Lamb slain is shown in Chapter 5 to be now alive and God's ally in bringing doom to Satan.

Chapters 6 and 7 deal with the breaking of the first six seals representing the loosing of a series of plagues, pestilences, famines, and war upon the inhabitants of the world while the saints and martyrs are taken to God. The intent is to give courage to those who are persecuted by portraying the martyrs beneath the altar in the protection of God. Following this there is a portrayal of a succession of cosmic disasters unleashed as God's judgment upon the earth.

From this state of affairs the faithful are seen as those saved from the disastrous judgment, released from the heat and burdens of earthly life. They are numbered as 144,000 which is evidently symbolic as a multiple of 12, this being the number of tribes of Israel. This number should not be taken literally any more than one should assume that the beasts are actual.

The bizarre symbolism of these chapters is evidently a means used to avoid identification of state personalities, direct reference to whom no doubt would have added to the persecution of the saints at that time.

The book proceeds to the ultimate vision of the New Jerusalem which is poetically described in the closing chapters.

This book has received many varying interpretations as to detail.

Some parts, such as chapters 12, 17, and 18, have received elucidation in modern revelation (see Doctrine and Covenants 5:3, 32:2, and Book of Mormon I Nephi 3, II Nephi 5:31; 12:22).

The main value is that in reading it with the background of its times in mind one has a sense of faith and confidence in God's grace and power, that God is guiding his church and mankind to his ultimate purposes. This is not necessarily to disagree with many private interpretations on detail but to suggest concentration on the major purpose of this most interesting book. It would take a book to analyze the detail.

71. Revelation 13:6

QUESTION

Concerning Revelation 13:6: "And he opened his mouth in blasphemy against God, to blaspheme 'his' name, 'his' tabernacle, and them that dwell in heaven," to whom do the quoted words refer? To God or to man?

ANSWER

According to a lesson I remember from my school days the rule of proximity would apply in interpreting this text, thus indicating that the word "his" following closely after the word "God" would indicate it is a pronoun standing for "God." Also the fact of blasphemy being referred to connects "his" with "God," blasphemy being primarily a reviling of God or sacred things such as the tabernacle or holy place.

72. Armageddon

QUESTION

What is the meaning of Armageddon, and when is it to take place?

ANSWER

The only exact scriptural reference to Armageddon is in Revelation 16:16. Doctrine and Covenants 85:35 refers to a great battle after the millennium which is called "God's great battle." There is no doubt that the latter is in intent identical with the former.

There is no other meaning to be gleaned from the text as amplified in Doctrine and Covenants 85 than that this is portrayed as a post-millennial struggle.

The word "Armageddon" had meaning for the Hebrew saints of the New Testament as it was reminiscent of great battles of their history in which God's people were involved with apparently overwhelming hosts of the heathen on the plains of Megiddo. The last great battle according to Revelation 16 will end in favor of God's people. The apocalyptic book of the Revelation of John catches up this concept of final victory in this word. Thus the battle of the forces of righteousness versus the forces of evil is symbolized by the word Armageddon. This is the first and only use of the word Armageddon in the scripture.

Some commentators feel that the significance of John's prophecy has been taken too literally and that the tension between good and evil is all that is implied with the resultant triumph of God. Whether one chooses to interpret this text literally or not, the underlying contest is very real.

In these latter days students of religious history see the world lining up into two great camps—those who are for God and those who are for evil. This last great issue which has yet to climax is well described as the "Battle of Armageddon."

73. Book of Revelation Fulfilled

QUESTION

A friend asserts that everything revealed to John on the Isle of Patmos and contained in the book of Revelation has been fulfilled. Is this true? I have always understood that at least chapters 12 and 14 have been fulfilled.

ANSWER

The book of Revelation is known as an apocalyptic work. It was written upon the theme that the forces of righteousness will eventually overcome all evil and the kingdom of God will be set up. This truth was of vital importance to the saints in the days when this writing was done. This most interesting document was undoubtedly of great importance and the meaning clear to those of that period. The sometimes bizarre symbolism would be more easily interpreted by them than by those of later generations.

Some have claimed to give a much more detailed interpretation and have often indulged in speculation. I am of the opinion that the book of Revelation should be first read for the basic message of the prophet of the triumph of truth and righteousness culminating in the conditions so wonderfully portrayed in the last three chapters.

This is important, for unless we approach it in this way we become entangled in a web of detail, preoccupied with the minutiae of every feature of dragons and other weird forms used as symbols. This basic principle of reading for the overall meaning holds for other apocalyptic literature also.

Nevertheless, to keep the particular problem of the question in view I should say that some portions of this work are used as a basis for some of the revelations to the church through Joseph Smith, Jr. Doctrine and Covenants 5:3 and 84:1-4 are undoubtedly built upon the premises of the book of Revelation, chapters 12 to 18. These chapters are concerned with the prophecy of the departure of the early Christian church from the true gospel principles. A beautiful "woman clothed with the sun" is the symbol of the church, the "wilderness" the unfruitful years of apostasy, the "dragon" evil, a "woman clothed in scarlet" an imposter in the place of the first.

The elders of the church have correctly presented this as prophecy fulfilled in many respects, although individuals may have been over-concerned with symbolic details.

It probably would be helpful to say that the book of Revelation had a vital message for the saints living at the time it was written, some of it foreshadowed events that are now history, and some of it pointed to a consummation of divine purpose yet to be realized.

74. Myths

QUESTION

I have been concerned with the use of the word "myth" in the writings of religious texts with reference to studies of the scriptures. I have not believed the word to be in place when referring to scripture. Please discuss.

ANSWER

Probably the writers you refer to are unwise in their choice of a word because of the loose connotation in present usage in the average mind today. The word is often used to imply the fanciful in the sense that a story is purely imaginative and without any real basis in truth.

Accurate, scholarly use of the word "myth" does not imply this. When used in connection with religion and scripture it is used to describe a story told in such a way as to embody a truth which is more important than the story itself. The historicity of the events in the story is not necessarily provable nor need it be. The concept embodied in the legend is the vital thing.

Many people have become confused when studying the scriptures, particularly the Old Testament, because they have regarded them as precise statements at all points, historically and scientifically accurate. This is not sustained because a more thorough analysis often reveals inconsistency of data, whereas the revelation of truth for which the scriptures are preserved remains constant.

Thus, to classify a story as a myth is not necessarily to destroy its importance. It often enhances its value because liberty can be taken with detail to throw light on the truth involved, using allegory and even personification of nature to achieve this.

I think the problem lies in the misuse of the word rather than any reflection upon scripture in its basic revelation of divinity.

75. Age of Earth

QUESTION

How does one reconcile the theory that the earth and its inhabitants are approximately 6,000 years old, as some figure it to be from biblical history, with scientific findings that the earth and its inhabitants are millions of years old?

ANSWER

I do not reconcile the two theories. I am not one of those who believe that the earth is only 6,000 years old. I do not know how long it took to bring the earth on which we live to the state where it would be fit for the habitation of man, nor do I believe this can be accurately figured from the Bible unless one interprets the Old Testament account in such a literal way as to regard the days of Genesis as actual twenty-four-hour periods. To do this presents more problems than it solves.

The "days" of Genesis may represent periods of time, but at least it is clear from the Genesis account that the days are not solar days as the phenomenon of the sun is not a fact until the fourth "day."

That man is stated to have been created in the sixth period does not necessarily imply an instantaneous event. Sometimes people are misled into taking a textual detail and building around it a philosophy of creation which is inconsistent with what we know of God today. God is consistent. This is emphasized in texts like "I am the Lord, I change not" (Malachi 3:6). The creation of human bodies today is a process and requires a period of time, so in my attempts to understand the record of God's works in past ages I reason from what I know of his action today.

In the Hebrew account of creation I note a logical sequence of preparatory developments so that all that was necessary for subsistence of man was there prior to his coming. I note also that the body of the first man was formed and that due to a divine breathing into his nostrils he "became a living soul," which marks a point in time as well as in quality.

Reverently we must say that it is not necessary to present the scripture as a scientific paper on the *modus operandi* of creation. Of all things it is definitely not that. The purpose of Genesis is to reveal God as the creator and to testify that man need not remain out of contact with him and that God moves first to make this communication. This is the great meaning of the Garden of Eden story wherein it is recorded that our first parents "heard the voice of the Lord" and responded. Thereafter man was not alone and knew that though not yet worthy of God's continual presence he might find salvation and thus become worthy.

Many people accept this view, though some do not, but after studying scripture, and in the light of some scientific findings, I look for the revelation of God's will in the recorded words of these scriptures, and not for a scientific treatise. I find this revelation of God consistent with his purposes. I refuse to get entangled in theories of billions of years (which tend to be beyond my finite comprehension), but on the other hand I do not find it necessary to squeeze the creation of this marvelous universe into six days of twenty-four hours each, or of 6,000 years.

As a result of our growing knowledge from explorations like John Glenn's orbital flight, our concept of time may have to be radically revised. The report of three sunrises in five hours certainly does give us food for thought! One wonders what Moses or Elijah would have said to describe this phenomenon! Surely one of old spoke better than he knew when he said "a day is as a thousand years" with the Lord.

There is no room for chance in my concept of creation. To me it speaks of definite purpose—the purpose of a beneficent God.

76. Gospel

QUESTION

What is the actual meaning of the word "gospel"?

ANSWER

Gospel comes from an old Anglo-Saxon word "God-spell." This literally means to tell about God. The word has been given the popular meaning of "good tidings," "good news," or "glad tidings." This usage is based on New Testament texts such as Luke 2:10 and Romans 10:15.

77. Field White for Harvest

QUESTION

What does the statement, "The field is white already for harvest" mean?

ANSWER

This simply means that the crops are ripe and in a condition to be gathered. I presume your difficulty is with the word "white."

Recently in traveling from Independence, Missouri, to a northern wheat state, I had occasion to leave before dawn. Driving along the highway in the freshness of the morning, I noticed the fields of ripening wheat—they were glistening white. This changed with the full light of day, but your question was answered in my own mind. I can imagine that the prophet had this experience, and as inspiration is somewhat colored by the vocabulary of the prophet, he used the words of Jesus in John 4:37 in clothing his perception of the world ready for the harvesting.

Reapers are needed, and the call is to all who have a will to labor. Read the whole of Doctrine and Covenants, Section 11.

78. Sanhedrin

QUESTION

What was the Sanhedrin? Was the apostle Paul a member of this body? I have been told one had to be married to belong to the San-

hedrin. Is there any evidence regarding this that would indicate Paul was married?

Reference to a good encyclopedia will give you more information on the Sanhedrin than space here will permit. A brief answer is that this was a judicial council of elders among the Hebrews. It was the supreme rabbinic court in Jerusalem. The word is a Hebrew version of the Greek "Syedrion" which means "assembly." It was used for the Aeropagus in Athens.

There was the "Great Sanhedrin" and smaller sanhedrins. The first comprised seventy-one members and the second, trial courts of twenty-three members. There was the Mishnaic Sanhedrin comprised of scribes who concerned themselves with interpretation of the Torah (Pentateuch).

The council as described in the Gospels was composed of Pharisees and Sadducees, serving as a secular state council of the high priest. Jesus was brought before this priestly state council. Pontius Pilate sanctioned this council. The Romans executed the sentence. The Sanhedrin was dissolved about A.D. 70. Other forms have been revived through the centuries.

I have never been able to discover any evidence that Paul was a member of the state Sanhedrin. He was a Pharisee and is referred to in Acts 8:1 as consenting to the death of Stephen. I doubt if this is a sufficient clue to membership in the Sanhedrin at Jerusalem.

I have not found evidence of the rule that members of these councils must be married, although, as they were composed of the elders (seniors) and other important persons, it may be deduced that most were.

Authors of historical novels have presented the idea that Paul was married. This is a deductive approach which reasons mainly from certain convictions as expressed by Paul and his obvious intimate acquaintance with feminine characteristics. This is not necessarily so, and I feel the authors have used their literary license too freely at this point. One such work may be quoted *And Walk in Love* by Henrietta Buckmaster, Collancz, London, 1956.

This author overstates her case and implicates Paul in an adulterous relationship which, of course, is quite unfounded and unjust. We cannot depend on such sources. However, they serve to color a possibly erroneous idea which is regrettable. There is no direct statement in scripture that Paul was married or that he was not married. The consensus seems to be that he was not. It is immaterial.

79. Selah

QUESTION

Is the word "selah," found frequently in the Psalms, intended to be read aloud when the psalm is publicly used?

ANSWER

The best information that I can find on this question indicates that the word *selah* is not intended to be spoken. The word was placed in the text of the psalm or at the end as an indication for emphasis. There is a sense in which it was used to indicate that at that point there should be an increase in emphasis by the accompanying music. It is thus a musical or liturgical sign. Being a sign for certain action or response it, therefore, was not intended to be read. Evidently the translators kept the word in the text as explanatory, knowing it had no grammatical connection with the text proper.

80. Kingdom of God Within

QUESTION

Please explain, "The kingdom of God is within you" (Luke 17:21).

ANSWER

A marginal alternative to "within" is given as "among." Another rendering is "in the midst of." Joseph Smith, Jr., expressed it in the Inspired Version as "the kingdom of God has already come unto you." The preceding verse states, "The kingdom of God cometh not with observation." The Pharisees expected a setting up of state power under the Messiah. Jesus said that the kingdom is first a spiritual phenomenon which finds place in men's hearts. In this sense it must be "within." It had already come and was in their midst but had not been perceived. See also Luke 19:11, 12; Acts 1:6-8.

81. Saint

QUESTION

Please give a correct interpretation of the term "Saint."

ANSWER

Psalm 50:5 reads: "Gather my saints together unto me; those that have made a covenant with me by sacrifice."

This text illustrates the Old Testament usage of the word. The basic meaning of the Hebrew from which the word saint is translated is one "set apart" or "holy." Such a person is consecrated to the purposes of God. A saint is therefore one who has covenanted with God to strive toward fulfillment of His standards. Thus the term becomes a description of members of the church.

Paul used it this way in a number of places and repeatedly says in addressing the members, "called to be saints." He gives his delineation of high ethical standards in the letter to the saints at Ephesus, particularly in Chapter 5. In short, the saints are God's people expressing their love for one another in a practical social way and moving always toward that high calling in Jesus Christ.

The medieval church developed the practice of declaring some person a saint a century or so after his demise. This was done as a posthumous honor for those who in the retrospective consideration of the high councils of the church were adjudged worthy of emulation. This is termed canonization and is still featured in the Roman Catholic Church. The emphasis of scripture in both Old and New Testaments is upon a covenant relationship in the fellowship of God's people.

82. Dispensations

QUESTION

Please explain Matthew 20:1-16. Do the various hours represent different dispensations? What relation has "for many are called, but few chosen" to the rest of the text?

ANSWER

This parable has been the subject of different interpretations. The first you have suggested, and the second applies it to the stages of a man's life, and on this some have based a belief in deathbed repentance.

Probably we get into difficulty in an endeavor to make a too detailed application. Parables are used to teach a central truth, and we get help in the consideration of this parable if we look for that truth. For instance, in the parable of the ten virgins there is a central meaning and that is "be ready and in a condition to meet our Lord at all times." To specify meanings for virgins and lamps and oil may be of some help, but if the detail obscures the thought of readiness we miss the great lesson.

Now in the parable of the vineyard the central truth to me is that man's reward is God's gift and that we do not actually merit our pay by anything that we do. Paul says salvation is "not of works, lest any man should boast," and explains that it is the gift of God (Ephesians 2:8-10). This is undoubtedly a reversal of the viewpoint of the laborers in the parable. The master dealt with them justly and according to his loving understanding. Those chosen in the eleventh hour had been standing all day because no one had hired them. It was not their fault. They received the same reward.

This in no way makes nonapplicable a parallel of the world's history being likened to a day. Christ came in the meridian of time and we are in the eleventh hour, but it is not necessary to this premise to align Matthew 20:1-16.

To the second part of your question, I would say that I can see no relation to the lesson. It is interesting to note that these words are not found in the manuscripts of the Sinaiticus, Vaticanus, or Coptic versions. It is thought by some, therefore, to be an insertion transposed from Matthew 22:14. The absence from the oldest manuscripts seems significant. It was retained in the Inspired Version. That it is out of context is obvious; however, the meaning of the quote itself is not under question, but its relevancy here is.

83. Word "Destroy"

QUESTION

What significance is attached to the word "destroy" in Matthew 10:28?

"And fear not them which kill the body, but are not able to kill the soul: but rather fear him which is able to destroy both soul and body in hell."—King James Version.

Does this have any relationship to the second death in Revelation 20? Does it mean that some will cease to exist?

ANSWER

In this text Jesus Christ is emphasizing that his work is not defeated even though his followers may be persecuted to the point of death. He is encouraging his disciples by reminding them that though the body may die the essential person lives on. Flame and sword are powerless to defeat one who knows this, and his behavior is conditioned by his faith. Man is more than a body. Jesus said that he that loses his life for His sake shall find it.

The word soul has several meanings in the New Testament. In this text it undoubtedly means spirit. I do not feel that the word destroy as used here means annihilation of the soul. It has been supposed by some that the one referred to as having the power to destroy the soul is Satan. This is not so in my opinion; I believe it refers to the all-powerfulness of God. Satan is the motivator of the persecution which resulted in many martyrs giving their lives, assured that immortality was a fact. The import of this passage then is not to fear evil but to act in the fear of the omnipotent Father of all in whose hands alone rests the destiny of souls even to their relegation to hell if they are found unfitted for his presence.

The second death of Revelation 20 also must be interpreted in this perspective. Death does not mean annihilation but separation. The last enemy that shall be destroyed is death; that is, Satan will lose his power to separate men from God. In the last analysis, only by our own acts can this occur.

The only difference between the Inspired Version and the King James Version is the substitution of "who" for "which" in the former.

84. Reign of Death

QUESTION

Please explain the meaning of Romans 5:14: "Death reigned from Adam to Moses, even over them that had not sinned after the similitude of Adam's transgression."

ANSWER

The New English Bible renders the passage thus:

"But death held sway from Adam to Moses, even over those who had not sinned as Adam did, by disobeying a direct command—and Adam foreshadows the Man who was to come. But God's act of grace is out of all proportion to Adam's wrongdoing."

On this passage there has been considerable discussion. It has been said that Paul did not explain fully what he intended to say and that we must supply the completion after he digressed. Probably he intended to convey the idea that the great love of God outweighs by abundant grace all the natural results of sin, and though physical death followed transgression, salvation came by Christ. The law was of God before Moses codified it, and though those who had gone before had no specific knowledge of it, in the very nature of its immutability death was the continuing result. Lack of knowledge does not remove the results of sin, yet though all men were not willfully disobedient to a direct command the result was in effect. There was, however, no responsibility, for where there is no knowledge of the law there can be no accountability.

It must be borne in mind that what Paul is really doing is contrasting the results of righteousness in Jesus Christ with the sin of Adam. Thus Christ, who came in the meridian of time (Doctrine and Covenants 36:9 c), performed the works of grace for all men who lived both prior to and after his coming. The last enemy to be destroyed is death (I Corinthians 15:54), and men will be judged only by their own acts when they know good from evil.

Paul as usual is using as an illustration the Hebrews' awareness of law and their concept of justice, but like all those attempting to make analogy complete he gets into difficulty in detail. Nevertheless one can see what he is emphasizing—the saving grace of our Lord Jesus Christ.

85. Corban

QUESTION

Please explain what is meant by "Corban" in the following:

"But ye say, If a man shall say to his father or mother, It is Corban, that is to say, a gift, by whatsoever thou mightest be profited by me; he shall be free."—Mark 7:11, K.J.; 7:13, I.V.

ANSWER

This word was used originally to cover any kind of offering. It came to mean in later Judaism anything that was set apart or dedicated to the service of God. By using the statement "It is Corban," even if it were an impulsive or rash declaration, the article was considered set apart and it could not be used for any other purpose.

A reprehensible practice arose among the Jews in which a person who wanted to avoid the use of money for some implied obligation to another, such as his parents, was allowed to be relieved of his filial obligations by making the declaration. Jesus said the Pharisees and scribes were using this technique where it was to their own advantage, but by so doing they were breaking a more important obligation of the law—that of honoring one's father and mother.

86. Garments

Please explain Deuteronomy 22:5—"The woman shall not wear that which pertaineth unto a man, neither shall a man put on a woman's garment; for all that do so are abomination unto the Lord thy God." Does this apply to slacks and such clothing?

ANSWER

No, it could not refer to slacks in particular because when the text was written slacks or trousers were not worn by either men or women in Palestine.

When interpreting scripture, one should always seek the meaning in terms of principle rather than of a concise rule. Paul stated, "The letter killeth, but the spirit giveth life" (II Corinthians 3:6).

Then again, what is exclusively man's apparel? What is male attire in one country may be female attire in another. The intent of the scripture with which you are concerned is to counsel against posing as a member of the opposite sex. This is for the protection of both sexes. Of course, the text should not be used as a weapon to defend or condemn any particular fashion. Read verse 8 of Deuteronomy 22 and you will find a rule about a battlement being obligatory when building a house. Obviously this applied to local customs and buildings, and was for safety's sake only. The principle in verse 5 also is based on local customs which I hope is clear from my comment.

87. Significance of Forty

QUESTION

Is there any real significance to the number forty as it occurs in Genesis 8:36, Exodus 24:18, and Luke 4:2? Is this number representative in the same sense that seven indicates perfection or completeness?

ANSWER

The literature of the Hebrews and of many other cults abounds in the use of numbers in a symbolic sense. We find many analogies in the use of numbers between the Hebrew scriptures and the old writings of the Egyptians, Canaanites, Hittites, etc. Numbers seem to have been used to convey concepts developed among ancient peoples.

The use of specific numbers was not necessarily intended to convey exact mathematical information. "One" was used in the Hebrew-Christian text to indicate unity as portrayed in God, Christ and God, the church, marriage, etc. Where in modern language we would say "a large number" intending to leave the exact figure unstated, the older cultures preferred to use the exact.

Thus Christ is to come with ten thousand of his saints, and the faithful in another text are reported to be one hundred and forty-four thousand. Following this rule "few" may be indicated by the definite number two, possibly three, or by both, "two or three." Right up the scale of numbers this applies. There are many examples of the use of "four," "seven," "forty," "seventy," and so forth. The underlying concept is difficult to ascertain on many occasions. "Three" holds the concept of completeness—beginning, middle, and end—as does seven. Among ancient Egyptians and Babylonians "four" was a significant number originating, it is thought, from the concept of the four compass directions. Multiples of four therefore take on significance and we have forty days, forty years, forty thousand, and so on. Forty years in Hebrew culture was a generation—hence forty years in the wilderness, illustrating a period of crisis or difficulty or period of a fast or punishment as well as the keeping of a watch.

The reason behind these numbers is not easy to ascertain, but they conveyed something to their users—subtle meanings that have been largely submerged in time with only the usage remaining. One would be superstitious to attach significance to any given number today. The only interest in their historical sense is in the possible help they might give in ascertaining what they were meant to convey at the time. They hold no magical insights or powers. As stated, their significance is difficult to discern today.

88. Agreeing with Adversary

QUESTION

Please explain the meaning of Matthew 5:27, 28—

"Agree with thine adversary quickly, while thou art in the way with him; lest at any time thine adversary deliver thee to the judge, and the judge deliver thee to the officer, and thou be cast into prison.

"Verily I say unto thee, thou shalt by no means come out thence, until thou hast paid the uttermost farthing."

—and a similar text in III Nephi 5:73-75.

I have always considered the meaning to be that one should not let difficulties develop to a point where they will bring greater distress than if dealt with early. One should not allow dissension to grow and thus widen the gap between brethren. If the law given concerning offences is kept (see Matthew 18:15) much pain and suffering of soul is avoided. A quarrel seldom extends without wrong occurring on both sides, and the sooner reconciliation is achieved the less there is to reconcile. These texts hold the idea of a judge and penalty which surely will be involved if brotherliness is not practiced. While we are human there will be offenses but saintly reaction enables brotherliness to be maintained.

The results of disagreement are perhaps minor at the onset compared with the greater price paid in the long run of unadjusted problems. Hence the reference to payment of the uttermost farthing.

89. Contradictory Texts

Two texts in the New Testament confuse me. First, Matthew 15:12 states, "Every plant which my heavenly Father hath not planted, shall be rooted up." Then Luke 9:50 states, ". . . for he who is not against us is for us." Are these not contradictory?

These texts are not contradictory. They have different applications. Both statements must be read in context. In the first instance the reading of the earlier verses shows that the disciples had informed Jesus that the Pharisees were offended by him when he answered their criticism of his disciples for not performing certain washings. Jesus in turn reprimanded them for not giving honor to the commands of God regarding respect to parents, thus making the commandments of no effect themselves. He said that it is not what and how a man eats that is important but what issues from his heart. Jesus' followers were overly concerned about the reaction of the Pharisees to his rebuke, but the Master assured them that in the long run only that which was planted by God would survive. It was not to be their particular responsibility to take the initiative in the rooting up but to "let them alone" because their unsound teachings would fall. Verse 14 says that because they were blind they would fall into the ditch. On another occasion he advised not rooting up the tares until the final separation of good and evil at reaping time.

The second text is concerned with another point. It cannot fully parallel Matthew 15:12 because that refers to the Pharisees who were at this point enemies of God's law. The text in Luke is undoubtedly pointed toward a narrow concept of the disciples concerning their authority as ordained representatives of the Master. They had taken the attitude that God could work only through them. Previous verses indicate preoccupation with their own status, and Jesus gave them an example of humility in placing a little child before them. The idea behind this teaching was the same that was expressed by inspiration through the late E. A. Smith at the Lamoni Conference of November, 1917: "I have many spiritual forces at work that you know not of."

There is, however, a common principle invoked in both texts: the pursuance of positive righteousness and the effecting of one's commission through constructive activity guarantees the ultimate success of the kingdom. Attacking or criticizing others, whether they be persons or groups, is a time-wasting occupation that prevents the fulfillment of our mission. This comment does not ignore the fact that at times it is necessary to point out error that truth may be the better understood.

90. Christ's Message Universal

QUESTION

Why did Christ say, "I am not sent but unto the lost sheep of the house of Israel"? If his message is universal, is this not contradictory?

ANSWER

The person to whom the statement was made (Matthew 15:21-27) was not of Israelitish descent. She is described as a Canaanite by Matthew and as a Greek by Mark (Mark 7:26). Christ was in the area of Tyre and Sidon when he spoke these words. He had gone there for rest and not primarily for ministry. He did not deny the blessing of healing which the woman sought, but he emphasized that his primary mission was to Israel. This was the plan—to commence the gospel proclamation in Israel. This was his primary task.

Jesus cleverly turned the request into an opportunity to demonstrate that it is not nationality or race that counts. He took the Jewish saying, "It is not meet to take the children's food and give it to the dogs" and put it to his Jewish followers in the form of a question. This no doubt brought home a lesson his followers needed to learn.

Christ at that time knew that the church would have to delay its foreign missionary task until it was endowed with power. One of the marks of Pentecost was breaking the barriers of tongues and race. Peter had to receive a vision before the fact that God was no respecter of persons was fully brought to his realization (Acts 10:34, 35).

No, the text does not deny the universality of the gospel, for the fact that Christ healed the woman testifies to this. However, he was content to initiate the work of salvation and to leave the wider responsibility of going into all the world to the church that he instituted, which was to be known by his name.

91. Christmas Tree Tradition

Does the text of Jeremiah 10:3, 4, refer to the Christmas tree tradition? If so are we not involved in a practice which is not approved in the scriptures?

ANSWER

Jeremiah 10:3, 4, reads as follows:

"For the customs of the people are vain; for one cutteth a tree out of the forest, the work of the hands of the workman, with the axe. They deck it with silver and with gold; they fasten it with nails and with hammers, that it move not."

These words have no reference whatsoever to the Christmas trees which are decked with ornaments in the traditional style. Jeremiah is here proclaiming against the worship of idols. If you examine the text carefully you will see that the prophet is speaking of idols that are carved from wood and decked with precious metals. These, being only gods of wood and metal and made by the hands of humans, in comparison with Jehovah are worthless, the prophet says.

Later verses state that these idols of wood have to be supported by fastening with nails with the use of hammers and even have to be carried wherever they must be taken. Jeremiah tells the people to note that they can bring neither evil nor good, and therefore exhorts them not to fear them.

96

Verses 6 through 25 present a wonderful contrast between the heathen idols and the all-powerful Jehovah. The Revised Standard Version gives Jeremiah 10 in metric form, and a lovely poem or hymn is the result.

Since this text has no reference to the Christmas tree tradition it obviously is no basis for regarding the decking of a Christmas tree as contrary to scriptural pronouncement.

92. Game of Chance

QUESTION

Acts 1:26 states that the successor to the apostle Judas was chosen by casting lots. Does this mean that Matthias was chosen to this important work by something like the throwing of dice as in a game of chance?

ANSWER

The text in full reads:

"And they gave forth their lots; and the lot fell upon Matthias; and he was numbered with the eleven apostles."—Acts 1:26.

The procedure involved cannot be exactly determined. Undoubtedly "casting lots" was a custom of great antiquity among the Hebrews. It has been suggested that the text may simply mean that a vote was taken. This, of course, is to read a modern meaning into an ancient practice.

References to the practice by both the Hebrews and pagans are to be found in the Old Testament. The pagan usage was to cast lots to obtain oracles (Esther 3:7). This is the light in which the practice first appears among the Israelites, but it differs from pagan magic in that the priest inquired of Jehovah upon the basis that he would guide the casting. Other gods were false. The method was either to cast stones upon the ground or to draw them from a bag or pocket in the ceremonial vest which the priest wore. Actually this procedure was known by the Hebrews as seeking guidance through Urim and Thummim. The Old Testament practice involved a simple choice between two alternatives (I Samuel 23:9-12; 30:7, 8).

Joshua 18:6-8 describes how the inheritances of seven of the tribes were selected by the casting of lots. Here is seen the origin of calling a piece of land "a lot." Verse 6 states that the lots were

97

cast "before the Lord our God." Deuteronomy 18:10-12, in condemning all forms of divination, does not include lot casting.

It is interesting to note in scripture that the last account of an occasion when lots were used to determine God's will is in Acts 1:26, the basis of your question. After this, reliance is placed on the Holy Spirit (Acts 13:2). This is a natural development as with greater spiritual insight dependence on mechanical means becomes unnecessary. Between the occasions Acts 1 and 13 the endowment of Pentecost intervened. A parallel might be seen in that after the Melchisedec priesthood was in effect in the Restoration, revelation came not by means of the interpreters but increasingly by intelligent study and prayer (Doctrine and Covenants 9).

God evidently dealt with the early saints in terms of their own understanding. Before the Pentecostal endowment the lots method evidently was considered valid. It was not magic but God in action seen through a medium which they could understand.

93. Wine Fermented

QUESTION

What would be Paul's reason for advising Timothy to cease drinking water and instead to use a little wine for his stomach's sake? Was the wine in those days fermented?

ANSWER

I give the text in full:

"Drink no longer water, but use a little wine for thy stomach's sake and thine often infirmities."—A.V., I Timothy 5:23.

The rendering in the Inspired Version is the same, but the verse is removed from its position between verse 22 and 24 and placed as verse 25. This is an interesting fact because Moffatt makes the comment that this verse is either a marginal gloss or misplaced. Joseph Smith in his study of the Authorized Version text evidently came to the conclusion that it more naturally followed verse 25 of the Authorized Version. Moffatt renders the verse in the margin:

"Give up being a total abstainer; take a little wine for the sake of your stomach and your frequent attacks of illness."

The Revised Standard Version gives the following:

"No longer drink only water, but use a little wine for the sake of your stomach and your frequent ailments."

I believe there is no basis for assuming that the wine of the time was nonalcoholic. It would appear to the contrary that it was alcoholic. It is helpful to note that Paul makes mention of Timothy's frequent ailments which obviously have to do with his stomach. In those days wine was considered medicinal as well as a beverage and was frequently prescribed for a variety of ailments. Paul was vigorous in his opposition to gnostic asceticism, a heresy with which he took every opportunity to deal. Purity, he says, is not due to such observances (verse 22).

Paul does not intend to uphold wine as an alcoholic beverage for pleasure. His emphasis here is on health, and when an ascetic cult or belief denies what is medicinally helpful he does not hesitate to counsel the saints to accept the prescription.

The question of the medical opinion as to the use of wine as a medicine in modern times is not here in question. At least it was believed to be of value in Paul's day.

The use of this text as an excuse for modern indulgence in alcoholic beverages is fallacious. The argument for abstinence from alcohol as a beverage rests upon more solid ground than a text reflecting the customs of the first century after Christ. The social consequences of alcoholic drinking are evident in our day. This is apparent without resort to scripture, but when we have the counsel of modern revelation in addition to our own observations of its tragic and evil results we may be sure that the use of alcoholic beverages is not saintly.

Doctrine and Covenants 119:3 d states: "Avoid the use of tobacco and be not addicted to strong drink in any form."

There have been many arguments concerning the text in Timothy as to the necessity of drinking, some because of the unhealthful water in the Bible lands. These may have their merits, but to see the instruction in the light of the facts here given is to see it in the setting and circumstances surrounding it.

94. Lord of the Sabaoth

QUESTION

What is the meaning of the phrase "Lord of the Sabaoth"? Is this a reference to the day of rest? How is the word Sabaoth pronounced?

The pronunciation is Săb'ĭ-ŏth. The original Hebrew meaning of this is "army host." A free interpretation is "host of heaven." There are a number of texts in scripture which use the latter "hosts of heaven." It is difficult to be specific as to what is referred to because on different occasions it may have slightly different meanings.

An ancient pagan concept was that all the heavenly bodies were animated by spirits and were thus "heavenly hosts," celestial bodies. Sometimes the references imply angels, and in others, the armies of the Lord.

Briefly, it may be said that "Lord of the Sabaoth" means the lordship of Jehovah over all the powers of heaven and earth. The early Hebrew idea was not always that there was only one God but that Jehovah was over all. There was room in primitive Hebrew thinking for other gods, but not for one in supremacy other than the God of Abraham, Isaac, and Jacob. The Hebrews grew in their concepts of divinity until Jehovah was understood to be the only true God.

The word "Sabbath" comes from a different Hebrew root, meaning "to cease, to abstain, to desist from, to terminate." Thus the day on which the Hebrews were commanded to rest was termed the Sabbath. This terminated the work of the preceding six days. According to Genesis, God ended his work on the Sabbath. This is the Jewish connotation. Other religious cults have institutionalized the Sabbath, e.g. Babylonia.

"Sabaoth" appears twice in the scriptures Romans 9:29 and James 5:4. The word "Sabbath" occurs scores of times as reference to a good concordance will quickly show.

The Book of Mormon

95. Book of Mormon Editions

QUESTION

In what years were the editions of the Book of Mormon in the early church published?

ANSWER

The first edition of the Book of Mormon is known as the Palmyra edition. It was printed in 1830 by E. B. Grandin of Palmyra, New York.

The second edition was published in 1837. In the preface of this edition it is stated that many errors had been detected and corrected. Joseph Smith did the reviewing himself, assisted by Oliver Cowdery. It was printed in Kirtland, Ohio, by Oliver Cowdery and Company for P. P. Pratt and J. Goodson.

The third edition was published in 1840 at Nauvoo, Illinois. It was printed by Robinson and Smith from stereotype plates made by Shepherd and Stearns of Cincinnati, Ohio.

In 1841 an English printing was made in Liverpool from the 1837 edition, and in 1842 a second printing from the stereotyped plates was made in Nauvoo.

These are the only editions published in the lifetime of Joseph Smith, Jr.

96. When Arranged in Chapter and Verse Style

QUESTION

At what point or time was the Book of Mormon arranged in chapter and verse style? Was the 1830 edition arranged as we have it today? Who did the arranging? Did Joseph Smith check the work?

ANSWER

The first edition of the Book of Mormon (Palmyra, 1830) was arranged in chapters. The text was arranged in paragraphs, many of which were long. Paragraphs were unnumbered. This applies to each of the early American editions. Parley P. Pratt published an edition in England in 1849 which made some changes in the length of paragraphs. Another edition was published in England in 1852 by F. D. Richards in which the paragraphs were numbered for the first time, the length of the paragraphs remaining the same.

J. O. Wright and Company published an edition in New York in 1858. This was taken from the third American edition and had no numbered paragraphs. Before the Reorganized Church was in a position to publish the book on its own press the work published by Wright and Company was used, a number of unsold copies being purchased from the publishers. This edition is known also as the Z. Brooks edition.

In 1874 an edition was printed at Plano, Illinois; the third American edition was the source. About thirty editions were printed at Lamoni, Iowa, from the plates of the 1874 Plano edition with printing dates from 1880 until the authorization of the present edition by the General Conference of 1906. At that Conference the following resolution was passed:

"Whereas, There are several editions of the Book of Mormon extant, differing in divisions of chapters and paragraphs, thereby rendering it impossible to prepare concordance and works of reference, therefore,

"Resolved, That we recommend . . . the appointment of a committee . . . to investigate and prepare a uniform plan for the divisions of chapters and verses, and, if thought advisable, to prepare or adopt a system of references."

—*Journal of History*, Volume 14, page 29

This was done, and what is known as the Authorized Version appeared in 1908.

The editorial committee had the advantage of being able to compare with the original manuscript which came into the possession of the Reorganized Church in 1903.

The versification of the Authorized Version of 1908 has remained unchanged. The Utah church has changed the arrangement of chapters, but the Reorganized Authorized edition maintains the chapters as in the original manuscript, though as stated the paragraphs have been rearranged into verses of a size suitable for easy reference.

A previous attempt to versify was made in 1892 when a large edition (7 inches by 10 inches) was published. The arrangement of the Authorized Version is a marked improvement on this.

Considerable information is available in the preface of the Authorized Version to which I suggest you refer.

97. Who Has Original Manuscript

QUESTION

Who has the original manuscript of the Book of Mormon?

ANSWER

The Reorganized Church has the only complete manuscript in existence.

There were two original manuscripts. The first was as dictated to various scribes when it was translated from the original plates. These scribes included Joseph's wife, Emma, Oliver Cowdery, and others. Oliver Cowdery made a second copy before any manuscript was taken to the printer. Thus before printing there were two manuscripts.

One of these was placed in the cornerstone of the Nauvoo House, and the other was in the care of Oliver Cowdery. The one placed in the cornerstone was uncovered when the Nauvoo House was remodeled by Major Bidamon. It was found to have deteriorated due to moisture. Part of this was given to Joseph Smith, son of the founder, and part was given to the Utah church president. The part given to the son soon disintegrated, and the other part was partially preserved in Utah. Leaders of the Utah church claim that a further portion of 130 pages came into their hands.

The manuscript kept by Cowdery remained intact through many situations. On his death it was given to his brother-in-law David Whitmer. After Whitmer's death it was kept by his family until George Schweich brought it to the Reorganized Church in whose possession it remains.

This copy has several handwritings which indicates that it is at least a portion (approximately two thirds) of the first copy. Some of this copy bears the printer's marks, which indicate that parts were in the printer's hands. It is in a good state of preservation and in a

Kansas City bank vault for preservation and security. A photostatic copy is used for reference.

98. Title and Testimony

QUESTION

In my Book of Mormon there is a two-paragraph statement on the page immediately preceding the testimonies of the three and the eight witnesses. Did Joseph Smith write this or was this material taken from the plates? Also, where did the title "Book of Mormon" originate?

ANSWER

In his "History of Joseph Smith," published in *Times and Seasons,* Volume III, Number 24, October 15, 1842, page 943, Joseph Smith made the following statement, which needs little by way of added comment to answer both of your questions:

". . . Therefore, in order to correct an error which generally exists concerning it, I give below that part of the title page of the English version of the Book of Mormon, which is a genuine and literal translation of the title page of the original Book of Mormon, as recorded on the plates.

"THE BOOK OF MORMON

"An account written by the hand of Mormon,
upon plates, taken from the plates of Nephi.
"Wherefore it is an abridgement of the record of the people of Nephi, and also of the Lamanites; written to the Lamanites, who are a remnant of the house of Israel; and also to Jew and Gentile: written by way of commandment, and also by the spirit of prophecy and of revelation.
"Written, and sealed up, and hid up unto the Lord, that they might not be destroyed; to come forth by the gift and power of God unto the interpretation thereof; sealed by the hand of Moroni, and hid up unto the Lord, to come forth in due time by the way of Gentile; the interpretation thereof by the gift of God.
"An abridgement taken from the book of Ether, also; which is a record of the people of Jared; who were scattered at the time the Lord confounded the language of the people when they were building a tower to get to heaven: which is to shew

unto the remnant of the house of Israel what great things the Lord hath done for their fathers, and that they may know the covenants of the Lord, that they are not cast off forever; and also to the convincing of the Jew and Gentile that Jesus is the Christ, the eternal God, manifesting himself unto all nations. And now if there are faults, they are the mistakes of men; wherefore, condemn not the things of God, that ye may be found spotless at the judgment seat of Christ."

The remainder of the title page is, of course, modern.

The two paragraphs referred to in your first question were part of the title page to the original 1830 Palmyra edition of the Book of Mormon. They were also printed as part of the copyright certificate on the reverse side of that page, over the inscription of R. R. Lansing, clerk of the Northern District of New York, in keeping with copyright laws.

Since the 1830 Palmyra edition, these paragraphs have undergone a number of minor changes in punctuation, capitalization, and grammar as they have been included in various editions. Note that in the above *Times and Seasons* transcription the material was printed in three paragraphs instead of the otherwise customary two.

Joseph's statement from *Times and Seasons* leaves no doubt as to the origin of the title. The title came from the plates from which the rest of the book was taken.

99. Literal Translation

QUESTION

Was the Book of Mormon a literal word-for-word translation of the characters?

ANSWER

Various opinions have been held about this. Early statements were made not based on firsthand acquaintance with the facts or by direct observation. It is often hard at this distance in time to decide what is primary and what is secondary testimony.

I regard Emma Smith as a most reliable witness, even to her last years. Her memory like her handwriting remained remarkably firm. It was she who wrote of a second instrument other than the so-called Urim and Thummim. It was she who said Joseph "translated" with the plates wrapped up and at a distance from him. David Whitmer speaks of a visual presentation indicating verbal detail. I personally think this was not from direct observation because he could not have seen the transcription in the darkened interior of the hat of which he and Emma speak.

Passages used in the Book of Mormon and also in the Inspired Version differ so greatly that I fear one cannot hold to a verbal accuracy in detail. In Isaiah 48 there are more than fifty differences between the Inspired Version and the Book of Mormon text. These are problems of the inclusion of French and Latin words and strange grammatical construction. One does not have to take the position that truth is always expressed in the same words. After intimate contact with the manuscript, I am of the opinion that the most plausible theory is that the work was conceptual rather than plenary. There are difficulties in both positions. It is significant that when asked by Hyrum Smith before a council to state how the work was done, Joseph Smith declined to say more than that it was done through the instruments "by the power of God."

I do not wish to be dogmatic but merely to state a well-considered opinion.

100. Translator or Author

QUESTION

I notice in comparing my present Book of Mormon with an original 1830 Palmyra edition that Joseph Smith had been variously described as a translator in the former and as author and proprietor in the latter. Please explain why this is so.

ANSWER

In June, 1829, when Joseph Smith registered the Book of Mormon title page with the clerk of the Northern District of New York he no doubt read that portion of the law which spoke of "securing to *authors and proprietors* copies of their maps, charts, and books." He saw that the terminology did not include translators as such, since the original (if contemporary) author would be secured under copyright protection, not the translator.

However, Joseph was faced with the fact that all the original authors of this compilation of books were dead and therefore not subject to copyright statutes. It is easy to see how he would use the very language of the law itself in describing his connection with the Book of Mormon on its title page of the 1830 edition. To be consistent, this same phrase, "author and proprietor," was repeated in the copyright certificate on the reverse side of the title page and also in the testimony of the eight witnesses.

Reference to the preface of the 1830 edition clearly demonstrates that there was no confusion in Joseph's mind as to his relationship to the Book of Mormon. The word "translate" or some form of it is used four times in describing Joseph's work on this body of scripture. This preface, which includes portions of Section 3 of the Doctrine and Covenants, leaves no doubt that Joseph wanted himself to be known as a translator, not as an author, as the title page, copyright certificate, and testimony of eight witnesses described him.

The title page and the testimony of the eight witnesses, printed in the second edition of the Book of Mormon (Kirtland, 1837) describes Joseph as a translator. He has been so described in every subsequent edition to date.

Perhaps one reason for the change was that by 1837 publishers were no longer printing such lengthy copyright certificates in their books, including the language of the law, as had been the case in 1829. There was no reason for Joseph and the witnesses to continue referring to him as author and translator, since by 1837 publishers on the reverse side of the title page were simply inscribing, "Entered according to Act of Congress." In the absence of this indirect influence or pressure to be consistent with the language of a law no longer printed in books, the editors of the Book of Mormon logically described Joseph, on the title page as well as in the testimony of the eight witnesses, as translator—a designation he chose repeatedly to use in the 1830 preface.

101. Book of Mormon Copyright

QUESTION

I see the church histories, Doctrine and Covenants, and the Inspired Version of the Holy Scriptures are copyrighted. Where would one go about finding the copyright on the Book of Mormon translated by Joseph Smith, Jr.? Is it in the copyright office of the Library of Congress, Washington, D. C.? A listing on the Library of Congress Catalog of printed cards gives the imprint date of the third European edition of the Book of Mormon as 1852. What about the copyright?

ANSWER

When the Book of Mormon was registered under the United States copyright law of the period, it was done under the Acts of 1790 and 1802. These statutes required registration, imprinted notice, published announcement, and deposit of a copy of the work in a public place.

In 1831 the copyright laws were amended in certain minor details, although the basic requirements were similar. Extra provision was made for the depositing of a copy of a book with the Secretary of State. This was a federal office. The requirement, previously held for the printing in full of the copyright statement as found on the back of the title page of the 1830 edition of the Book of Mormon, was relaxed by this 1831 revision and merely required a statement as found in the 1837 edition of the Book of Mormon. This reads:

"Entered according to the act of Congress, in the year 1829, by Joseph Smith, Jr. in the Clerks office of the Northern District of New York."

The earlier acts required a statement by the author and proprietor with a full description of the work. These words do not appear in texts after 1831.

For details of the copyright laws of the United States, I suggest you write to the United States Government Printing Office, Washington, D. C., where you may obtain a copy of a brochure on the studies of a subcommittee of the judiciary on patents, trademarks, and copyrights, printed in 1960. The only place I know you can have ready access to the first document of copyright is in the first edition of the Book of Mormon, where it is printed in detail.

The only reason I can suggest that the Library of Congress Catalog gives only the imprint date of the third European edition is that probably that was the first edition lodged there under the act of 1831. The 1837 edition was issued before the expiration of fourteen years, which period was covered by the initial copyright which was not lodged in the State Department. I have found no record of a renewal of copyright by Joseph Smith or his assigns. This application must have been made within a period of six months prior to the expiration of the first registration; if not, the copyright would have lapsed and the book would have come within "public domain." One extension of fourteen years only was allowed, after which a work was in "public domain." The application for renewal of copyright could be made only by the author or his assigns.

English copyright, after the act of 1838, required registration at Stationers' Hall, which was the guild of printers. English law provided recognition and copyright protection only if this registration had been made.

An examination of all editions of the Book of Mormon, 1841 through 1854 in particular, published in England indicate they were registered at Stationers' Hall. All editions in Nauvoo are under the copyright of 1829.

108

The first edition printed in the United States after Nauvoo, 1842, was published after the copyright had expired, even taking into consideration any possibility that there was a renewal which we have not been able to discover. This first American edition after Nauvoo, 1842, was the Huntley edition of 1858.

102. Why Not Records in Other Continents

QUESTION

If the ancient inhabitants of America left a record such as the Book of Mormon, why did not the people of Africa, Asia, and other continents leave records? Do we expect any to be discovered?

ANSWER

There are millions of unanswered questions beginning with the word "why." Why God chose to work through certain channels may be unexplainable though we may attempt some solution in our own thinking. History seems to indicate that God chose a people as a nucleus and that the process of his kingdom is one of growth by expansion—that is, by spreading the gospel to the nations of the earth.

The fact that the Book of Mormon people were of the house of Israel makes the two records—the Bible and the Book of Mormon—one. Perhaps one could say that the four records comprising the Old and New Testaments with the records of Joseph and of the Jaredites comprise a simple line of a sacred interpretation of history.

Who knows but what other records of God's dealings may yet be found, such as the discovery of the Dead Sea Scrolls version of already existent records? The idea of other people having records was no doubt in the mind of the early leaders of the church. This led some to a hasty acceptance of some parchments in other forms of writing such as what is known today as the Book of Abraham. Because of this susceptibility, attempts were made to impose fraud on the early leaders as in the case of the Kinderhook plates, but fortunately no attempt to translate them was published. I raise this as a speculation, as an attempt to answer, but I do not think it necessary to God's plan. I feel that the plan of God was one of gradual growth of his kingdom in the hearts of men, starting with the chosen people, down through the Christian dispensation, and finally until the "earth shall be full of the knowledge of the Lord, as the waters cover the sea." Because of this belief I do not look for the specific revealment of records from Africa and Asia. Some may consider that the sealed portion of the plates hold some mysteries, but it would appear that they contained matters of import regarding the same lineal lines as the rest. I do not know.

It seems the important thing is that we recognize our obligation to take the revealed gospel into all the earth—and in this we have hardly begun to respond. God desires this because he is no respecter of persons.

103. Belief in Book of Mormon

QUESTION

Is it necessary for me to believe in the Book of Mormon to be saved?

ANSWER

I find no scripture or support in logic for the view that one must believe in the Book of Mormon *per se* to obtain salvation. This would also be the answer had you asked whether it is necessary for one to believe in the Bible to attain salvation.

However, I hasten to add that insofar as the eternal truths necessary for one's salvation are contained in the Book of Mormon or the Bible, then acceptance of those truths is essential. The mere assent to a principle, however, does not save a person. The gospel as revealed in the texts mentioned suggests a way of life which, if followed, will lead on to perfection.

Since Joseph Smith stated in answer to Mr. Wentworth, editor of the *Chicago Democrat* in 1842, that we believe that the Bible contains the word of God, we have always taken this position with regard to the Bible and Book of Mormon.

Salvation is not in the books but in the practice of their eternal truths. As to the value of the Book of Mormon teachings, the text itself suggests a personal seeking, through prayer, for the truth of the principles taught. Belief in the historical fact of the Bible or Book of Mormon is quite different from belief in and compliance with the principles taught therein.

104. Urim and Thummim

QUESTION

When do the words "Urim and Thummim" first appear in Latter

Day Saint church literature? Did Joseph Smith use them at the time he was translating the Book of Mormon?

ANSWER

To the best of my information and knowledge, the first occasion in which the words "Urim and Thummim" appeared in our church literature was in *The Evening and the Morning Star*, Volume I, Number 8, Independence, Missouri, January, 1833. The pages of this publication were not numbered, but the reference appears on the second page of this issue. Had the pages been consecutively numbered in Volume I, the page would be No. 58. I give the reference in sufficient context to be helpful:

> "The Book of Mormon, as a revelation from God, possesses some advantage over the old scripture: it has not been tinctured with the wisdom of man, with here and there an Italic word to supply deficiencies—It was translated by the power of God, by an unlearned man, through the aid of a pair of Interpreters, or spectacles—(known, perhaps, in ancient days as Teraphim, or Urim and Thummim) . . ."

The article from which this is taken is unsigned but evidently appeared under the sponsorship of the editor, W. W. Phelps. Though opinions may be held that Phelps or some other wrote it, undoubtedly it is the official explanation of the coming forth of the Book of Mormon. The caption of the article is "The Book of Mormon."

The next use of the term "Urim and Thummim" was in the *Messenger and Advocate*, October, 1834, published in Kirtland, Ohio. It did not appear in any text of the earlier revelations until the first edition of the Doctrine and Covenants, 1835. Consequently we do not find it used in the partial printing of the book that was to be known as the Book of Commandments.

It is interesting to note that the writer of the reference of 1833 which I have given made a parenthetical explanation of the Interpreters, stating that they were "perhaps" what was known of old as "Teraphim" or "Urim and Thummim." Later the words in question were used generally to describe the instrument used in translation. Joseph Smith himself used the term when describing the events of his early spiritual experience when he commenced publication of his history in 1842. Apart from the fact that he must have approved the insertion of the words in the 1835 Doctrine and Covenants edition of the early revelations, we have no direct record of his using the words earlier than his history published in 1842.

111

The use of the word "perhaps" indicates an uncertainty as to whether Interpreters and Urim and Thummim were identical, especially as the word "Teraphim" is also given as an alternative. A "Teraphim" was a small idol of Babylonish culture, and Ezekiel 21:21 includes it as among the methods used for "divination." Zechariah 10:2 speaks of it as a source of false prophecy.

Some have felt that in their efforts to identify the means used by Joseph Smith the description Urim and Thummim was wrongly accepted. Their concern would seem justified if the Interpreters were considered in the same light as the Teraphim. Whether the term was correctly applied or not is not so important, but it seems there is no evidence that the term "Urim and Thummim" was in use in the immediate years following the discovery of the plates.

105. Doctrine and Covenants and Urim and Thummim

QUESTION

It was stated by the teacher of our church school class that the first few sections of the Doctrine and Covenants were received through the Urim and Thummim. Is this a fact? If so, will you cite authoritative references?

ANSWER

Your teacher was correct in his statement. You will find reference to this in *A Commentary on the Doctrine and Covenants* by F. H. Edwards, page 67.

This statement is based upon a study of the "History of Joseph Smith" which appeared in sequence in issues of the *Times and Seasons,* Volume III, published in Nauvoo in 1842. It is generally accepted that the revelations so received are sections two through sixteen. Section 1 was given at Hiram, Ohio, on November 1, 1831, as a preface to the first book of revelations and commandments about to be printed.

There is frequent mention in *Times and Seasons,* Volume III, of the fact that the Urim and Thummim was used up to June, 1829, when it is believed to have been given up with the other sacred things. David Whitmer bears testimony of this in his book, *Address to All Believers* (page 32).

There is no mention of this instrument after Section 16 (June, 1829) and the next dated revelation is March, 1830 (Section 18). The following references state definitely that certain sections were received through the Urim and Thummim: *Times and Seasons,* Volume III, page 786 (Section 2); page 801 (Section 3); page 832 (Section 6); page 853 (Section 7); page 866 (Section 10); page 885 (sections 12, 13, 14). Because of the methods being clearly stated in these instances and the fact that the last reference to the instruments was in June, 1829, it is logical to conclude that the same procedure applied to all communications up to that date. After 1829 it is not so indicated.

It should be mentioned, however, that in the English publication, *Millennial Star* (July, 1842, page 47), a statement is made that the Book of Abraham was being translated by the Urim and Thummim. In our opinion this is a misstatement as no corroboration is found in *Joseph Smith's History* or in the *Times and Seasons,* then under his control in 1842.

106. Interpreters or Directors

QUESTION

In the latest RLDS edition of the Book of Mormon, Alma 17:56 reads: "And now my son, these directors were prepared, that the word of God might be fulfilled . . ." A Utah church edition, Alma 37:24, 25, uses the word interpreters instead of the word directors. Which is faithful to the original manuscript?

ANSWER

The original manuscript in possession of the Reorganized Church uses the word "directors" in the text you refer to. A comparison with the 1830 edition and all others published by the early church and the Reorganization shows the word "directors" to be used without exception.

All the Utah church editions up to 1920 followed the same rendering of the text, and it was at that time that the alteration to "interpreters" was made.

In the manuscript the word "directors" is plainly written and there is no indication of indecision, afterthought, or revision which is sometimes evident as a result of proofreading. One such occasion was when the scribe had written *Messiah* and the translator had said *Mosiah.* This necessitated the word "Mosiah" being written above the erroneous word. Nothing of that kind appears in the case of the question you raise.

113

107. Spaulding Manuscript

QUESTION

In church school class the "Spalding manuscript" was mentioned. What is it, and if there is a manuscript, is it in the possession of the Reorganized Church? Is it available in printed form?

ANSWER

The so-called Spalding manuscript is a romance written by Reverend Solomon Spalding (sometimes spelled Spaulding) who was born in Connecticut in 1761. He died in 1816 at the age of fifty-five. He was engaged in several secular occupations, mercantile and industrial, following a period as a minister and as a teacher. He had a leaning to literary work and when living in Conneaut, Ohio, wrote a story claiming to be a history of the wars between the Indians of Ohio and Kentucky. He appears to have shared his work with his neighbors as he wrote it, so that a number of people were able to pretend to have familiarity with the text. He hoped to reestablish his impaired financial position by publishing the story, but the publication did not materialize.

Later, opponents of the Book of Mormon were to accuse Joseph Smith of plagiarizing this work of Solomon Spalding, the accurate title of which was "The Manuscript Story."

E. D. Howe of Painesville, Ohio, seems to have been the first to publish this accusation of plagiarism in his book, *Mormonism Unveiled,* in 1834. D. P. Hurlbut, an associate of Howe, joined in gathering stories to support this charge.

Because the manuscript was not printed, the public had little chance of refuting the testimony of those who declared the Book of Mormon to be a copy, and for many years the story was used to discredit Joseph Smith.

In 1884 a Mr. L. L. Rice discovered the Spalding story manuscript in a large collection of books and papers originally owned by Howe and sold in 1839-40. Howe had borrowed it and never returned it to the author. This in itself would indicate Howe's knowledge that his claim was false. The collection of material had by this time (1884) been transferred to Honolulu. Mr. Rice eventually deposited his find with Professor Fairchild for the library of Oberlin College, Oberlin, Ohio, where it is today.

Later Mr. Rice was to write in a letter to Joseph Smith III (March

28, 1885): "I am of the opinion that no one who reads this manuscript will give credit to the story that Solomon Spalding was in any wise the author of the Book of Mormon."

In a letter to Joseph Smith III, dated May 14, 1885, Mr. Rice also said, "My opinion is from all I have seen and heard, that this is the only writing of Spalding."

A letter to C. J. Hunt from Professor James H. Fairchild, Oberlin College, February 27, 1892, and now in the Reorganized Church archives states, "There is no reasonable basis for a claim that the Book of Mormon originated in this manuscript."

Later the manuscript was made available for publication, and the Reorganized Church published it in 1885. It is out of print now, but many copies are in private libraries as well as in the Church Historian's Office at the Auditorium in Independence, Missouri.

No longer do informed people present the arguments invented by Hurlbut and Howe.

108. Book of Mormon and Isaiah

QUESTION

How could the Book of Mormon record contain the Book of Isaiah if, as I have read, a large portion of Isaiah was not written until after the Book of Mormon people left around 600 B.C.?

ANSWER

The problem occurs only for those who accept the modern view of certain biblical scholars that Isaiah is not the work of a single writer. At least two writers are considered by these as responsible, Isaiah and Deutero-Isaiah. However, believers in the historicity of the Book of Mormon cannot consistently hold this view because, as you state, Deutero-Isaiah was not in existence at the time the Book of Mormon text was carried from the old world to the new.

Belief in the historicity of the Book of Mormon leaves no room for belief in several authors of Isaiah and vice versa. I have heard arguments to allow belief in both, but they appear to be two irreconcilable positions. To accept one is to reject the other. This is definitely involved in your acceptance of the historicity of the Book of Mormon. If you decide that it is not literally historical, you raise many problems with relation to the means by which the record came to us. All I can say is that the position of those who believe in the multiauthorship of Isaiah is at odds with the position of the Restoration that the Book of Mormon was translated from actual records engraved on plates. This claim has always been made by the church and is its official position. Therefore, it would seem that one must choose between the two positions.

109. Missing Verse

QUESTION

In comparing my 1874 Lamoni edition of the Book of Mormon with my 1953 Independence edition, I find that in the sixteenth chapter of Alma of the 1953 edition, verse 157 does not appear in the text of my 1847 edition. Please explain this later addition to the Book of Mormon text.

ANSWER

A thorough examination of all the editions and printings of the Book of Mormon, from whatever press, between the years 1830 and 1907 discloses that the verse to which you refer was always omitted from the text.

However, this omission was not noticed until the Reorganized Church, having gained possession of the original manuscript several years earlier, was in 1908 in the process of publishing the Authorized Edition of that year. Of course when the error of the years was noticed there was only one course to pursue: to begin printing from that time forward the hitherto omitted verse. Therefore, since 1908 every printing and edition of the Book of Mormon by our church has included Alma 16:157.

Prior to 1908 every printing of the Book of Mormon by the Reorganized Church was reprinted from the third American Edition (Nauvoo, 1840). In those printings the missing verse would have been included as a portion of Alma 16:23. This earlier, more lengthy type versification included all of what is now Alma 16:153-165, excluding, of course, verse 157.

110. Melchisedec Priesthood

QUESTION

In Alma 2:28 the priesthood under the administration of the Mosaic Law is referred to as "the high priesthood of the Holy Order of God." Was Alma endowed with the Melchisedec priesthood while the people were living under the Mosaic Law?

The statement is clearly affirmative. The affirmation of Alma is that he held the Melchisedec priesthood. Alma (3:3) tells how that priesthood came to his father: "I, Alma, having been consecrated by my father Alma, to be a high priest over the church of God, he having power and authority from God to do these things . . ."

This authority is from the source of all authority and requires no further validation.

There is no problem if you see the church in the Western Hemisphere as distinct from the Old World. If Lehi held the Aaronic priesthood when he left Jerusalem there is nothing to prevent the greater priesthood from being bestowed as Alma stated did occur in his case.

It would appear that Christ and his atonement were taught to the church in the New World and the people were clearly told that "The law of Moses availeth nothing, except it were through the atonement of his blood" (Mosiah 1:113).

The people of Nephi were not under the Mosaic Law in the same sense as it appears the Hebrews were who were left behind. They were looking forward to Christ as we look back. They worshiped Christ and lived according to the "law of liberty," obeying the old law "inasmuch as it shall be expedient" (II Nephi 11:57), which means in the sense that we are obligated today to keep the law to the degree that the spiritual intent of the law requires. Thus we are not under obligation in the ceremonial aspects of the old law. These have been caught up in the spiritual implications of the gospel. A full reading of II Nephi 11:43-58 will clarify this further.

111. Metals in 399 B.C.

QUESTION

In Jarom 8 there are several terms mentioned such as machinery, iron, copper, brass, and steel. Were these words and metals known in 399 B.C.?

ANSWER

The existence of large buildings in ancient America is an established fact. That machinery, simple or complex, was used is obvious, and the use of the word is necessary to intelligent description of the building procedure. That Joseph Smith should use current English words to convey the meaning is logical. As far back as Genesis 4:22, the Bible makes reference to iron and copper. This is descriptive of metals known much earlier than 400 B.C. There is record of iron being found in an Egyptian pyramid five thousand years old.

The brass of the Bible and Book of Mormon was probably bronze. Brass is mentioned as early as Exodus 25:3. The older versions use the word "brass" consistently, but the Revised Standard Version retains the word only when used as a simile for stubbornness and hardness of heart, etc. This version gives "bronze" when referring to the metal alloy.

The word "brass" constitutes no real problem in the Book of Mormon. Brass is a copper alloy, and any such metal was covered by that word in the Authorized Version. No one has objected, except on highly technical grounds, to the use of the word in this version. Why, therefore, should one object to its use in the Book of Mormon?

On the question of steel being an appropriate word, I note that a metallurgical authority states it is very difficult to draw a line between iron and steel. Joseph Smith could have used the word "steel" to describe any alloy of iron that was harder than pure iron.

If we accept the view that Joseph Smith was using words within his comprehension to express the text of the Book of Mormon, we have no difficulty. Undoubtedly this was so in the case of the use of the word "adieu" which certainly was not used in 400 B.C. Smelting of other metals in ancient America is a demonstrable fact, and it is hardly likely that some combination of iron and an alloy would not have appeared in the process. It seems that Joseph Smith used the common word "steel" to describe hardened iron.

112. Binder Rings and Book of Mormon

QUESTION

Did the idea of rings incorporated in the modern loose-leaf binder originate with one of our members using the principle of the Book of Mormon plates?

ANSWER

The answer to this has appeared in various columns before but as the question often arises I am printing the facts again.

The idea that the loose-leaf principle came from the rings of the plates is erroneous. This arose because people heard that Brother William Pitt had taken out the patent. His son Fred D. Pitt when interviewed on this subject in 1957 stated that his father, a machinist and inventor, invented the ring which would snap open and shut. This was patented by the Irving-Pitt Manufacturing Company.

The method of holding leaves together by rings is quite old and did not come first from the discovery of the Book of Mormon record.

113. Daughters of Zion

QUESTION

Who are being referred to as the daughters of Zion in II Nephi 8:54?

ANSWER

The second verse of the chapter from which this text is taken clearly states that the writer, Nephi, is writing words from Isaiah. He states that his "soul delighteth in his words." In verse 16 we find the clue to Nephi's interest and his reason for including so much of the Old Testament prophet's writing. He says, "Now, these are the words; and ye may liken them unto you, and unto all men."

These words concerning Judah and Jerusalem are applicable in principle to all men. Nephi is deeply concerned, as was Isaiah, about the righteousness of God's people. Observing the low state of morality, the preoccupation with things of tinsel and show, the inequalities and pride among brethren, the prophet is inspired to point out the destiny of a people who so conduct themselves. In the verse you mention he is making particular reference to the women of the nation and calls them the "daughters of Zion." Later in the passage he personifies the city itself to which the same standards of criticism and prophetic insights are applied.

It may be appropriate here to emphasize the value of seeing scripture more in the light of the basic principle being illustrated than to seek to identify persons or fix the time of events. This does not exclude the concept of prophecy involving at times the pinpointing of an event in the future, but it does serve to keep the real reason for the study of history and prophecy in view, *viz*, that men may know how to live in harmony with the divine intent.

114. Polygamy Reference

QUESTION

What is meant in reference to polygamy in Jacob 2:38, 39?

"Wherefore, this people shall keep my commandments, saith the Lord of hosts, or cursed be the land for their sakes.

119

"For if I will, saith the Lord of hosts, raise up seed unto me, I will command my people: otherwise, they shall hearken unto these things."

ANSWER

I assume your question to be rooted in the claims of some Utah Mormon advocates of polygamy that it was possible for God to command his people to practice plural marriage. It would be impossible for God to command something to be done which he has described in a few lines before as an "abomination," a "gross crime" and "iniquity" which caused great suffering in families, especially wives and children.

"Behold, David and Solomon truly had many wives and concubines, which thing was abominable before me, saith the Lord.

"Wherefore, thus saith the Lord, I have led this people forth out of the land of Jerusalem, by the power of mine arm that I might raise up unto me a righteous branch from the fruit of the loins of Joseph.

"Wherefore, I, the Lord God, will not suffer that this people shall do like unto them of old.

"Wherefore, my brethren, hear me, and hearken to the word of the Lord: For there shall not any man among you have save it be one wife; and concubines he shall have none: For I, the Lord God, delighteth in the chastity of women.

"And whoredoms are an abomination before me: thus saith the Lord of hosts.

"Wherefore, this people shall keep my commandments, saith the Lord of hosts, or cursed be the land for their sakes.

"For if I will, saith the Lord of hosts, raise up seed unto me, I will command my people: otherwise, they shall hearken unto these things."

—Jacob 2:33-39.

If you analyze the verses given you will note the following:

1. God said that David and Solomon's polygamy was abominable (verse 33).

2. God led the people from Jerusalem to raise up a righteous branch (verse 34).

3. God would not suffer the new nation to follow David and Solomon's example (verse 35).

4. One man was to have only one wife (verse 36).

5. A curse on the land is threatened if polygamous practices are followed (verse 38).

6. It was God's intention to raise up a righteous seed and he would command his people to this end (verse 39).

7. Should he not so command (which he did) in the absence of those instructions, they would continue to hearken unto these things written about David and Solomon (verse 39), thus following the iniquitous practice. Therefore his command was for chastity.

The need of a righteous seed in contrast to that which had occurred in the old world was stated to be by monogamy and not polygamy.

A correspondent has suggested that in verse 39 the last word "shall" would have been better translated "will," and that lack of erudition led the translator to use "shall." "Shall" is permissible, but if defined as command it is obviously out of harmony with what goes before. This is a very helpful comment. In support, page 713, verses 98 and 99 of the Book of Mormon are quoted. Research in the Book of Mormon manuscript shows that a word-perfect translation was not had, and so "imperfections" in minor detail are found. Without a doubt the meaning of Jacob 2:32-39 is that God disapproves of polygamy, and that enlightened peoples practice monogamy. Polygamy is defended only by groups with some weakness of a historical nature or those who have a leaning toward "iniquity." Then again it could be plain ignorance.

The principle of monogamy was reiterated in 1835 in the Doctrine and Covenants statement on marriage. This church believes in a God who is at least consistent.

115. Identity of Persons

QUESTION

Could you please inform me if there are two different persons by the name of Ammon in the Book of Mormon?

ANSWER

There are two persons named Ammon in the Book of Mormon. You will find the first reference in Mosiah 5:4, 17, where mention is made of "Ammon, . . . a descendant of Zarahemla." In Mosiah 11:203 you will find reference to one "Ammon, . . . [one] of the sons of Mosiah." Ammon, the son of Mosiah, was of the Nephites. The people of Zarahemla were descendants of the colony led by Mulek. The two persons by the name of Ammon are clearly of different lineal descent.

116. Gazelem

QUESTION

In the Book of Mormon Alma 17:55 states: "I will prepare unto my servant Gazelem, a stone, which shall shine forth in darkness unto light, that I may discover unto them the works of their brethren . . ." Is Gazelem the Brother of Jared's name? If not, what was it?

ANSWER

I presume you see a possible connection of the name Gazelem with the Brother of Jared because in Ether, chapters 1 and 3, stones of a luminous and miraculous nature are associated with him, as well as in the text you quote. I see no need to connect these two passages in such a way as to indicate that the unstated name of the Brother of Jared was Gazelem. A number of texts both in the Bible and Book of Mormon mention stones and artifacts of this kind; therefore these two texts are not necessarily related.

According to the texts available there seem to have been various kinds of objects used as media for divine direction. These were of different patterns and forms and were used for varying purposes, ranging from the simple decisions through the Urim and Thummim of the Old Testament (see I Samuel 28:6; Numbers 27:21) to the instruments of guidance and direction in the Book of Mormon (see Alma 17:77-80; Mosiah 5:73, 83; Ether 1:93), and later to the different instruments used by Joseph Smith in bringing forth the Book of Mormon and other revelations to the church.

Now the fact that Doctrine and Covenants 77:2 b uses the name Gazelam for Joseph Smith has led some to the supposition that Alma 17:55 refers prophetically to him and his latter-day revelatory work of the Book of Mormon. Though this is disproved by the fact that Gazelem was to precede Helaman, the modern use of this ancient name indicates that Joseph was a latter-day Gazelam or seer, who had an instrument prepared. It should be noted that the Doctrine and Covenants spells the name with an "a" while the Book of Mormon spells it with an "e". The similarity of the work done by Gazelem of the Book of Mormon to that done by Joseph Smith is apparent.

In my opinion the identification of the Brother of Jared with Gazelem is ruled out by the fact that the revelation given to Helaman in Alma 17 indicates that Gazelem was to be presented with a stone at a time when it became necessary to reveal the fact of the destruction of the Jaredites because of their wicked works. Gazelem must have lived after the destruction of the Jaredites for this revelation to be made and to be of any value.

The name of Jared's brother remains obscure while Gazelem is one of those like many others in scripture whom we know only as a name without any degree of biographical record.

117. Synagogues

QUESTION

Helaman 2:13 and Alma 13:24 contain references to synagogues. Historians say that synagogues did not exist until the exilic period. This period was later than the records the people of Lehi took with them to the New World. How could the Nephites have known the word let alone describe the nature of the buildings?

ANSWER

One of the facts that is impressed by a study of the manuscript of the Book of Mormon is that a literal word-for-word translation cannot be substantiated. It is obvious that the vocabulary of the translator was a modifying factor in the choice of English words.

The word synagogue is used to denote a place of assembly and worship, and Joseph Smith no doubt used the word to convey this meaning. (See Webster for various uses.)

You do find difficulty if you take for granted that the exact Hebrew word for synagogue was on the plates or that the Book of Mormon is a literal translation. Without doing violence to the meaning, Alma 13:21 could be translated thus: "And Alma and Amulek went forth preaching repentance to the people in their temples, and in their sanctuaries, and also in their other places of assembly which were built after the manner of the Jews." The description "after the manner of the Jews" is not necessarily restricted to the word synagogues but applies to all the structures mentioned.

The date of the origin of the synagogue is obscure, but it is generally conceded that no synagogues have been discovered which give any indication of being preexilic. In the light of this, the explanation I have offered seems feasible.

118. Latin in Book of Mormon

QUESTION

In Alma 24:79 I find the last word to be "etc." Is this not from Latin? Was Latin known in 63 B.C.?

123

"Etc." is an abbreviation of two Latin words "et cetera," literally meaning "and the rest." This question presents a similar problem to that of the word "adieu" being a French word for "farewell," which also appears in the Book of Mormon. The difficulty is dissolved if you accept the fact that literal verbal translation is not sustained by a study of the methods by which Joseph Smith stated he produced the English text of the Book of Mormon. If you examine sections 8 and 9 of Doctrine and Covenants, you will see that concepts rather than words are primarily involved. These sections do not deal with simple revelation as some have supposed but are dealing directly with Oliver Cowdery's desire and failure to translate. Hence the words coming freely to Joseph Smith in his dictation will be those with which a young man of his period and schooling would be familiar; both Latin and French were used as indicated.

This view makes unnecessary a discussion as to the existence of Latin in 63 B.C. Latin is quite an ancient language. Old Latin was spoken by the Romans prior to 75 B.C. and is known as "preclassical." Classical Latin dates from 75 B.C. to A.D. 175. Modern Latin dates from about A.D. 1500. It seems unnecessary to prove or disprove that the Latin expression was known in ancient America.

If we are disturbed by the idea that the text is largely conceptual rather than literal, we have greater problems to solve. Hence the hypothesis that the work involves expressions of concepts expressed mainly in the culture of Joseph Smith is the one I lean toward. Some students, particularly one eminent Utah writer, have felt convinced of Hebrew and Arabic phrases being present in the text, these being quite outside the vocabulary and usages of Joseph Smith. These are perhaps quite sound conclusions to some, but this leaves us with words like "etc." and "adieu." I, too, am still an explorer into the *modus operandi* of the production of this unique document, the Book of Mormon.

119. French in Book of Mormon

QUESTION

In Jacob 7:29 the word "adieu" is used. Is this not a French word? What does it mean?

ANSWER

"Adieu" is definitely a French word. It has its counterpart in the Spanish "adios." The meaning of the word is simply "farewell" and is so used in the Book of Mormon. Your difficulty appears to be in the use of a French word in an English version of the Book of Mormon.

Joseph Smith stated that he performed this work "by the gift and power of God." This did not displace his own intellectual processes, for it is apparent that his own vocabulary was involved in the English text. It is not claimed to be perfect English, but the basic content and concept of this ancient record is expressed in the language of the modern seer's times. If we take a literal word-for-word approach we have problems of grammar, punctuation, and words such as adieu.

Probably this word was well known to Joseph Smith in his youth because of the proximity of his area to the French Canadian border at that time. Our everyday language includes other non-English words which naturally have found their way into our current writings and translations.

To have contact with the manuscript of the Book of Mormon and to note the many adjustments to the text made by Joseph Smith himself (see 1837 Book of Mormon preface) is to realize that the wording is related to the mind and speech of the "author and translator," as he described himself in the original edition of 1830.

120. Activities by Church

QUESTION

What archaeological activities are operated or participated in by the church? Can you give me data of the comparison between archaeological findings and the Book of Mormon?

ANSWER

The only official activity sponsored by the General Church centers in the committee appointed by the World Conference. This committee, known as the Executive Committee of the Society of Archaeological Research, reports its activities to the Conferences at intervals (see General Conference Resolution No. 950).

There is no text available compiled by this committee, but several individuals have had works published by Herald House which could form a basis for the study of the comparisons in which you are interested. There are *America's Lost Civilizations* by H. I. Velt, 1949; *In the Land of the Feathered Serpent* by P. M. Hanson, 1949; *The Sacred Book of Ancient America* by H. I. Velt, 1952; and *Jesus Christ among the Ancient Americans* by P. M. Hanson, 1959. These are out of print but should be available in many private libraries.

The following three are published by the Utah church but usually are available through Herald House, Independence, Missouri: *America*

Before Columbus by D. Farnsworth; *Archaeology of the Book of Mormon* by Milton Hunter; and *Evidences of the Book of Mormon* by D. Farnsworth.

Paul M. Hanson, previously in active leadership of the committee, did considerable work and on-the-spot research. Several committee members both past and present have investigated this study as related to the Book of Mormon.

121. Contradiction of Command

QUESTION

What is your understanding of II Nephi 1:115 which contains the statement that Adam sinned that men might be? Is this a contradiction of the command to multiply?

ANSWER

The statement in Nephi has deep philosophical import and could be approached from many angles and, moreover, take considerable space. First, we must consider your dual question as one. Are we assuming that the sin was in multiplying? Surely we cannot believe this!

I suggest that if Adam had not been disobedient or, as the scriptures put it so well, tasted of the tree of knowledge, there would have been no real man in a moral and spiritual sense. Our first parents were in a state of innocence which corresponds with the state of childhood. A man is not good merely because he can do no wrong. Only when free choice is exercised do we become real persons. Once we, like the first humans, were immature as a child is. Maturity brings responsibility, and choice becomes determinative.

I personally have never been able to avoid the conclusion that the story of Eden is allegorical. The story is in the best Hebrew form of religious and philosophical interpretation; therefore we must look for the spiritual meaning. It was a conscientious effort of the Hebrews to place on record an answer to the obvious waywardness of man as compared with the divine intent. Note I Nephi 1:101 where Lehi says, "I Lehi according to the things which I have read, *must needs suppose* . . ." Here we have an *interpretation* by Lehi. The whole context must be read in this light.

My approach to the problem is summed up thus: Had Adam and Eve remained in immaturity, not having the experience of choosing for themselves, they would have been as children. They thus would

126

not have moved on to their adult role. The story is colored by the Hebraic idea of sex; that this ancient concept is inadequate in this connection is evident by the fact that a paradox is apparent in the command to multiply and the sexual implication of the "transgression." What is called "the fall" in Hebraic literature denotes the gap between man in his present state and the divine intent that he should dwell with his Creator in positive righteousness.

The Doctrine and Covenants

122. Selection of Revelations

QUESTION

Upon what basis were the revelations of the Doctrine and Covenants selected for inclusion in that book?

ANSWER

The basis for the selection of documents for publication in the Doctrine and Covenants is set out in a preface to the 1835 edition signed by the selection committee consisting of Joseph Smith, Oliver Cowdery, Sidney Rigdon, and F. G. Williams.

I print the whole of the preface as a matter of interest and a basis for further study.

> "We deem it to be unnecessary to entertain you with a lengthy preface to the following volume, but merely to say, that it contains, in short, the leading items of the religion which we have professed to believe.
>
> "The first part of the book will be found to contain a series of Lectures as delivered before a Theological class in this place, and in consequence of their embracing the important doctrine of salvation, we have arranged them into the following work.
>
> "The second part contains items or principles for the regulation of the church, as taken from the revelations which have been given since its organization, as well as from former ones.

"There may be an aversion in the minds of some against receiving any thing purporting to be articles of religious faith, in consequence of there being so many now extant; but if men believe a system, and profess that it was given by inspiration, certainly the more intelligibly they can present it, the better. It does not make a principle untrue to *print* it, neither does it make it true not to print it.

"The church viewing this subject to be of importance, appointed, through their servants and delegates the High Council, your servants to select and compile this work. Several reasons might be adduced in favor of this move of the Council, but we only add a few words. They knew that the church was evil spoken of in many places—its faith and belief misrepresented, and the way of truth thus subverted. By some it was represented as disbelieving the Bible, by others as being an enemy to all good order and uprightness, and by others as being injurious to the peace of all governments civil and political.

"We have, therefore, endeavored to present, though in few words, *our* belief, and when we say this, humbly trust, the faith and principles of this society as a body.

"We do not present this little volume with any other expectation than that we are to be called to answer to every principle advanced, in that day when the secrets of all hearts will be revealed, and the reward of every man's labor be given him.

"Kirtland, Ohio, February 17, 1835"

The first part referred to in the above were seven theological lectures. These were later published separately and do not now appear in the current edition of the Doctrine and Covenants.

123. Historical Background to Preface

QUESTION

What is the historical background to the statement in the preface to Doctrine and Covenants, Section 7, which says "translated from parchment, written and hid up by himself [John]"?

ANSWER

There is only meager data on this. It consists of the exact words you quote which were first printed as an introduction to the revelation of April, 1829, in the preparation for the Book of Commandments.

This was never published as a complete work although some 169 pages were printed before the destruction of the press.

This introductory statement was reprinted in the first edition of the Doctrine and Covenants, 1835, and this appears to be the basis on which it is in the present edition.

I have discovered no elaboration of this reference in any early publication nor do any of the commentaries deal with it.

Times and Seasons, Volume 3, page 853, tells of a difference of opinion arising between Oliver Cowdery and Joseph Smith over whether John the apostle died or continued, and they agreed to settle it by the Urim and Thummim. A revelation (Doctrine and Covenants 7) was received. The text states it to be from a translation from a parchment bearing John's testimony. It does not, however, imply that a piece of parchment was in the hands or possession of Joseph Smith and Oliver Cowdery. What was written was by revelatory process. It is obvious that the only text in their hands from which John 21:22 could project controversy was the New Testament. A free paraphrasing could be: "John elaborated on this in a document which he hid away: a translation of the contents of which reads as follows." Then follows Section 7.

124. Sections 22 and 36

QUESTION

How did sections 22 and 36 of Doctrine and Covenants become included in that book? Is there record of endorsement by a conference?

ANSWER

These two sections were first included in the Doctrine and Covenants by the Reorganization in 1864. At a semiannual conference of the church on October 8, 1863, a resolution was passed as follows:

"Resolved, that this conference authorize the committee of Publication to publish the Book of Doctrine and Covenants with such corrections in arrangement as may be necessary."

Evidently the committee interpreted its functions rather broadly, and because both of these documents had appeared in print as revelations in the days of Joseph the Martyr it included them in the book.

There is indication that Joseph III was considering the problem of variations in the text of the various printings of these documents.

He wrote the Board of Publication in 1896 that he did not know how they came to be included but surmised that Isaac Sheen inserted them as valuable. He also stated it was unimportant to him whether they were included or not. Probably he considered their inclusion in the Holy Scriptures (I.V.) sufficient.

The text of both appeared in the Inspired Version of 1867, Section 22, as a prefatory document, and Section 36 as a part of Genesis (Chapter 7, verses 1-78).

In any case their authority as being accepted by the church is based on General Conference Resolution 215, September 13, 1878, which states that we recognize

". . . the Holy Scriptures, the Book of Mormon, the revelations of God contained in the Book of Doctrine and Covenants, . . . as the standard of authority on all matters of church government and doctrine. . . ."

The book in use at that time contained these sections. By General Conference Resolution 214 they would stand approved as they are part of the Inspired Version of the scripture.

125. Sections Added in 1844

QUESTION

Which sections were added to the Doctrine and Covenants in 1844? How many if any were approved by Conference action?

ANSWER

The following sections were included in the Doctrine and Covenants for the first time in 1844:

1. Revelation to Thomas B. Marsh given at Kirtland, Ohio, July 23, 1837. Section 104 in 1844 edition; Section 105 in RLDS Authorized Edition.

2. Revelation on tithing given at Far West, Missouri, July 8, 1838: Section 107, 1844 edition; Section 106 in RLDS Authorized Edition.

3. Revelation on Nauvoo Temple, etc., given at Nauvoo, Illinois, January 19, 1841. Section 103, 1844 edition; Section 107, RLDS Authorized Edition.

4. Two letters written by Joseph Smith, September 1 and 6, 1842. Sections 105 and 106, 1844 edition; sections 109 and 110, RLDS Authorized Edition.

5. Statement on "The Martyrdom of Joseph and Hyrum Smith." Author not given.

None of these sections were approved by a General Conference of the church at the time of publication in 1844. However, they have since been considered as coming under what has been called a "blanket motion" passed by the General Conference of the Reorganization in 1878. This action is General Conference Resolution 215 and reads as follows:

> "That this body, representing the Reorganized Church of Jesus Christ of Latter Day Saints, recognize the Holy Scriptures, the Book of Mormon, the revelations of God contained in the Book of Doctrine and Covenants, and all other revelations which have been or shall be revealed through God's appointed prophet, which have been or may be hereafter accepted by the church as the standard of authority on all matters of church government and doctrine, and the final standard of reference on appeal in all controversies arising, or which may arise in this Church of Christ (see 222)."

It has been contended by some that this resolution applied only to revelations which had been or would thereafter be accepted by the church and that the additions of 1844 do not come under that category.

The fact remains, however, that when the RLDS edition was authorized by the semiannual conference of 1863 the committee proceeded upon the basis of the 1844 edition. Later question was raised as to whether the resolution of 1878 (215) quoted here covered the Doctrine and Covenants as then existing, etc., and clarification was made in the Conference of September 29, 1879. General Conference Resolution 222, paragraph 1, reads:

> "Whereas, Certain rumors had obtained currency that the church had not at any time so attested the Book of Doctrine and Covenants, and the later revelations given to the church, by vote and affirmation, that they should form with the Bible and Book of Mormon a standard of reference in case of controversy and difference of opinion upon questions of doctrine and practice in the church; therefore to remedy this defect, if it existed, the resolution referred to was introduced and passed."

Whatever personal opinions may be, this is the Conference action.

132

126. Section 66

In the list of contents of the Doctrine and Covenants (my edition is 1934) which gives comparative tabulations of various editions beginning with 1835, there are two sections 66 given for the 1835 printing. One is listed page 192 and the other page 195. Can you straighten this out for me?

ANSWER

The explanation of this anomaly is that the numbering of the sections in the 1835 edition was in error at this point. The section on page 195 should have been number 67. Both of these sections were contained in the original attempt to print the early revelations in what was to have been the "Book of Commandments." This work was never completed, the last chapter being number 65. This chapter also was not fully printed when the printing press was destroyed; or, if so, the last part was destroyed, as none of the later bound copies have anything after page 160.

The sections you are concerned with were 54 and 55 in the incomplete Book of Commandments. The 1835 edition renumbered the sections. The error in numbering was obviously noted when the printing was too far advanced; this was remedied in the next edition of 1844. Renumbering has occurred subsequently as the table in the front of the present editions shows, the two sections 66 becoming 52 and 53 in all Reorganization editions (that is, since 1864 to the present time).

127. Civil War Revelation

QUESTION

Was the revelation on the Civil War ever published in the Doctrine and Covenants? If so in what edition?

ANSWER

It has not appeared as a numbered section in the Reorganized Church editions, but it has been printed as a supplementary document in certain editions. These editions were 1894, 1897, 1901, 1905, and 1906. This practice was discontinued in later editions because, as a document, it was never approved on the same basis as the contents of the 1835 edition and as later revelations were endorsed by General Conference vote.

The committee chosen to prepare and select documents for inclusion in the 1835 edition evidently were of the opinion that it did not carry any principle or teaching in harmony with the purpose for which the Doctrine and Covenants was being compiled. It is a definite prophecy and, being uttered and later printed before the fulfillment of the details contained therein, stands on its own merits in relation to the subsequent historical record. It contains neither a doctrine nor a covenant. The Utah church first published it in the *Pearl of Great Price* in England in 1851 and later gave it place in editions of the Doctrine and Covenants as Section 87, commencing with 1876. The date attributed to the document is December 25, 1832. There appears to have been no printing of it at that time, although the substance appeared in the church periodical of the times, the *Evening and Morning Star*, January, 1833. It can be read in the RLDS *Church History*, Volume 1, page 262.

128. Incorrect Printing

QUESTION

Recent access to the 1835 edition of the Doctrine and Covenants has made me aware that the statement on marriage, Section 111, was incorrectly printed and I find a correction on a page of errata at the back of this work. Yet in our current text revision to the erroneous text is noted. What is the reason for this?

ANSWER

The document is identical in all publications except for a sentence in the last paragraph. The 1835 edition used these words:

"We believe that all persons who exercise control over their fellow beings, and prevent them from embracing the truth, will have to answer for that sin."—Pages 251-252.

Following the index of contents this correction is printed on page XXIII:

"We believe that husbands, parents and masters who exercise control over their wives, children and servants, and prevent them from embracing the truth, will have to answer for that sin."—Page XXV.

The latter version was followed from 1844 until as a result of the work of a committee appointed in 1910 to consider reversification and correction of typographical and clerical errors, the 1911 and all subsequent editions have followed the first wording found within the body of the text; this was the subject of the errata note.

The committee consisting of the First Presidency, Historian, and Board of Publication reported to the 1911 Conference that the work of preparing an authorized version was proceeding.

In the 1912 Conference Minutes the committee reported:

"We your committee on correction of typographical errors, etc., of the Doctrine and Covenants, herewith submit our report. We have done the work assigned us, and the book as corrected is now in print. . . ."

Research has revealed no recorded reason for detailed corrections or for the reversion to the original wording of page 251 of the 1835 text.

I can only attempt to envision what would appear a logical step of clarification of the principle in relation to the times. By the early twentieth century the dependent status of wives had greatly lessened, and full citizenship of the wife as an individual apart from the husband had been or was in the process of being achieved. Slavery had been abolished in the United States of America and the relationship of servant and master greatly liberalized.

The corrected version of 1844, therefore, no longer was realistic in particular detail and so what was in the first instance a variation of the verbal text became later a more factual statement. It carries a broader interpretation and adheres to the original principle and intent. This section is not a revelation but an affirmation of principle and is binding today as then.

129. Error in Date

QUESTION

RLDS "Church History," Volume 3, page 126, states that the Nauvoo edition of the Doctrine and Covenants was issued during the summer of 1845. This is not in harmony with a statement in the "Saints' Herald" where the date given is 1844. Which is correct?

ANSWER

There were three printings of the Doctrine and Covenants in Nauvoo, Illinois—1844, 1845, and 1846. The only previous printing was the first edition in Kirtland, Ohio, in 1835.

The 1844 or second edition was printed by John Taylor under the original copyright by Joseph Smith, Jr., in 1835. The 1845 or third edition was published by John Taylor also but was printed under copyright of Newell K. Whitney and George Miller. This was actually printed from the plates prepared for the 1844 (second) edition. It is strictly, therefore, not an edition but a printing, but we use the description because the title page carries that wording. The 1846 (fourth) edition was also a reprint of the plates of the 1844 edition and is known as the fourth *American* edition (the first English edition was published by Wilford Woodruff in Liverpool in 1845).

130. Error in Date

QUESTION

In a question answered in the "Saints' Herald" is the statement that the edition of the Doctrine and Covenants in the minds of those attending the 1878 Conference was the 1844 copy. Should not this read 1864?

Yes. This was a typographical error originating on my desk. Readers should note the correct date. I am pleased to have the opportunity to comment further because of factors involved other than concern about the additions of John Taylor in 1844.

The 1864 edition of the Reorganized Church was the result of Conference action in 1863 in Iowa. This was the book in use at the time of the resolution referred to in 1878 and would be the one in the minds of the members of the Conference. This is important for other reasons which I will state. Sections 22 and 36 appeared in the Doctrine and Covenants for the first time in 1864.

The resolution of 1863 simply provided that the Conference "authorize the committee of publication to publish the Book of Doctrine and Covenants, *with such corrections in arrangement* as may be necessary." Note that the authorization does not specify but was evidently taken to apply to the 1844 edition. The committee appears to have gone beyond what was authorized in adding sections 22 and 36 and evidently this was a factor in the resolutions of 1878 and 1879. *The corrections in arrangement* authorized resulted in the sections being printed in order of the dates of the revelations up to January 19, 1841. One exception was that the appendix (November 3, 1831) was placed after Section 107 which is the last revelation by Joseph Smith included. Also, the two letters of 1842 (sections 109 and 110), Section 111 on marriage, Section 112 on "Governments and Laws in General," and Section 113 on the martyrdom were all given place after the appendix (Section 108).

John Taylor, who printed the 1844 edition, had already eliminated the minutes of the General Assembly which outline the procedures followed for approval of the Doctrine and Covenants on August 17, 1835, and which form part of the 1835 text. For some reason the 1863-64 committee of the Reorganization did not correct his omission. This was first corrected in the 1911 edition, and the document is now 108A of the RLDS text. It is omitted from the Utah Mormon text.

Though not following a consistent rule in that some sections not revelations were left in chronological sequence and the others referred to placed after the appendix, the 1864 printing was a much improved arrangement and formed the basis of all later compilations of the Doctrine and Covenants.

131. Editions

QUESTION

Were paragraphs 16 and 17 as found in Doctrine and Covenants 17 contained in the "Book of Commandments"? If not, how is their absence in the first printing to be explained?

ANSWER

Paragraphs 16 and 17 of Section 17 were not in the original printings of either the *Evening and Morning Star* or the later uncompleted work known as the *Book of Commandments*. It should be remembered that Section 17 containing the "Articles and Covenants of the Church of Christ" is not a simple document originating on any one date but is a compilation of a number of documents. In the reprinting of the Doctrine and Covenants the two paragraphs in question were added. The propriety of this has been questioned, and this may be the basis of your inquiry.

Since the *Book of Commandments* was never actually published due to the destruction of the church press in Independence in July, 1833, the church moved to produce the Doctrine and Covenants. A committee was appointed to prepare the material to this end. While doing this the committee found a number of inaccuracies, omissions, and other errors. The new project offered an opportunity to make quite a number of changes in the Doctrine and Covenants of 1835. This is evident when it is compared with the partial printing of the earlier work which was to be known as the *Book of Commandments*.

In addition to the data about which you inquire, revelations which were in manuscript form but had not yet been typeset or printed were included.

In the possession of the church historian is the manuscript copy from which the last page printed for the intended *Book of Commandments* was taken. This contains fifteen lines of script more than appeared on the page printed from it—and in addition one complete and one part of a further revelation. The printed page (160) concluded with the word Ephraim. This, of course, was due to the interruption of the procedure by the mob which destroyed the press.

I cite these facts to give reason for the statement of Editor Cowdery of the recommenced *Evening and Morning Star* in Kirtland, Ohio. He stated:

> "There are many typographical errors in both volumes, and especially in the last, which we shall endeavor carefully to correct, as well as principle, if we discover any. It is also proper for us to say, that in the first 14 numbers, in the revelations, are many errors, typographical, and others, occasioned by transcribing manuscript; but as we shall have access to originals, we shall endeavor to make proper corrections."—*Evening and Morning Star*, Volume II, page 384.

W. W. Phelps, editor of the *Evening and Morning Star* in Independence before the press was destroyed, had already published the following in June 1833:

> "We have again inserted the articles and covenants according to our promise in a previous number, for the benefit of our brethren abroad who have not the first number of the first volume. As there were some errors which had got into them by transcribing, we have since obtained the original copy and made the necessary corrections."—*Evening and Morning Star*, Volume II, page 196.

132. "Gods, Even the Sons of God"

QUESTION

Please explain Doctrine and Covenants 76:5 h, "They are gods, even the sons of God."

138

This text is more easily interpreted if we place it alongside other scriptures which use similar words. Jesus quoted Psalm 82:6 and his words are recorded in John 10:34-36. The Psalmist said, "I have said, Ye are gods; and all of you are children of the Most High. But ye shall die like men, and fall like one of the princes."

Two views are taken by commentators on the Old Testament text in Psalms. One is that the word "gods" means humans standing in relation to their fellows as judges under divine authority. Both *Abingdon Bible Commentary* and *Dummelow's Commentary* (single volume) present this view.

In relation to the passage in Psalms, *The Interpreter's Bible* gives the view that the Old Testament people used the term gods in harmony with their early concept that Jehovah was superior to all gods. They later discarded the idea of acceptance of the existence of other gods at all, having had intimate experience with the only true God. This commentary also refers to the view I have just given conceding that in Psalm 82:2-4 reference is made to judicial iniquity which, of course, would involve human beings. It further states, "Such an interpretation lies behind the use of verse 6 in John 10:34."

I would say the word "gods" is used in this sense in the Doctrine and Covenants text you mention.

133. Meaning of "Seal"

Please explain the meaning of the word "seal" as it is used in Section 1, paragraph 2 c, d, and e, of the Doctrine and Covenants.

On reference to a good Bible concordance such as Cruden's you will find a number of texts using the word "seal" and its variations. Actually the word has a number of meanings both as a noun and as a verb, although there is a similarity between them. It is, however, used in the Old Testament and other scriptures in two main ways. One is to close or bind up so that a book or covenant cannot be reopened while the seal is upon it. The other meaning is to place the stamp of authority upon a document or covenant. This appears in older times to have been a symbol on a royal ring which was used to stamp authoritative documents. Thus it was a sign of authority.

The prophet Joseph Smith was deeply immersed in the culture and verbal expression of the Authorized Version and in the study of the Hebrew way of life and expression. Therefore, when he revealed in documentary form what he sensed as prophetic vision, this language and cultural interest are often marked.

An apocalyptic expression was also characteristic of Joseph Smith's revelations, and though it would be inaccurate to say that his concept of the finality of the righteous and the rebellious was wholly deterministic, there is this element in his expression in Doctrine and Covenants, Section 1, paragraph 2.

The whole purpose of this section is to make a proclamation calculated to challenge the peoples of the earth to action which would determine their salvation or the opposite. This method was used by the Old Testament prophets, and it is used even by modern evangelistic preachers. Therefore, the first meaning of "seal" (closing the book because the die has been cast) is here implied. Men who refuse to believe and who are rebellious seal their fate in the very nature of things.

The other aspect, that of authority, is also involved in this paragraph. One is reminded of the language of Jesus as recorded in the Authorized Version, Matthew 16:19, with regard to binding and loosing by the apostles. Section 1 is undoubtedly given to proclaim an authoritative message, one with the seal of the King of Kings upon it, and this is the criterion by which men are saved or lost. In this sense the rebellious and unbelievers are sealed up unto the day of wrath. One needs to consider other texts which offer salvation to the repentant to place this statement in perspective. This removes undue emphasis upon a wholly deterministic interpretation. If you consider Doctrine and Covenants 1 with Matthew 16:19 and Mark 16:15, 16, it becomes meaningful at this point.

134. The Angel Raphael; Book of Enoch

QUESTION

In Doctrine and Covenants 110:21 b the name of an angel Raphael appears among others. What is known of this personage?

In researching the question above the reference to Enoch, Chapter 20, is given. I have examined several versions of the Bible and cannot find this book. Where is it, and is it authentic?

Research reveals very little concerning this figure. Apart from the reference you quote, the name appears only in apocryphal and pseudepigraphical literature. The apocryphal reference is in the Book of Tobit. This book is in the Roman Catholic Bible and some other version but is not in the King James or Revised Standard versions.

The angel Raphael is a prominent character in the pseudepigraphical book of Enoch, of which manuscript copies were discovered in the middle ages and later centuries in the Greek language. The original Semitic text has disappeared. It supposedly originated about 100 B.C. It was first translated into English in 1821 by Laurence.

An equivalent for the word Raphael is Azarias. Raphael means, "God Heals" and Azarias "Jehovah Helps." According to this book he is listed among the seven holy angels whose names are given as follows: (1) Uriel, (2) Raphael, (3) Raguel, (4) Michael, (5) Saraguel, (6) Gabriel, (7) Remiel. These were said to present prayers before God (see Enoch, Chapter 20). Each had a special role to fulfill in serving mankind before the throne. Raphael's function was to bring healing to the spirits of men. St. Raphael's day is celebrated by some Catholic communions as a feast on October 24. Raphael has been associated by some with the angel who troubled the waters of healing as recorded in John 5:4.

Because this information comes from such sources I do not offer it as factual but as tradition has recorded it.

The Book of Enoch is not to be found in standard biblical texts. It is what is called by some a pseudepigraphical work. Translations of this work were discovered in the Middle Ages. They were then in the Greek language, but the original Semitic text had been lost. It is supposed to have dated from the first century before Christ. The fact that it is classified as pseudepigraphical means that in the opinion of scholars it is not a genuine writing of the person whose name is ascribed to it. To describe the Book of Enoch in this way is to say that it was not written by Enoch and therefore is a fake or fictitious.

Various works have been attributed to Adam, Enoch, Moses, Isaiah, and other ancients. Opinions naturally differ on which texts come under this heading, and this is why Roman Catholic Bibles include works which non-Catholic versions do not.

The more recent scholarly opinion is that such books should be listed simply as apocryphal, or in other words "books outside the Canon." Thus there may be many reasons for excluding a book other than its alleged false authorship. Many of the canonical books are pseudonymous—that is, having been ascribed to names other than the original writer—but they find their place in the Canon because in the judgment of the compilers the texts contain authentic material of value.

The text of this book may be found in a work by R. H. Charles. D. Litt., D.D., under the title *The Book of Enoch or I Enoch* translated from the editor's Etheopic text and from some fragments in Greek. The only edition listed (1912) still in print is the same as the one in the Historian's Library at the Auditorium. It may be ordered from Oxford University Press, 1600 Pollitt Drive, Fair Lawn, New Jersey.

The Hebrew People

135. Age of Noah

QUESTION

Is there any explanation for the discrepancy of dates given in different chapters of Genesis concerning the age of Noah at the time of the flood? According to Genesis 7:85 and 11:7 Noah would be 594 years old. In Genesis 8:33 he is stated to be 600 years. The Inspired Version contains the same reckoning as the Authorized Version.

ANSWER

It may be that the two accounts were recorded at different times and by different narrators. If one thinks of the Bible as a plenary document dictated verbally in detail, then one has difficulty in reconciling conflicting records, which by the way are quite numerous. Many students are of the opinion that many of the books as we now have them are composite documents, and in compiling them those editing did not always harmonize the parts.

This is rather more reassuring than disturbing to me. If seen in correct perspective these are natural variations. If there are errors they are human.

After close examination of the manuscript of the Inspired Version, I am of the opinion that only those matters which Joseph Smith under inspiration saw as of importance were corrected. The matter of the age of Noah at a given time would be a minor point in the light of saving principles and may not have been pointed out.

143

136. Cain's Offering

QUESTION

Why was Cain's offering not acceptable if he brought the best of what he had? If the Lord's direction was for the firstfruits of the flock and Cain did not raise animals, did he err in not raising some, or in not going and buying some to make an offering?

ANSWER

A key to your question is found in Genesis 5:9, Inspired Version, "If thou doest well thou shalt be accepted, and if thou doest not well, sin lieth at the door." The reason for the rejection of the offering of Cain was that he was disobedient (Genesis 5:4): "But, behold, also Cain hearkened not, saying, Who is the Lord, that I should know him?" In contrast Abel was obedient: "And Abel hearkened unto the voice of the Lord" (Genesis 5:5). The scriptures tell us again that Cain loved Satan more than God (Genesis 5:6). His sin was willful disobedience, "for he rejected the greater counsel, which came from God" (Genesis 5:10).

The text does not indicate the specific act of disobedience, but his disobedience made his offering unacceptable. A careful reading of the whole chapter will show that God was impartial in dealing with these two brothers and sons of Adam. Cain's disobedience led to murder.

137. Chosen Today

QUESTION

Are the Jews a chosen people today?

ANSWER

The word "chosen" may be too narrowly defined. A person or people may be selected for a specific purpose, but not necessarily on a basis of favoritism.

It seems that the Hebrew people misinterpreted their selection. They were chosen because of their knowledge of the true God in a heathen world to be the instrument through which the knowledge of God should come to all men.

Their rejection of the Messiah meant a failure in commission. Paul saw the "chosen people" as those who were a "choosing people" also, and he interpreted for us the universal concept of salvation. He removed the choosing from dependence upon blood heredity and placed it upon a basis of response and willingness. He said, "They are not all Israel, which are of Israel" (Romans 9:6).

To the saints of Galatia he said:

"For ye are all the children of God by faith in Jesus Christ. For as many of you as have been baptized into Christ have put on Christ. There is neither Jew nor Greek, there is neither bond nor free, there is neither male nor female; for ye are all one in Christ Jesus. And if ye are Christ's, then are ye Abraham's seed, and heirs according to the promise."—Galatians 3:26-29.

Thus when we speak of latter-day Israel in the Restoration sense we mean those who are covenanted in Christ, not by blood but by obedience. To use a Pauline expression again:

"But when the fulness of the time was come, God sent forth his Son, made of a woman, made under the law,

"To redeem them that were under the law, that we might receive the adoption of sons.

"And because ye are sons, God hath sent forth the Spirit of his Son into your hearts, crying, Abba, Father.

"Wherefore thou art no more a servant, but a son; and if a son, then an heir of God through Christ."—Galatians 4:4-7.

Whatever our racial heritage we must come into this chosen relationship to be counted God's people. Thus the obedient Hebrews are called in this age also. One of the stated purposes of the Book of Mormon was to do this—to bring both Jew and Gentile into the covenant family of God. The preface states:

". . . and also to the convincing of the Jew and Gentile that Jesus is the Christ, the Eternal God, manifesting himself unto all nations."

138. A Chosen People

QUESTION

Who are the chosen people?

ANSWER

This description is usually applied to the people of Israel. It certainly has no meaning of favoritism although they, with others, may have at times so believed. God has chosen to work through certain channels and individuals in history and, thereby, placed great responsibility upon such. Members of the RLDS church, too, have a special calling and in this sense are chosen, but when we interpret this as exclusive, we miss the mark. Peter answered this in Acts 10:34 where it is stated: "Of a truth I perceive that God is no respecter of persons."

139. Author of Pentateuch

QUESTION

I understand that many modern scholars hold the opinion that the Pentateuch was not actually written by Moses. Could you indicate the basis upon which they form their opinion?

ANSWER

This opinion is not by any means a new theory or a modern one as your question implies. I have before me a volume of *Saints' Herald* published in 1875 at Plano, Illinois, wherein is an article captioned "Past and Present" by J. W. Briggs. This writer makes a scholarly analysis of the Pentateuch and takes the position that the actual text came into being many years after the death of Moses. His research lists a number of incidents and facts which are in the text which had not occurred or were not yet true. The outstanding point of evidence is that the last chapter in Deuteronomy describes Moses' own funeral. Moses obviously did not write that record. Multiplication of similar details is unnecessary to make the point clear.

It is obvious that persons later than the time of Moses were involved in preparation of the records. Of course, the Pentateuch is known as the Five Books of Moses, not because he wrote them in detail but because he is the character that stands out so boldly in the development and national focus of the Israelites. Through Moses much of the law was given.

This is not to state that a great deal of the record is not the teachings of Moses as he presented them to the people on occasions. Most students do not take the position that these words have come down to us in exact terms, but that they have passed through many hands and a great number of translations. This alone can explain differing versions of the same incident in the Pentateuch.

The statement of Joseph Smith, Jr., found in the document traditionally known as "the epitome" that "in the Bible is *contained* the word of God in so far as it is correctly translated" may help in obtaining a sound perspective.

140. Leviticus and Dietary Provisions

QUESTION

How do we as a church regard the dietary provisions and laws mentioned in Leviticus 11?

ANSWER

This chapter of the Pentateuch in the Old Testament must be considered in the same way as any other regulations set up for the children of Israel. It must be remembered that the people to whom these instructions were given were a nation emerging from slavery and all that goes with it in lack of moral, spiritual, and intellectual opportunity.

We certainly cannot attempt to apply all the technical provisions of the Old Testament today in the way they were presented to these early people.

The lists of clean and unclean beasts and other creatures given in Leviticus were obviously guides to a local situation. This situation must be seen not only in the light of the creatures mentioned but also of their habits as related to their environment.

It is true that these privileges and taboos were enforced rigidly by their officers. They needed a disciplinary code spelled out in detail. Paul was later to speak of the Law of Moses as a schoolmaster to bring them to a position where they could appreciate the Christian concepts of life. He also spoke of this code in a way which relegated it to a position of no efficacy. To some who would have applied the rules of Moses he said, "Now therefore why tempt ye God, to put a yoke upon the neck of the disciples, which neither our fathers nor we were able to bear?" (Acts 15:10).

We may get some help by taking Leviticus as a whole. Most people would agree that the primitive rules of purification and others of one-time ceremonial procedures are not applicable to our time under Christian motivations. Regulations of dress and the provision for walls on the roofs of houses and so forth illustrate the local and particular purpose of certain levitical rules.

As often stated in this column we must look for principles rather than for rules to govern conduct. The rule requiring a parapet on a

147

house was related to the type of houses where the housetop was used and therefore needed a safety provision. This rule would be good today where the housetop is used as a place of living. In fact, we do usually require this where there are stairs leading to roof gardens and so forth.

Moses has been described as the "father of modern hygiene," and a broad view of his provisions reveals some basic principles that are unchangeable. Viewed in this light, much help can be obtained by studying his laws and the reasons for them. Unless, however, we see them thus we could be led into some ridiculous procedures in our time. In Deuteronomy 22:12 we find a rule of dress which requires a fringe to be attached. A little thought can suggest reasons for such particular rules as this, but they are not applicable to our day.

The laws of Moses still apply to us where the principle and purpose of a rule are true for our circumstances. Because of need in a particular circumstance and for a particular people many rules are made that are not universal.

141. Ark of the Covenant

QUESTION

What was the Ark of the Covenant? Please explain its significance.

ANSWER

There are a large number of references to this object in the Old Testament. In addition to being called the "Ark of the Covenant" it is referred to as the "Ark of Yahweh [God]" and in later priestly references as the "Ark of the Testimony."

In the earlier passages it appears to be a simple wooden chest, but later descriptions indicate a much more elaborate vessel ornamented with gold. (Compare Deuteronomy 10:1-5 and Exodus 25 and 37.)

In this receptacle were placed the tablets on which were inscribed the law. The ark was placed in the inner portion (the holy of holies) of the tabernacle. The tabernacle was a tent structure which was erected in the center of the Israelites' camp wherever they sojourned for the time.

The significance of the ark seems to have been to keep before the Israelites their relation to Jehovah and the need to obey his law. There is indication that at sometime it became, in their view, an extension or pervasion of Jehovah's personality, therefore the interpretation given by these people that when the ark was with them they were powerful and when absent they were unprotected as in the case of its capture by the Philistines.

Much ritual surrounded the ark and the tabernacle; the arrangement of the priestly groups and the various tribes around the tabernacle containing the ark was very particular.

It appears that the ark functioned symbolically as many scriptural objects do. It had no inherent power of itself, though then, as now, the people of God did not always look beyond the physical artifacts involved in their worship to the spiritual meaning intended. The children of Israel had to be led from more elementary concepts of divinity to the place where they could worship in spirit and in truth (John 4:20-24, A.V.)

We find no mention of the Ark of the Covenant in the historical books after it was lodged in Solomon's Temple (I Kings 8). It was thereafter no longer housed in a portable tabernacle as had been the case since Sinai. Its final fate is a mystery, although it probably was destroyed in the Babylonian invasion.

Church History

142. Gun in Carthage Jail

QUESTION

Did Joseph Smith take a gun to Carthage jail to defend himself? Did he use it when attacked? John L. Smith in a book, "Has Mormonism Changed," says that he did. Please comment.

ANSWER

In *Saints' Herald*, Volume 40, page 391, June 24, 1893, the following appears in an editorial (Editor Joseph Smith III):

"The 'squad' that attacked the jail has never been estimated by any writer at less than one hundred and forty; and from that to two hundred. The only weapon that any of the prisoners had was a small six barrel revolver, of the old time Allen's pattern; and that was one that was thrust upon Joseph Smith by one of his brethren, when leaving the jail the evening before the attack. This weapon was discharged from the open door at the crowd surging up the stairway inside the building after the guard was overcome and had ceased all show of resistance. It was not possible for one of the prisoners to fire upon those outside the building through the door, as there was but one door to the room they were in, and that opened into a hall inside the building. The door was not broken down, but was forced partially open, and the assailing party fired into the room through the half open doorway. The mob did not enter the room, but stood in the hallway; the cry that Joseph Smith had jumped out the window attracted them from the room to the outside of the building, Hyrum being already dead.

150

In *Journal of History* (Editor Heman C. Smith), Volume II, page 398, the following appears:

"The following account of the death of Joseph and Hyrum Smith by an eye witness, William M. Daniels, was published at Nauvoo, Illinois, in 1845, by John Taylor. There have been reprints of this pamphlet published recently, but fortunately an original copy has come to our hands from which we copy. Some of the language is scathing, especially that following the account proper, but considering the provocation at the time it is not to be wondered at."

Having made this explanation of the source of his material, Heman C. Smith gives the following from the Daniels account, page 410:

"A few hours previous to this a friend of General Joseph Smith put in his possession a revolving pistol which discharged six shots. With this in hand, he took a position by the wall at the left of the door. While this scene was transpiring, Joseph Smith reached his pistol through the door, which was pushed a little ajar, and fired three of the barrels; the rest misfired. 'He wounded three of them—two mortally . . .'"

An abridged copy of this appeared in *Saints' Herald*, Volume 99, page 585, June 23, 1952. The reference to the pistol was the same as in the previous quote.

If we read the last two quotations in relation to the editorial given here we have about as much information as is available.

It should be remembered that Daniels' account is an uncorroborated story. The original referred to in *Journal of History* is in the Historian's care.

143. Fate of Mob Which Murdered Joseph Smith

QUESTION

I read that every one of those participating in the mob which murdered Joseph Smith met death in a tragic way. Is this truth or rumor?

ANSWER

All those participating in the unlawful action which killed Joseph Smith are obviously unknown, but there have been several efforts to identify members of the mob. Five of these were eventually brought to trial. After a trial which reeked with prejudice and by a judge who, according to Governor Ford (*Ford's History of Illinois*, page 368), was under duress, they were acquitted.

Endeavor has been made to identify the members of the mob. Backenstos, who was Hancock County sheriff, listed sixty-one names of those who allegedly took part. Willard Richards, who was with the prisoners, offered sixteen names. In a Utah publication, *The Fate of the Persecutors of the Prophet Joseph Smith*, by N. B. Lundwell, Chapter 16, a number of persons are discussed in this connection who are alleged to have died violent deaths. Only two of these appear in the lists of Backenstos and Richards. Of the sixty-one previously mentioned, one third were either unemployed or in disreputable occupations.

Our opinion is that there is not enough evidence to make such a blanket statement. Some evidence offered is second- and third-hand. There appears to be no abnormal number of these suspected participants dying by other than natural causes. The end of life of the type of accused persons is often a natural result of their low style of living and the habits they have.

In short, research done by the staff in my department does not bear out the statement that all the mobocrats involved died tragically. That some did does not justify generalization.

144. Manuscript from Nauvoo House

QUESTION

Why was a part of the manuscript taken from the Nauvoo House given to the Utah church?

ANSWER

Major Lewis Bidamon, I understand, was responsible for the sharing of the manuscript found beneath the cornerstone in the Nauvoo House. Major Bidamon was the second husband of Emma Hale Smith, the widow of Joseph Smith, Jr. To the best of my knowledge he did not become a member of either the Utah church or of the Reorganization and, not being committed personally to either, acted in what he obviously felt was an impartial way, sharing a document with the two major groups interested.

The RLDS portion of twenty pages soon crumbled since they had been previously exposed to damp and frost. Officials of the Utah church endeavored to preserve theirs, succeeding only with a small portion.

Relevant, though not directly involved in your question, is the fact that the other complete manuscript held by the RLDS Church has a number of handwritings which leads to the view that it was considered the original. It is most unlikely that an original document of this importance would have been placed in a cornerstone with attendant hazards.

145. Nauvoo Legion

QUESTION

When was the Nauvoo Legion organized and how many soldiers did it contain?

ANSWER

On February 3, 1841, the Nauvoo City Council passed an ordinance providing for the organization of the Nauvoo Legion. The minutes of the actual organizational meeting of the legion appear according to the Journal of Joseph Smith (published by the Utah church as *History of the Church*, Vol. IV, p. 295) under the date of February 4, 1841.

The date given for the passing of the ordinance by the city council is printed as February 8. This must be a misprint, since the organization could not have taken place before passage of the ordinance providing for it.

According to the above reference, a bill for the establishment of the University of Nauvoo was passed on the same day, which was given as February 3, 1841.

Inez Smith Davis, in her *Story of the Church*, page 303, states that the Nauvoo Legion numbered over a thousand men.

146. Foundation Stone

QUESTION

When and under what circumstances was the foundation stone of the Nauvoo Temple laid?

ANSWER

There were four foundation stones laid for the Nauvoo Temple with great ceremony on April 6, 1841. It is estimated that the

153

attendance was at least ten thousand. A full account of the occasion can be found in *Times and Seasons,* Volume 2, Number 12, page 375, April 15, 1841. A few details from this account are interesting. The Nauvoo Legion, a military organization of the city, was present with all the customary grandeur of parade. A silk national flag was presented to Joseph Smith as Lieutenant General by the women of Nauvoo. I quote:

> "At 12 M the procession arrived upon the Temple ground, inclosing the same in a hollow square, with Lieutenant General Smith, Major General Bennett, Brigadier Generals Law and Smith, their respective staffs, guard, field officers, distinguished visitors, choir band &c. in the center, and the ladies and gentlemen citizens surrounding in the interior. The superior officers together with the banner, architects, principal speaker &c. were duly conducted to the stand at the principal corner stone, and the religious services were commenced by singing from page sixty-five of the new hymn book."

President Sidney Rigdon then delivered an oration after which the four stones were laid. The southeast stone was lowered into position by the architects under the direction of the First Presidency. Joseph Smith pronounced a benediction, declaring the stone representative of the Presidency. President Rigdon also pronounced a benediction.

After an adjournment of one hour the southwest and second stone was laid under the direction of the "President of the High Priesthood and his council and President Marks" with benediction by the president of the High Priesthood. The third stone on the northwest corner was representative of the twelve apostles who, being absent, were represented by the High Council. Elias Higbee pronounced the benediction. The placing of the fourth and northeast corner stone was supervised by the Bishopric, and Bishop Whitney offered benediction expressive of the place of the Aaronic priesthood.

Over five years later and after the death of Joseph Smith, Jr., the *Hancock Eagle* for April, 1846, announced the dedication of the Temple. Research indicates that though the main structure was erected it was not completed. What motive pressured Brigham Young, who had assumed leadership in Nauvoo, to plan this premature dedication is not clear. Possibly a superstitious fear of failing to follow out the instructions of Joseph Smith as given in Doctrine and Covenants 107:11-14 was the motivation. However, the announcement referred to was made immediately before the Young faction set out for the Great Salt Lake.

147. Nephi or Moroni in Vision

QUESTION

On page 159 in the book "Restoration—A Study in Prophecy" by Elbert A. Smith, why are both the names Nephi and Moroni given as the one appearing to Joseph Smith in vision? Which one was it?

ANSWER

The word "Nephi" appears first in *Times and Seasons*, Volume 3, page 753, and was repeated in the *Millennial Star*, a newspaper published in England. The use of the word "Nephi" instead of Moroni is an error there. In Doctrine and Covenants, Section 26:2 (1830) and in Section 110:20 (a letter written in 1842 by Joseph Smith) the name Moroni is given. The 1830 revelation was in the 1835 edition of the Doctrine and Covenants which was published after scrutiny by a committee, and endorsed by the church.

Further research has shown that the preface of the 1840, 1842, and 1858 editions of the Book of Mormon is signed "Moroni." The date 1840 antedates the reference in *Times and Seasons*, Volume 3, of 1842. Seeing that Moroni was used in 1830, 1840, and 1842 it is our opinion that the *Times and Seasons* reference is an error, it being the only place the word "Nephi" appears.

148. Revelation Designating Kirtland Edifice a Temple

QUESTION

Was the edifice in Kirtland designated a temple by revelation?

ANSWER

No. The first reference involving the word "temple" is in Doctrine and Covenants 35:3. This is actually biblical language as in Malachi 3:1 and is in no way specific as to location. Further reference is made in Doctrine and Covenants Section 42:10c which undoubtedly refers to the building up of Zion, the place of which had not been revealed at that time. This revelation was received in February, 1831. In Section 45:3a there is further reference to the word "temple," but this is simply a paraphrasing of Luke 19:44; 21:6-24.

Not until July, 1831, was there specific information as to the building of a temple, and this was with regard to an edifice in the

Center Place, Independence, Missouri (see Doctrine and Covenants 57:1 d).

The building in Kirtland was referred to in Doctrine and Covenants 85:36 as the "house of God." Some details for the building of the House of the Lord are found in Section 92:3. This structure was completed and dedicated early in 1836. As late as May, 1841, it was referred to as the "Lord's House" (see *Times and Seasons*, Vol. 2, p. 459). The original inscription on the building was "House of the Lord."

In later years the building was described as "Kirtland Temple," and the present custom of referring to it in this manner is one of usage. This may not appear to be significant, but it is important when the question of temple function is considered. Our viewpoint is that the purposes in Section 85:36 and in Section 92:3 e, f are clear and explicit. In the light of these texts, practices which were later indulged in by those failing to follow the early church patterns of worship are seen to be departures in principle.

149. Reorganization and Title to Kirtland Temple

QUESTION

Does the Reorganization at present have a clear title to the Kirtland Temple? If so, could you give particulars as to when and how it was acquired?

ANSWER

Yes, the Reorganization has clear title.

A full consideration of the factors involved in the ownership of the Kirtland Temple would require too lengthy a statement for this column. I will, however, endeavor to give the main points.

An action known as the "Kirtland Temple Suit" was instigated by the Reorganized Church of Jesus Christ of Latter Day Saints, which by its attorneys appeared before the Court of Common Pleas, Lake County, Ohio, February 23, 1880, asking for possession of Kirtland Temple. The church in Utah was named with other parties as defendants. These others were such persons who might have laid claim to ownership because of certain transactions over the property which had occurred since the death of the prophet, Joseph Smith. After the death of Joseph Smith the property was sold to satisfy certain debts of a personal nature. Through several persons in succession, the deed eventually came into the possession of Joseph Smith

III and Mark Forscutt, and this deed or title was held by them at the time the church took action for possession of the Kirtland Temple. This document is in the General Church Historian's file in the Auditorium. The reason the Reorganized Church took action to establish ownership when a deed was already held by Joseph Smith and Mark Forscutt, members of the church, is set out in *Joseph Smith III*, pages 287 to 291.

The result of the court action was that the Reorganized Church was adjudged the legal successor of the original church, but legal title was not granted to the Reorganized Church in that judgment. The judge stated that the legal title was held by the descendants of Joseph Smith but was held in trust for the church; therefore the previous sales of the property to others to satisfy personal obligations was wrong. Legally he felt unable to adjudge the Reorganized Church the owner, but in stating that the Reorganized Church was the legal successor, it becomes evident that Joseph Smith and his brothers were trustees, holding for the successor, the Reorganized Church. It is a quibble to argue, as some have, that the petition was denied the Reorganized Church. Technically, the church as such was not granted possession at that time, but in effect the decision in favor of the heirs of Joseph Smith as trustees for the original church made the Reorganized Church the legal owner of the Temple. The judgment states the position of successorship to be held by the Reorganized Church.

S. A. Burgess, who did much research in this matter, makes these points in an opinion now in the Church Historian's files:

1. The court decision leaves it that Joseph Smith, Jr., bought or held the Kirtland Temple property in trust for the church and not as a personal possession.
2. It was wrongly sold to pay debts.
3. It belongs to the original church and its successors.
4. Joseph Smith's heirs held legal title in trust for the church.
5. The judge found the Reorganized Church is that church in continuity or succession ("in legal language succession equals continuity."—S.A.B.).
6. The judge declined in view of statute to hold that the Reorganized Church had legal title.
7. His judgment indicated it had equitable title with legal title in the heirs of Joseph Smith, Jr., as trustees.

To have the title clearly and legally vested in the Reorganized Church of Jesus Christ of Latter Day Saints was thereafter a simple and legal procedure. There is no possible question as to the ownership of the Temple resting with this church, but it is not correct to say that Judge Sherman placed the legal title with the church at the time of the court hearing as it is sometimes said. That statement is open to objection on a technical point only. The Reorganized Church does own the Temple.

150. Difference between House and Temple

QUESTION

In reading Section 94 of Doctrine and Covenants I noted the command which says, "Verily I say unto you, that it is my will that an house should be built unto me in the land of Zion, like unto the pattern which I have given you; yea, let it be built speedily by the tithing of my people."

Is there a difference between a house and a temple, and has this command ever been fulfilled?

ANSWER

I see very little possible difference between a house of the Lord and a temple. What is now known as Kirtland Temple was originally "House of the Lord." However, in referring to the building to be erected in Independence, Missouri, the word "temple" was used in sections 57:1 d and 83:1, 2 of Doctrine and Covenants.

Paralleling these with Section 94:3, 4, we get the functions of a temple; i.e., a center of worship and instruction in matters of the kingdom of God.

Unfortunately events did not allow the fulfilling of the command to build. Later those who moved to Utah built what they called temples, in which secret, unscriptural practices have been featured. By this means the word "temple" has been colored to signify concepts foreign to original intent. Other religious groups use the word "temple" in the sense of a house of worship and learning.

The command to build a temple in Independence has never been implemented.

151. Church Political Paper in Ohio

QUESTION

I have been informed that the early church leaders at Kirtland, Ohio, published a weekly "political paper." I find no reference to this in our church's historical writings. Could you supply any information regarding this?

In *Church History*, Volume I, page 379, an excerpt of a letter from Joseph Smith at Kirtland to Bishop Edward Partridge at Liberty, Missouri, appears:

"We are now distributing the type and calculate to commence setting to-day, and issue a paper the last of this week, or the beginning of next."

This of course referred to the *Evening and the Morning Star*, terminated by mob action in Independence in July, 1833, and recommenced the following December. The entire letter quoted from was first published in *Times and Seasons*, Volume VI, pages 913-915, and contains the following item relating to your question:

"We expect shortly to publish a political paper, weekly, in favor of the present administration; the influential men of that party have offered a liberal patronage to us, and we hope to succeed, for thereby we can show the public the purity of our intention in supporting the government under which we live."

About fourteen months later, F. G. Williams, publisher of the *LDS Messenger and Advocate,* began printing a political paper called *The Northern Times*. It was published weekly between February and October of that year. Very little information is available regarding this periodical, since no known copies are extant today. One searches in vain for references to *The Northern Times* in the current papers of the 1830's. Thus the assumption is that this paper was of nominal political importance or influence.

In view of the exacting temporal demands upon the Saints toward the completion of the house of the Lord at Kirtland, it is probable that the paper never gained very wide circulation.

More significant than the fact of the existence of *The Northern Times*, however, is the attitude in evidence in December, 1833, on the part of Joseph Smith in his plans to publish this type of paper. He wanted the public to know of the Saints' basic political loyalty to the government of the land, which government had seemed so reluctant to honor the church's efforts to secure redress for their astonishing losses in life, civil liberties, and property.

152. John C. and James A. Bennett

QUESTION

In my study of church history I have encountered the names John

C. Bennett and James Arlington Bennett. It has been suggested to me that they are one and the same person. Please comment.

ANSWER

This has confused others, but it appears that they are two distinct personalities. Confusion has occurred even in periodicals of the times due, no doubt, to the similarity of names.

However, the surnames are spelled differently. John C. Bennett spelled his name with a double "t," while James Arlington Bennet ended his with one "t".

John C. Bennett, of dubious notoriety, held membership and priesthood in the church and high civic offices in Nauvoo until 1842 when he was expelled from the church for unchristian conduct. He later wrote a series of articles against the church which were subsequently published as a book, *History of the Saints*.

In this book, page 40, there is printed a letter over the signature of Sidney Rigdon and addressed to James Arlington Bennet, Arlington House, Long Island, attesting the character of John C. Bennett. Here, therefore, are the two names in the same letter, with the correct spelling of each.

In the *History of Joseph Smith* (Deseret Press), based on his own journal, is an entry obviously from a report from Brigham Young which is quoted as follows:

"Tuesday, 29 [August, 1843]—Elder Brigham Young paid a visit to James Arlington Bennett (sic), Arlington House, Long Island, and baptized and confirmed him next day."—Volume 5, page 556.

Niles Register, February 3, 1844, page 355, published a letter from James Arlington Bennet to Joseph Smith, Jr., dated October 24, 1843, in which Bennett referred to an encounter with Brigham Young, describing it as follows:

". . . a glorious frolic in the clear blue ocean; for most assuredly a frolick it was, without a moment's reflection or consideration. Nothing of this kind would in the least attach me to your person or cause. I am capable of being a most undeviating friend, without being governed by the smallest religious influence."

This certainly does not give the same interpretation of the alleged baptism as the report made to Joseph Smith, but it at least serves further to establish the identity of James Arlington Bennet as distinct from John C. Bennett. Surely Brigham Young could not have been referring to the expelled ex-Mayor Bennett of Nauvoo!

153. Scriptures in Other Languages

In Inez Smith Davis' "Story of the Church," sixth edition, second revision, 1959, page 600, the following appears:
"1851, Doctrine and Covenants published in Welsh . . . May 1, 1851, Book of Mormon published in Danish . . . 1852, Book of Mormon published in French, German, and Italian; also, April 6, in Welsh.
"1852, Doctrine and Covenants published in Danish."
Where and by whom were these seven books published?

ANSWER

The 1851 publication of Doctrine and Covenants in the Welsh language contained 111 sections and was translated and published by John Davis at Merthyr-Tydfil, Wales.

In 1851 the Book of Mormon was translated from English into Danish, as *Mormons Bog,* by Erastus Snow and Peter O. Hansen, and published by F. E. Bording, Copenhagen. This was the first publication of the Book of Mormon in a language other than English.

In 1852 the French translation of the Book of Mormon, *Le Livre De Mormon,* was made by John Taylor and Curtis E. Bolton, and published by John Taylor, Paris Rue De Tournon.

The first German translation and publication of the Book of Mormon, entitled *Das Buch Mormon,* translated by John Taylor and G. Parker Dykes, was published in 1852 by John Taylor at Hamburg, F. H. Nestler and Melle, printers.

The Italian edition of the Book of Mormon, *Il Libro Di Mormon,* was first published by the Utah church in London, England, in 1852.

The first Welsh edition of the Book of Mormon, *Llyfe Mormon,* was translated and published by John Davis at Merthyr-Tydfil, Wales. The title page bears the date of April 6, 1852.

The 1852 Danish edition of Doctrine and Covenants, containing 111 sections, was published by F. E. Bording, Copenhagen, Denmark.

All of the books referred to in your question were published under the auspices of the Utah Mormon church.

154. Jason Briggs and Zenas H. Gurley, Jr.

QUESTION

What disturbed Jason Briggs and Zenas H. Gurley, Jr., who withdrew from the church in 1886? Did they ever return?

They did not return as far as I am aware. There was no stain on their characters, and I find myself wishing that ways had been found to retain the valuable contributions that would have accrued.

Jason W. Briggs was a man with knowledge and insight beyond many of his contemporaries, and I fear some of his views—now quite acceptable to many scholarly members—were misunderstood as being opposed to faith. When we consider that articles found acceptance in the *Herald* of those years endeavoring to sustain the view that the world is flat, we sense some of the difficulties faced by an intellectual like Briggs. He wrote, among other works, a series of articles entitled "Past and Present" in which he dealt with the historical aspects of the Pentateuch which were disturbing to some who took an oversimplified stand on the textual accuracy of scripture.

Here is a valuable lesson to be learned from history—we must never dogmatically demand conformity, especially on matters of lesser detail. Joseph Smith III was concerned over the attitudes which caused these brethren to withdraw, but he did not succeed in having a better approach to the problem. Briggs was later to state that had some expressions of understanding been made prior to the action of withdrawal, it might not have been necessary for him to do so.

There were other matters which he considered important, and Zenas Gurley, Jr., shared his opinion. This is a point where we might ask the sad query, "What might have been under better circumstances?" A full statement on the withdrawal and all the factors involved is published in *Saints' Herald*, Volume 33, page 249.

155. First Publication of Follett Sermon

QUESTION

In your answer concerning the Follett sermon you stated that the first publication was in "Times and Seasons," August 15, 1844. Is it not true that there was an earlier publication of this material in a pamphlet, "The Voice of Truth," published by John Taylor in Nauvoo, dated June, 1844? I have a copy of this document.

ANSWER

Your question is a most interesting one, and as a result I did considerable further research, because my desire is to be accurate.

As a result I am still of the opinion that the date of August 15, 1844, is the correct one. Previous historians agree with this as does the statement of several Utah church scholars. If they could substantiate an earlier date it would be helpful to some of their theological contentions as it would bring the publication within the lifetime of Joseph Smith, Jr., with the natural conclusion that though the report was not verbatim it had the review of the author at the time.

There are several copies of *The Voice of Truth* in my files. The cover is of yellow paper and bears the following title:

"The Voice of Truth, containing the public writings,
portrait, and last sermon of President Joseph Smith.
Nauvoo, Illinois. Printed by John Taylor. 1845."

Inside the cover on the title page, the subtitle lists all the items expected to appear under the copyright. This is dated 1844, but it is significant that the Follett sermon is not listed as it is on the cover. On the following unnumbered page is this detail:

"Entered according to the act of Congress, in the
year 1844 by W. W. Phelps, in the clerk's office
of the district court of Illinois."

On the third page is a dedication in the form of a one-stanza poem. Below this appears the date—June, 1844. It is this item that may lead one to the false conclusion that the booklet was published in June, 1844.

The last item in the brochure is the Follett sermon and is captioned, "Appendix—Joseph Smith's last sermon, delivered at the April Conference, 1844."

It should be noted that it is included as an appendix, which is usually supplementary to the main body of material, and also that it is described as the "last sermon." This designation as the last sermon could not have occurred before the death of Joseph Smith. His death was not anticipated. This would indicate a later printing than June, 1844, as Joseph Smith, Jr., did not die until June 27.

That the date on the title page and the registration of copyright is 1844 is not significant because in those days the only requirement to secure copyright is the presentation of the title page.

On the back cover under "Errata" is found "Read 'and appendix' on title page," which indicates that the addition of the Follett sermon was not made until after the copyrighting in 1844.

When all these considerations are taken together it becomes evident that the earliest printing must have been *Times and Seasons*, August 15, 1844.

156. Joseph Smith and the Negro

QUESTION

In a magazine article discussing the Utah church attitude toward the Negro people this statement was made: "The Negroes' exclusion goes back to Joseph Smith . . . who wrote that the Negro, as a descendant of Ham, bore the curse that God had placed on the descendants of Cain." How much does this statement represent Joseph Smith's doctrines—if at all?

ANSWER

A pronouncement or an opinion of one such as Joseph Smith is not necessarily infallible. Nor does a statement claiming revelation become a matter of dogma immune from analysis or questioning by others. The fact that Joseph Smith is recognized by the church as having been inspired in his leadership does not commit the body to his view at all points.

Joseph Smith had the limitations inherent in his educational status and also by many concepts in the social milieu in which he was placed. He did not automatically become omniscient and all-wise because he had a special commission.

I make this qualifying introduction because Joseph Smith did make statements along the line of the quotation you have given. He followed the train of thought on the question of the colored people that most of his contemporaries did. The literal interpretation of the cursing of Canaan and Ham was not questioned by him in the 1830's. He wrote to this effect in the *Latter Day Saints' Messenger and Advocate* (Volume II, No. 7, April 1836). In this article he obviously misconstrued the source of the curse. It was not a divine curse but the curse by Noah uttered following a regrettable incident caused by Noah's drunkenness.

It is also a matter of record that Joseph Smith lived to change his mind. Instead of believing Negro slavery to be the design of God he proposed the liberation of the slaves of America by purchase and the granting to them of full constitutional rights. This is announced in his political platform when he sought nomination for the Presidency of the United States in 1844. He proposed a six-year period to effect this change which was to complete the program by 1850. Joseph Smith was killed on June 27, 1844, and therefore did not run for President. Thus he lacked the opportunity to amplify his reconsidered views on slavery, its cause, and its future as he saw it.

Your question deserves a frank answer because many people do not understand Joseph Smith's change of stand; they are ignorant either of his earlier interpretation or of his later position advocating abolition. I have no information that he changed view on the curse of God being the dark color, but we do know he proposed abolition. Evidence has been produced of the ordination of two Negroes to priesthood offices in the early Restoration movement. Both reports owe their origin to Utah church sources.

157. Nicolaitans

QUESTION

In the "Saints' Advocate" of July, 1883 (page 352), reference is made to a revelation in which Newel K. Whitney is rebuked for his association with the Nicolaitan band. Can you explain the nature of the Nicolaitans? Why should Whitney have had need to be ashamed of them?

ANSWER

It is not clear whether this reference involves a specific organization or is used as descriptive of a certain type of social behavior. The revelation you refer to appeared in *Millennial Star*, Volume 16, pages 183, 184, and involves various counsels to individuals and the church. Particularly noted are William Marks and Newel K. Whitney. Marks is spoken of with approval, but Whitney is counseled to be ashamed of his involvement in Nicolaitan behavior.

Beyond reference to "their secret abominations" there is little to indicate what Joseph Smith intended to convey. Undoubtedly it was not a complimentary reference.

Research on the word "Nicolaitans" which appears only once in the Bible (Revelation 2:6) fails to reveal a sure definition of what was involved in the reprehensible behavior of these people. The consensus appears to be that they were involved in idolatry, which in those times in particular involved immorality. Heathen feasts tended to foster licentious behavior. The word "fornication" in the early Christian Era also connoted unfaithfulness to God.

However, it is of interest to note that the Utah church has put Newel K. Whitney forward as the custodian of the purported revelation on polygamy. W. W. Blair described him as "the wet-nurse and guardian of the pretended polygamous revelation."

If this is true, as Utah literature would make it appear, Joseph

Smith may have been aware of a tendency to immorality and used the words "Nicolaitan band" to describe such people. It is true that Whitney went to Utah and endorsed polygamy. He died in Utah in 1850.

158. Adam-ondi-Ahman

QUESTION

What is the significance of Adam-ondi-Ahman? Are the theological and historical statements about this place valid? In what way was Joseph Smith connected with the existing legends?

ANSWER

I do not know what particular theological and historical statements you have in mind, so this is difficult to answer categorically.

As to the historical significance, Adam-ondi-Ahman is the name of a town developed by the Saints in Daviess County, Missouri, after their expulsion from Jackson County and later removal from Clay County. A stake was organized by the same name centering in this town.

Joseph Smith is credited, by the Utah church, with the statement that Adam-ondi-Ahman was so named "because it is the place where Adam shall come to visit his people." However, it was not until 1854 that such a statement was printed in the *Millennial Star* (Vol. 16, p. 125) which of course is a Utah Mormon publication. This same statement appears in the RLDS *Church History* (Vol. 2, p. 153), but it was quoted from Utah Mormon sources which have admittedly been edited under the careful supervision of the leaders of that church. This statement attributed to Joseph appears nowhere in the endorsed revelations of our church.

Somewhere a legend arose that when Joseph Smith and a party came upon a mound of stone near Gallatin, Missouri, he said that this was Adam's grave. However, extensive research through the years has failed to reveal the source of this legend. It is therefore more than likely purely imaginative.

We do know that this term originated in usage in March, 1832 (Section 77:3 e), in reference to the Holy One of Zion "who hath established the foundations of Adam-ondi-Ahman." In March, 1835, another use of the term indicated that Adam-ondi-Ahman was the name of a place where Adam blessed his posterity (Section 104:28 a). These texts obviously could have had no connection to the later place

166

name of the stake organized in June, 1838. It appears that from the vantage point of the previously mentioned old rock mound which was speculatively referred to as "an old Nephite altar," Joseph Smith in May, 1838, was moved to compare the matchless beauty of the valley spread out before him with the primeval state of creation.

John Corrill, once of Far West, later wrote in his history that "Adam-ondi-Ahman" meant "The valley of God in which Adam blessed his children." Such a name as this, given to the Mormon community endeavor in Daviess County in 1838, cannot logically be linked with a claim that it was intended to indicate the actual residence of Adam on this continent.

In my opinion legends tying the term "Adam-ondi-Ahman" as used in sections 77:3 e and 104:28 a (given in Kirtland, Ohio) with the town and stake of 1838 of that name are not justified beyond that indicated in the preceding paragraph. These legends are not theologically or historically authenticated. I know of no evidence in the Bible, Book of Mormon, or Doctrine and Covenants, nor in the findings of archaeological researchers that would justify the idea that Adam ever lived on this continent. A hymn written by W. W. Phelps, entitled "Adam-ondi-Ahman," was published in the *Latter Day Saints' Messenger and Advocate* in June, 1835 (Vol. 1, p. 144). The sentiment expressed by this author suggests a perfect condition of beauty and righteousness as was found in the days of Enoch. The hopes of the early Saints of establishing the Zionic city evidently influenced the naming of the modern town in Missouri.

159. "Profiles in Courage" Series

QUESTION

My children have asked several questions after seeing the television showing of General Doniphan in the "Profiles in Courage" series. Was the film correct in placing Adam-ondi-Ahman a little east of Far West, Missouri, and was Adam really there? Also was Sidney Rigdon accurately portrayed as a preacher using the word "extermination" in his sermon?

ANSWER

The film was a fairly accurate portrayal. Of course there were minor details which might be considered as dramatic license. The main facts were well presented. Adam-ondi-Ahman was correctly stated to be east of Far West, Missouri.

The legend concerning Adam grew out of some remarks attributed to Joseph Smith, Jr. The Utah church has made much of this. The Reorganization has not taken the legend seriously, whatever the basis of the remarks attributed to Joseph Smith. The name is mentioned in Doctrine and Covenants but only representative of a condition rather than an American location.

We have many things in North America, and an ancient history much deeper than many know, but I doubt if the Garden of Eden can be placed on this continent. This strains any interpretation of the facts.

Rigdon was correctly quoted in his speech with reference to the word "extermination." This may have been in Governor Boggs's mind when he issued his infamous "Extermination Order." In the light of history Rigdon's remark was unfortunate and undoubtedly inflammatory.

Judging by pictures available, the characterization of Rigdon was not too accurate in my opinion. He had more dignity than appeared in the film. Probably the purpose was to convey the idea of his not being the prime figure in the church. The main thing to keep in mind is that the film was intended to show the courage of General Doniphan. In doing this the producer dealt kindly with the Latter Day Saint pioneers and this was well done even if unusual.

160. Manuscript History by John Whitmer

QUESTION

Is there in existence a manuscript history by John Whitmer? I have been told that John Whitmer's history printed in the "Journal of History" (RLDS) is not a faithful copy. Would you state the facts?

ANSWER

Yes, there is a manuscript copy of a writing by John Whitmer. It is in the possession of the Reorganized Church. It came to us with other material (the Book of Mormon manuscript and some original transcriptions of early revelations to the church) from the family of David Whitmer in 1903. It consists of ninety-six pages of lined foolscap written in ink.

Concerning the second part of your question, it is important to state that nineteen chapters out of twenty-two were printed in the *Journal of History,* 1908, edited by Heman C. Smith, church historian at the time. It is unfortunate that the publication of this work did not contain an explanatory note as to why chapters 20-22 were not printed. The facts are as follows: John Whitmer was appointed by revelation in March, 1831, to be church historian and served the church until he was disfellowshiped in 1838. He served with distinction in several fields of ministry, including membership on the 1835 Doctrine and Covenants committee, as editor of the *Messenger and Advocate,* and as assistant president of a Missouri High Council, as well as commencing to write church history.

When leaving the church, he took with him the writings he had made. On page eighty-five of the manuscript he states, "Therefore I close the history of the Church of Latter Day Saints," and then after a few lines of request that his faults may be forgiven, pens three final words, "Farewell, March 1838." It is obvious that this was intended to be the conclusion, and the editor of the *Journal of History* so interpreted it and finished the printing there.

The supplementary chapters (20, 21, 22) were written in different ink and include items of which John Whitmer was not a witness. In commenting on some of the problems of Nauvoo (he did not reside there) he says, "According to the best information I could get," etc. This approach, coupled with the fact that the last three chapters were an afterthought and were written much later than his official connection as historian, raises the question of their accuracy.

It may be said that the accuracy of any dating could be doubtful. The manuscript appears to have been prepared after 1835, as reference is made to page numbers in the 1835 edition of Doctrine and Covenants. It contains statements in parentheses, such as (insert revelation here). This would indicate a preparation for printing from notes or diary after 1835 but before 1838. The last three chapters were very probably much later than this.

At least when the supplementary chapters were written, Whitmer was suffering (rightly or wrongly) from a sense of injustice.

161. Oliver Cowdery

QUESTION

Did Oliver Cowdery join the Mormon church shortly before he died?

ANSWER

In a letter published in the *Millennial Star* of January 1, 1849, George A. Smith states that Oliver Cowdery visited Council Bluffs with his family and was invited to address a gathering of the Saints on October 21, 1848, which he did. In the *Star* it is reported that Cowdery asked to be readmitted to the church by rebaptism. He had been "cut off" from the church by a high council in Far West, Missouri, in 1838.

The authenticity of this claim—that he was readmitted to the church in Council Bluffs—has been challenged and an accusation made that Cowdery was impersonated on that occasion. Though there are a number of occasions when *Millennial Star* made unjustifiable changes in reprinting documents, I see no reason to question seriously the basic testimony that Cowdery was there and acted as stated. The part of George A. Smith's letter dealing with this was dated October 31, 1848. The *Millennial Star,* published in Liverpool, England, on January 1, 1849, carried the letter only two months later. Oliver Cowdery lived another fifteen months after the publication of the letter and there appears to be no statement by him that the report was false.

Of course this report is used to produce one of the "three witnesses" to the Book of Mormon as a later witness supporting the tenets of that faction which eventually accepted Brigham Young as its president in Utah. This is not necessarily true, because if Cowdery did as the report states, there is no evidence that he knew of the degree of apostasy occurring or about to occur in that group led by a section of the Twelve. Thus, even if mistaken in the identity of the true church (the Reorganization did not even begin to take formal shape until 1852, which was over two years after Cowdery's death), he is not committed to the position of Utah by a formal entry into what he felt was the body with the authoritative line.

It is attested in George A. Smith's letter that he bore testimony of the belief that the Twelve had authority. This he may have done, but history shows that the Twelve overstepped their authority. We believe Cowdery would not have supported them in doing this had he remained with them and journeyed to Utah—which he never did.

There is evidence in letters in his own handwriting showing that he abhorred the immoral practices which became official in the group led by Brigham Young, and when stories reached him he stated he could not believe them. Evidently he later accepted the protests of innocence which continued to flow until 1852.

One thing is certain. Oliver Cowdery reaffirmed his testimony of the Book of Mormon not only at the time of his visit to Council Bluffs in 1848 but on his deathbed. That he renounced the church and the Book of Mormon is not true, and the evidence produced to prove that he did fails.

170

162. Sidney Rigdon

QUESTION

Did Sidney Rigdon ever unite with either the Mormons in Utah or the Reorganization after he published the "Messenger and Advocate" and became a leader of the group in Pittsburgh in April, 1845? Is there any record of his death?

ANSWER

Sidney Rigdon joined neither the Reorganization nor Brigham Young's group. In an editorial (*True Latter Day Saints' Herald,* Volume 20, page 48) Joseph Smith III wrote the following:

"His connection with the church began at an early date in its history; and continued till the death of Joseph and Hyrum, after which for a few years he led a portion of the saints into the Cumberland Valley. What there transpired is past; but the bond established over the minds of many was broken, and Elder Rigdon became apparently silent."

A group persisted, advancing the position that Rigdon was the rightful leader after the Twelve usurped leadership under Brigham Young in Nauvoo. This movement lost force and direction after the death of Rigdon. Rigdon died at Friendship, New York, on July 14, 1876, at the age of eighty-three, according to an obituary dated July 18, 1876, in the *Friendship Register,* Friendship, New York. Incidentally, Sidney Rigdon was an uncompromising opponent of Brigham Young's espousal of polygamy and claimed that his opposition was the cause of his rejection by the false leaders whom he says were by that time practicing this iniquity.

163. Martin Harris

QUESTION

What finally became of Martin Harris? Did he go to Utah and embrace polygamy?

ANSWER

I give the following data concerning Martin Harris. He was born May 18, 1783, in Eastown, New York, and baptized shortly after April 6, 1830, being ordained a priest in June of that year. He was ordained a high priest on June 3, 1831, and traveled with Joseph Smith, Jr., and others to Missouri, arriving in July.

He returned to Kirtland, Ohio, and became a member of the first high council February 17, 1834. He was not sustained as a councilor at a conference in September, 1837. He was one of the committee chosen to select the first Council of Twelve Apostles in 1835. According to a report he had brief association with J. J. Strang and went to England on a mission. Later he appears as being affiliated with the movement of David Whitmer in Kirtland, Ohio.

According to a publication entitled *Ensign of Liberty*, Volume I, pages 56, 57, he was "immersed, confirmed, and reordained" on February 13, 1847. He lived in Kirtland, Ohio, until 1870, when he went to Utah where his son lived. He died at Clarkston, Utah, in 1875 at the age of 92.

Martin Harris reaffirmed his testimony of the Book of Mormon, in the production of which he shared as a scribe and with monetary assistance.

In a report of an interview by Elder Simon Smith (who visited Harris on his deathbed) which was published in the *Saint Joseph, Missouri, Herald* of April 16, 1884, Harris denied that Joseph Smith, Jr., sponsored polygamy or that it was a doctrine of the church in his lifetime. According to an article in *Autumn Leaves*, Volume 1, page 182 (1888), Harris was invited to preach in Utah; he denounced polygamy in the sermon. He based his denunciation of the doctrine on the statements in the Book of Mormon. I find no claim or record of rebaptism in the Utah church.

164. Church Action against Some of Early Church

QUESTION

What action did the early church take against Oliver Cowdery and Martin Harris, witnesses to the Book of Mormon? What was the feeling of the Reorganization toward them and Sidney Rigdon? Were they ever branded as liars and cheats by the church?

ANSWER

One of the values of accurately recorded history is that those who come later may review events in perspective, which the passing of time allows. Most people of any maturity often feel that if they could have a chance to remake decisions in the light of greater experience they would do somewhat differently. An organization such as the church is no different in this respect. That is the value of record. The persons you mention were involved in difficulties with the Presidency and others in the 1830's, and Rigdon even later.

No action was ever taken by the church in Joseph Smith, Jr.'s, day or by the Reorganization with reference to Rigdon, and he was in the Presidency at the time of the martyrdom. The Brigham Young faction took action against Rigdon after Joseph's death. This was motivated by obvious factors involved in Young and Rigdon's claims to leadership.

Oliver Cowdery fell from Joseph's favor over some land deals and other matters in Far West and was castigated in church publications. Cowdery was excommunicated at Far West April 12, 1838. The Whitmers, along with a number of others, also disagreed with the leadership and ended outside the church. Martin Harris remained in Kirtland and did not figure in Far West or Nauvoo. His inactivity after the church migrated to Far West, Missouri, in 1838 has been alleged by some to be evidence of apostasy. The *Elders' Journal* of August, 1838, included the name of Martin Harris among a group of dissenters in Kirtland, Ohio, who were accused of "all kinds of abominations." He eventually died in Utah Territory, where he lived from 1870 to 1875.

What I am saying is that we are not in a position to judge too harshly either the official criticism or the reaction of the person you mention in those days of turmoil and stress. The lives of each of these men evidenced integrity in the years that followed, and none ever retracted his testimony previously given of the Book of Mormon.

165. "Pearl of Great Price"—What

QUESTION

What is the book, "The Pearl of Great Price"? Does the Reorganization accept it?

ANSWER

The Pearl of Great Price was first published in England by F. D. Richards in 1851. This was seven years after the martyrdom of Joseph Smith. Its title page contained the following description: "A choice selection from the revelations, translations, and narrations of Joseph Smith."

It was a pamphlet containing fifty-six pages and included twelve selections. This work was revised and altered on several occasions. Following the English edition of 1851 the work was revised and re-published in Salt Lake City, Utah, in 1878. At this time was added the spurious document purporting to be "A Revelation on the Eternity of the Marriage Covenant, including Plurality of Wives" commonly known as the "Polygamy Document." This is Section 132 in the Utah Doctrine and Covenants.

In 1880 the Utah church canonized *The Pearl of Great Price*, placing it as equal with the Bible, Book of Mormon, and Doctrine and Covenants. It remained in the form of the 1878 edition until 1902 when it was again revised. Certain documents which were also in the Doctrine and Covenants were among those omitted from this edition, the reason being given that they were redundant. The revision presented an opportunity for the removal of the document of "Plurality of Wives" although this was retained in the Utah Doctrine and Covenants as Section 132. There were changes of format in *The Pearl of Great Price* in 1921 and after. The last action of the sponsoring church endorsing the book was in 1902.

It has never been accepted by the Reorganization as authoritative. This is not to say that all the material in it is spurious, but unless the material was from original authoritative sources we do not accept it as governing in faith or doctrine. For instance, the Book of Abraham, though published in *Times and Seasons,* is not accepted as scripture. It was translated as an effort of scholarship and published as a matter of information. There is no evidence that it is what it purports to be.

166. Temple Lot in Independence

QUESTION

Which particular area of ground in Independence is the Temple Lot? Does the Reorganized Church own it?

ANSWER

Early in the year 1831 the church purchased a parcel of land about three fourths of a mile west of the courthouse. This land comprised about sixty-three acres. The purchase was made by Bishop Edward Partridge, and there is no doubt that it was purchased in trust for the church.

On August 3, 1831, the officials of the church dedicated a portion of this property as a site for the temple. We have this description written by Parley P. Pratt in his autobiography when describing an incident seven years after the dedication, while under guard with Joseph Smith as prisoner.

"With him we walked to the westward and visited the desolated lands of the Saints, and the place which, seven years before, we had dedicated for the building of the Temple. This was a beautiful rise of ground, about half a mile west of Independence center."

This identifies the place where the dedication was held as that area bounded by Lexington on the north, Walnut on the south, River on the east, and Bowen on the west. It should be remembered that it was a knoll or rise on the total area of sixty-three acres (plus). No boundaries were named in the dedication and it seems that the purchase was made to include the lot.

The actual place of dedication seems to have been that piece now possessed by the Church of Christ (Hedrickites). The Reorganized Church contested the ownership, and judgment was given to it in 1894. This judgment was appealed, and though the court decision was not reversed in law the Reorganized Church was denied possession on the grounds of laches, a legal provision implying that the claimants had rested too long before claiming their rights.

A rumor persists that that body has conditional tenure. This, of course, is an error.

The people who now possess the section in dispute are a God-fearing and good people. Though there are differences of opinion, relations between the two groups are cordial as both stand for high moral principles.

167. "Joseph Smith and His Progenitors"

QUESTION

Did the Reorganization publish the book "Joseph Smith and His Progenitors"? Is the book "History of Joseph Smith" by Lucy Mack Smith and published in Salt Lake City the same work?

ANSWER

The Reorganization first published Lucy Smith's book in 1880. This was not the first printing. The first was made in Liverpool, England, in 1853, for Orson Pratt by S. W. Richards under the title

Biographical Sketches of Joseph Smith, the Prophet, and His Progenitors for Many Generations. This is a volume of 297 pages, approximately 6 x 3¾ inches. It appears that this publication was not approved by the Utah president, Brigham Young, and by his instruction was, according to a later president of that church, J. Fielding Smith, "suppressed or destroyed." The order for this according to Mr. J. Fielding Smith was given on August 23, 1865, the reason given being inaccurate historical data.

The Utah church claims that Lucy Smith dictated the manuscript to an amanuensis, Martha Coray, who made a second copy. She took one to Utah. Orson Pratt obtained the other on his way to England and published it as stated in 1853. The Reorganization reprinted from this edition.

In 1901 the Utah church published a revised version in serial form in *Improvement Era* (Volume 5). This version was supposed to have been printed from the copy Mrs. Coray took to Utah, designated as the original. Brigham Young's statement in *Millennial Star* (Volume 17, page 297), however, does not indicate that what he had was the original. He stated:

> "I have had *a written copy* of those sketches in my possession for several years, and it contains much of the history of the Prophet Joseph. Should it ever be deemed best to publish these sketches it will not be done until after they are carefully corrected."

Comparison of the 1901 serial and a later reprint edited by Preston Nibley under the title *History of Joseph Smith by His Mother, Lucy Mack Smith,* with the 1853 edition reveals many changes, additions, and omissions. On casual reading, one finds no basic reason for these variations except possibly in a correction of a few dates. The Utah claim is that a committee "personally familiar with the family and thoroughly conversant with church history" revised the book by comparison with the "original." This has raised questions as to its reliability to some who are familiar with the "thorough revisions" of other documents made under the direction of Brigham Young. The method of its writing does not make the work one of documentary reliability and thus a comparison of texts may not be of primary value, although when associated with other works of more documentary nature its study is helpful.

168. History of Joseph Smith

QUESTION

Is the "History of Joseph Smith" as published in the "Millennial Star" authentic?

ANSWER

The *Millennial Star* was an English publication commenced in 1840. Much of the material in the periodical was reprinted from other church journals published in America. After the death of the prophet Joseph Smith it continued to be published in England and became an organ of the church in Utah. It is still published as a monthly journal, though it has varied from a weekly to a semimonthly and now to a monthly publication.

In 1852 the *Millennial Star* began reprinting the "History of Joseph Smith," taking the text mainly from the *Times and Seasons* of Nauvoo and from a source which the Utah church claims is a diary of Joseph Smith. This series of reprints concluded May, 1863, but included events only to August 8, 1844.

There is no means of checking the entries purportedly from "the diary" because that has never been made available to us for original research. It has never been published in photostat other than by printing a few facsimiles of certain pages as evidence of its existence.

However, the *Times and Seasons* issues of relevant dates are available. Research involving comparisons between the *Millennial Star* version of the history and the *Times and Seasons* has been made, and the results are disquieting.

In the *Millennial Star* (May 2, 1863, Volume 25, No. 18, page 279) we find the following statement made upon the conclusion of the reprinting of the history in question and over the signatures of George A. Smith and Wilford Woodruff:

"The history of Joseph Smith is now before the world, and we are satisfied that a history more correct in its details than this was never published. . . . Moreover, since the death of the Prophet Joseph, the *history has been carefully revised under the strict inspection of President Brigham Young,* and approved by him."

It has been argued that these changes were editorial and mainly incidental to good grammatical expression. However, further research shows extraordinary liberty being taken with the text. There is not space in these columns to give extensive quotations, but one reference is indicative of the type of changes made. In *Times and Seasons* (Volume I, No. 7, pages 99-104) a letter signed by Joseph Smith and four others appears. This letter from Liberty Jail, Missouri, was reprinted under the caption "History of Joseph Smith" in *Millennial Star* (Volume 17, pages 52-56). A careful comparison shows deliberate tampering with the original text. Many complete lines are interpolated altering the sense of whole paragraphs. The word "God" has been changed to "Gods"; "the council of Heaven" to "the council of the Eternal God of all other Gods." One cannot escape the conclusion that these changes were made "under strict inspection" to harmonize with false doctrines that were then being taught by Brigham Young concerning "plurality of Gods," etc.

Those interested in more detailed research on this document will find a comprehensive comparison in *Saints' Herald*, Volume 43, No. 23, under the title "An Important Document Change."

These and other changes of more than grammatical significance sustain the statement that the "History of Joseph Smith" and other documents in the *Millennial Star* purporting to be from the originals are not authentic and cannot be relied upon as statements of fact.

169. Authentic Pamphlet

QUESTION

Is the pamphlet "Correct Account of the Murder of Generals Joseph Smith and Hyrum Smith at Carthage," by William M. Daniels what the title purports to be—that is, authentic?

ANSWER

This was originally published in Nauvoo, Illinois, by John Taylor in 1845. John Taylor was in charge of the *Times and Seasons* printing press at the time of the martyrdom. He stood with the Brigham Young faction and was later president of the Utah Mormon church. It would appear by the title and cover page that Taylor did not sponsor this in his official capacity as these pages carry the following:

Published by John Taylor
For the Proprietor
Nauvoo, Illinois
1845

Although it is not stated, it is presumed that William M. Daniels is the proprietor and sponsor referred to. The pamphlet has been reprinted a number of times; among those who reprinted this work was Daniel Macgregor, one-time minister of the RLDS Church. Some of these are in the possession of church members, and the Historian has several copies as well as originals.

In general outline it may probably be considered a fairly authentic account. However, in that it is a statement by one claiming to be an eyewitness but with no corroborative testimony, it stands alone. Some details have been questioned, such as the alleged bursting of light from the heavens and the murderers standing paralyzed because of the phenomenon. The account is certainly given in a most dramatic style and by one who states at the end of the pamphlet that his life has been in danger because of his testimony. It is not certain what motives originally impelled Daniels to publish it, but it obviously appeared on a privately sponsored basis. The author shows considerable animosity to those he names as responsible for the murders and a definite bias in favor of the Saints. It is a most interesting document, but as evidence on details it stands simply on the testimony of a single witness. In the *History of Illinois* Governor Ford discredited the pamphlet and claimed that the writer was later expelled by the Mormons.

170. Utah Church History

QUESTION

Recently I have been reading a seven-volume work, "History of the Church," published by the Utah church. It is presented as taken from Joseph Smith's journal. If this is so, I have been mistaken on our history at a number of points. Can this publication be relied on?

ANSWER

When Joseph Smith was killed on June 27, 1844, a group of the Quorum of Twelve assumed control of the church administration, and thus many of the records of Joseph Smith's office passed into the hands of the group led by Brigham Young. Emma Smith and others retained certain documents and manuscripts, but the Young faction retained many records. Among them, it is claimed, was Joseph Smith's journal.

Because of an understandable reluctance on the part of the Utah church authorities to make the original journal available for reference, some people have expressed a doubt as to its actual existence. However, there is little doubt that it was taken with other records to Utah. Assuming its existence, the careful student needs to beware of accepting the published work as being authentic in all parts, especially where the text differs from other statements of Joseph Smith published during his lifetime.

I personally am wary of accepting any statement in the work under consideration which involves Utah doctrine which is not borne out by other documentary evidence from credible sources. My serious doubt about the integrity of the work is based upon a statement in the preface to Volume I, page vi, which states:

> ". . . since the death of the Prophet Joseph, the history has been carefully revised under the strict inspection of Brigham Young, and approved by him."

Only the first 240 pages of Volume I appeared in print prior to the death of Joseph Smith; therefore the rest was not available for his scrutiny. Many variations appear within these 240 pages from earlier printings. The preface, while admitting many changes, goes to great pains to affirm the correctness of the final copy.

Heman Hale Smith, in an article entitled "Proper and Improper Uses of History" (*Journal of History*, Vol. II, pp. 78-88) gives the results of his research showing 1,802 changes in Volume I of the Utah work alone, some involving both the insertion of whole paragraphs and the deletion of others. This research was done by comparison with authentic publications in the prophet's lifetime.

The Utah history increased the volume of material stated to be a letter from Liberty Jail by approximately 1,000 words as compared with that published during Joseph Smith's lifetime (*Times and Seasons*, May, 1840).

A most discriminating study must be made of any data appearing in the work you are concerned about, especially where matters discussed reflect upon the principles and practices of the church under Joseph Smith, Jr.

171. Name of Graceland College

QUESTION

How did Graceland College get its name?

ANSWER

The story of the development of Graceland is told in the book, *Through the West Door*, by Dr. Roy A. Cheville.

"In 1895 the college committee made this succinct report. It clarifies the question of the origin of the name of the college. The surveyor engaged for plotting the college grounds had been fascinated by the lay of the land. Its 'graceful' topography had prompted him to speak of it as 'Graceland.'"

Then follows the committee's report, in which paragraph five states:

"The college grounds have been named 'Graceland' by the committee, but no name or style of title has been agreed on for the college."

Today as one stands on the hillcrest and views the landscape with its many buildings, paths, and lawns, one can't help appreciating the appropriateness of the committee's choice of the name "Graceland."

172. Israel Smith and the Lepers

QUESTION

Upon two occasions I have heard it said that when Brother Israel Smith visited an island where five of our members who had leprosy lived, "he prayed for them, they were all healed, and their bodies made whole." Is this true?

ANSWER

The answer to your question is fully given in the book entitled *Adventures of a South Sea Missionary*, pages 114, 115, by F. Edward Butterworth. The words you quote are not actually in the account of the visit of President Israel to the leper island. Five persons were hospitalized there at the time of his visit. The emotional impact on Brother Smith, because of his realization of the sufferers' plight, was quite evident to the missionary in charge, Brother F. Edward Butterworth, and Brother Horahitu who had accompanied him to the island. The author of the work quoted said that the appreciation and lifted hope of the sick ones was evident as Brother Smith said he would pray for them.

Within five years none of the five lepers needed to remain on the island, and the belief of those concerned was that a miracle had occurred in their lives. Those intimately involved alone know the full circumstances, but there is no inference in the text or justification for one that a pronouncement of healing was made on the island.

181

Those involved many years later stated it was their belief that here was a miracle. The lepers had not had to return, which so often is the case of those with remissions of this disease.

There is a Latin phrase, *post hoc, ergo propter hoc,* which translated means "after this, therefore on account of it." A careful and enlightened person avoids oversimplified deductions from coincidental happenings and attributing one happening to be the result of another. It is a fact that treatment continued and Brother Smith continued along with others to pray. A number of factors are in evidence here: faith, hope, continued treatment, and prayer.

I have made more comment on this than just to answer "yes" or "no" because the words you quote as being repeated are not actually in the text, and the statement is not justified as simply stated. I am merely give you a setting in which to view the happy sequel to the visit.

Salvation

173. Meaning of Grace

In Ephesians 2:8, 9 we are told that we are saved by grace, not by works lest any man should boast. Does grace mean unmerited favor?

Often the concepts of salvation by grace and salvation by works are placed in a position of contradiction that is not justifiable. One gains insight by reading Romans 4:4, both Authorized and Inspired Versions.

"Now to him that worketh is the reward not reckoned of grace, but of debt."—A.V.

"Now to him who is justified by the law of works, is the reward reckoned, not of grace, but of debt."—I.V.

In the second rendering the problem is approached exegetically, that is, interpretively. What is being said is that if one approaches salvation on the basis of performing sufficient acts to earn it, he fails to appreciate that our whole existence and life is due to the divine favor, the grace of God.

174. Retaining Salvation

A friend quoted I Corinthians 6:12 as evidence that a Christian cannot lose salvation no matter what he does. What is the meaning of this text?

Different translations give this text with varying wording. I presume you quote from the King James Version:

"All things are lawful unto me, but all things are not expedient: all things are lawful for me, but I will not be brought under the power of any."

The New English Bible gives the passage as follows:

"I am free to do anything you say. Yes, but not everything is for my good. No doubt I am free to do anything, but I for one will not let anything make free with me."

What is meant by both these versions is that a man does not lose his agency by becoming a Christian. He may still do anything others do if he so chooses, but if he does he returns to the bondage of his past sins. One may do many things under the law of the land that a Christian dares not do and retain his Christian status. I suggest you read verses 8-10 of the same chapter to your friend and point out that they state that those who do the things written in these verses "shall not inherit the kingdom of God." Paul reminds his readers in verse 12 that if one does these things he comes under their power, and that means spiritual death.

Joseph Smith inserted the negative so that this passage in the Inspired Version reads, "All these things are not lawful." However, though this is true by the Christian law it is still true that the things referred to may be legally permissible but not expedient or wise. Paul certainly is not arguing for the right of a Christian to return to the ways of the world and still reap the fruits of righteousness. A man under grace should not do the things inveighed against in I Corinthians 6; if he does he is no longer under grace and will become subject to the underlying principle that "whatsoever a man shall sow that shall he reap."

175. "Savior" and "Savor"

In the tract, "Baptism for the Dead," by Charles R. Hield and Russell F. Ralston, on page 11 of the 1960 edition this statement is made: "The word of God plainly states that man is not the savior of his fellow man. Christ is the only Savior!" Doctrine and Covenants,

Section 100:2 *c, d, contains this phrase: "For they were set to be a light unto the world, and to be the saviors of men; and inasmuch as they are not the saviors of men, they are as salt that has lost its savor." Please explain.*

ANSWER

The word "savor" as a noun means "a taste or smell or quality." In the statement of Jesus, "Ye are the salt of the earth but if the salt has lost its savor wherewith shall it be salted" (Matthew 5:13), the word is used in the sense of "flavoring or preserving." The word "savior" means "one who saves, preserves or delivers from destruction, etc." The word "savor" comes from the Latin root *sapor* while the word "savior" comes from the Latin word *salvatore*. In Section 100:2, the two words are used to emphasize the part that each human must play in relation to others, and particularly the responsibilities of Saints to others.

Joseph Smith used the two words in the same paragraph, possibly being unaware of their different roots, but using something that is still common to both words, that is, the quality of "preserving." Ultimately there is only one savior, Jesus Christ. If we fail to share our saving knowledge of the gospel of Christ with those who have need, we are responsible. Ultimately the Savior will be available to all God's creatures, but each has a cooperative part in the plan. No man will be condemned by God because of anything anyone else might or might not do! God has chosen to save the world through Jesus Christ, and Christ has shared this task by sending his followers into the world as ambassadors. I see no basic contradiction.

176. Fullness of the Gospel

QUESTION

Do we believe that the Book of Mormon contains the "fullness of the gospel"? Does the Bible do likewise? If so, is the Book of Mormon necessary to salvation, or is the Bible sufficient?

ANSWER

The Doctrine and Covenants states "with Moroni, whom I have sent unto you to reveal the Book of Mormon, containing the fullness of my everlasting gospel" (Section 26:2 a).

It is necessary to be clear as to what is the basis of salvation. This is unequivocally "belief on the Lord Jesus Christ." This involves obedience to Christ.

It would be untrue to hold that persons who lived prior to the compiling of the New Testament did not obtain salvation. The point is that salvation is not conditioned by belief in a book which, after all, is but a record.

These sacred records grew over years. The Book of Mormon parallels the Bible somewhat in time and of course in teachings. In fact, its primary value is as a witness that Jesus is the Christ. The truth is independent of a witness but is established in the minds of men by testimony. Witnesses are confirmatory.

These records are thus aids to faith and understanding and to expansion of our knowledge, but the gospel is not found only in the written word. It comes by the power and assurance of the Holy Spirit (Gal. 1:12).

The Doctrine and Covenants, as another teacher and witness, adds to our understanding of God's laws and the function of his church.

Faith in the Book of Mormon as a mere book is not essential to salvation, but faith in the Lord Jesus is. The Book of Mormon testifies of him: "And the Book of Mormon, and the Holy Scriptures, are given of me for your instruction; and the power of my Spirit quickeneth all things" (Doctrine and Covenants 32:3 d).

Water Baptism

177. Authority

QUESTION

In Acts 19:4 we read that Paul told certain people who had been baptized "unto John's baptism" that theirs was the baptism of repentance. In verse 5 we read, "When they heard this, they were baptized in the name of the Lord Jesus." Does this baptism in the name of the Lord Jesus refer to baptism by immersion? If so, by what authority had John baptized these people if it was necessary for them to be rebaptized by Paul?

ANSWER

You will most likely find the answer to your problem by reading more of the context in Acts 19 than you have quoted in your question. If you do this, you will note that the first question Paul asked those who are described as disciples was, "Have ye received the Holy Ghost since ye believed?" Their answer indicated that they were totally ignorant of the Holy Spirit. Paul immediately questioned the nature of the baptism they had received and they gave the answer, "John's baptism." It would appear that Paul seriously doubted whether what had occurred had been truly a baptism according to the authority and teaching of John, because he stated that John had informed his hearers of the Holy Spirit that would be received through Christ who should follow him.

Matthew 3:38 reads, "I indeed baptize you before he cometh, that when he cometh he may baptize you with the Holy Ghost and fire." Had it been John who baptized these people they would not have been ignorant of the Holy Spirit. The record does not so state, but the only conclusion I have been able to reach in the light of the principle involved is that a person whose name has not been recorded, being convinced of the necessity of baptism after hearing John preach, proceeded to perform baptisms.

Had John personally done the baptizing, the baptisms would have been authoritative. That Jesus accepted baptism by John is evidence that his priesthood was recognized by God who endorsed it openly by the sign of the Holy Spirit resting upon Jesus in the form of a dove. (This will be clear if you read the rest of Matthew 3, particularly verses 41-46.)

John's priesthood must have been of the Aaronic Order, because he intimated that he did not have the power to bestow the Holy Spirit for which he said they would have to wait for Jesus Christ who should come after him.

178. Consent Necessary

QUESTION

Doctrine and Covenants 111:4 states that a woman should not be baptized without the consent of her husband. Why is not the consent of a wife required likewise? Is this not an outdated approach built upon the concept that a woman is a chattel? Should one adult be able to deny the privilege of baptism to another?

ANSWER

Section 111 is a revelation given August 17, 1835, and as all other documents, should be studied in its historical setting. The laws of this country as well as of others of that time gave a husband certain legal rights in relation to his wife. The Saints were counseled to be obedient to the laws of the land. Understanding of human rights had not developed to that of the present, and the church respected the laws of the time. The world movement toward recognizing women's rights was definite but slow. Though granted in some other countries earlier, it was not until 1919 that the United States granted women the right to vote. Many countries were less advanced.

This church has been one of the advanced organizations in this respect. The General Conference of 1868 passed a resolution which affirmed the right of women to vote in the democratic phases of church procedure. This was many years ahead of state action.

A careful reading of Section 111 reveals a spirit of mutuality in

188

marriage and also of the unity of the family, including the rights and responsibilities of children to parents. As to a husband being in agreement before a wife is baptized, it appears to me that if interpreted in the light of the modern status of women in free countries, the principle applies equally to both parties. Because the church recognizes its mission to bind and not separate families, it counsels that "oneness" of the marriage be respected. This concept removes any suggestion of one being a chattel or possession.

If one partner should hinder the free exercise of the other's human rights, he or she assumes responsibility. Certainly no one, husband or wife, should attempt to assume control over another's soul. Should domestic strife be occasioned over religion, the church believes that it should not influence a partner to action which is disrupting to the marriage. The responsibility then rests where it belongs.

179. Require Spoken Vow

QUESTION

Is it the usual practice to ask a baptismal candidate the question, "Are you willing to serve Jesus Christ through good and evil report while life shall last?" If this is not so, how can a candidate be said to have entered into a covenant to serve God at baptism? Is there any General Church ruling on this matter?

ANSWER

It is not general practice to ask publicly the question with which you are concerned. Doctrine and Covenants 17:7 makes it obligatory that the prospective candidate give evidence of repentance and good intention. This evidence should be "before the church" and would not imply a statement such as you quote. To witness "before the church" would imply "before the officers responsible" rather than a specific gathering or meeting.

It would seem that the fact that the Lord gave specific instruction as to the words to be used covers the position, and had other words been required, they would have been included. Doctrine and Covenants 17:21 states:

"Baptism is to be administered in the following manner unto all those who repent: The person who is called of God, and has authority from Jesus Christ to baptize, shall go down into the water with the person who has presented him or herself for

189

baptism, and shall say, calling him or her by name: Having been commissioned of Jesus Christ, I baptize you in the name of the Father, and of the Son, and of the Holy Ghost, Amen. Then shall he immerse him or her in the water, and come forth again out of the water."

The baptismal rite itself constitutes the symbol of the covenant and should be simply engaged in as instructed in the law referred to. Any adornment that tends to become ritual should be discouraged so that the scriptural ordinance remains significant. The rite of baptism seems to require no spoken vow. General Conference has not acted to endorse the specific or similar words which you use in your question.

180. Forgiveness of Sins

QUESTION

When our sins are forgiven by the Lord at baptism, do we still have to answer for them at the day of judgment? When the presiding elder at a Communion service says under the influence of the Holy Spirit that our sins are forgiven, do we still have to answer for them at the day of judgment? If the answer is yes, of what value is forgiveness? Are our sins forgiven each time we properly repent? If not, what is the value of repentance? How does all this apply to forgiving one another?

ANSWER

The answer to this problem is dependent upon what is meant by forgiveness. Forgiveness is primarily a matter of relationship, and this is independent of the results of law. Repentance clears the way for forgiveness, and it should be remembered that restitution is a part of true repentance. Forgiveness opens the channels for relationship to be restored to that which existed prior to the circumstances which called for repentance.

Baptism certainly marks the first step in the new life, but one starts from where he is and then works toward final salvation. The way that has been closed by sin is now open. Provided one continues in the way, God will not hold past sins against him. Those sins may still involve burdens and require continued effort to overcome and to remedy the results of those sins. However, God does not continue to judge us on the basis of preregenerate actions. Baptism opens the door to eternal life but does not complete the journey.

190

We err if we see "eternal judgment" solely as an event in time and fail to see it as a principle of life. The fact that God has forgiven us does not fit us for celestial glory. It is not for us to pass judgment as to who will be fit for his presence, but we do know that it will be the quality of the soul achieved that will condition our destiny and not merely the imposition of a final penalty or reward that will exclude us from or admit us to his glory.

Our sins are forgiven each time we properly repent, but to keep on sinning on this basis may well leave us at a point very near our condition at the time of baptism. That status is no guarantee of salvation.

I know of no scripture that entitles a minister to offer forgiveness outside of the exercise of the principle of baptism, which is conditional upon repentance prior to and continuously thereafter. Repentance and continued obedience alone guarantee forgiveness and enable the Holy Spirit to witness our acceptance by the heavenly Father. There is no point of higher significance for such a realization than when fully repentant, and in the attitude of humble recommitment, we come to the Communion service and partake of the emblems.

The application of the principle of forgiveness in our dealings with each other simply involves the truth that if we do not forgive each other we have no claim on the forgiveness of God. Forgiveness cannot be an act varying with situations but is a continuing and functioning principle. It is a part of life, not a theological term.

181. Baptize Tobacco User

QUESTION

If a tobacco user asks for baptism and confesses to the minister that he cannot yet get along without smoking should his request for baptism be complied with?

ANSWER

Neither the scripture nor the church has made nonsmoking a condition of membership and therefore if the person desires baptism and qualifies in all other respects he should not be denied baptism. The fact that he wishes to commit his life to the Lord is the step which he should be encouraged to take. It is well for the minister concerned to counsel with the candidate, making sure that the stewardship of the body is understood to be part of a saintly responsibility and therefore that one should continue to endeavor to come into harmony with all God's will.

If the candidate sincerely desires to discontinue the habit which has control of him the very fact of his being obedient to the baptismal requirement will bring to him strength to overcome this as well as other weaknesses.

Smoking is not endorsed as desirable in a Saint, and we are counseled to avoid it (Doctrine and Covenants 119:3), but it is not a condition of membership. A man will not be ordained to priesthood office if he is addicted to the use of tobacco, however.

This answer is not intended to be a weakening of the standards of Sainthood. While a member fails to progress to a point where he can control the habit, he delays his usefulness and also misses the joy of total commitment to the higher purposes. The fact that he knows his present weakness should indicate this to him and stimulate him to a determined effort to surmount the problem. There are a number of weaknesses that each has not necessarily conquered prior to baptism. That is why Paul said, "Let us go on to perfection." If the intention of the candidate is clearly to overcome, God will accept his offering and grant him power as he sincerely strives upward.

182. Infant Baptism in New Testament?

QUESTION

Is there any evidence of what is termed "infant baptism" in the New Testament period of the church?

ANSWER

There is no evidence that infants were baptized in the New Testament period. Although there are some who reason from a few texts referring to the baptism of a household that herein is implied the baptism of infants, this is at best suppositious.

The household of Lydia mentioned in Acts 16:14, 15 was most probably an adult household including those engaged with her in business as "a seller of purple."

The Greek from which the English word "baptism" is translated indicates the mode of immersion. This practice is most unsuitable for infants, which is shown by the later and continuing practice in some sects of sprinkling.

Evidence that immersion was the method by which converts were initiated into the Christian communion abounds. Roman Catholic authorities admit to this while attempting to justify a change in method.

That immersion of those having arrived at an age of decision was the New Testament concept is shown by Jesus' sayings which refer to baptism as a birth (John 3:5, 6) and as a death and burial (Luke 12:50).

The Pauline treatment of baptism expands on this concept and in certain passages makes the rite a symbolic representation of death, burial, and resurrection in Christ (Romans 6:11).

The strong emphasis on belief and acceptance of Christ as a prerequisite of baptism further precludes the possibility of infant baptism being endorsed or practiced in the New Testament period (Acts 2:37, 38, 41; 8:12; 16:14, 15).

Some have sought to distinguish between the baptism of proselytes and those of already Christian families. This process of reasoning is inverted and reaches the conclusion which is based on an assumption that subsequent practice was the original. The evidence that infant baptism was not a practice when the New Testament was being formulated seems conclusive.

183. Scripture Support for Infant Baptism?

QUESTION

Is there any scripture to support the practice of infant baptism?

ANSWER

No scripture supports the baptism of any but those who are of an age and condition to make their decision for Christ. Baptism is a symbol of a voluntary and rational acceptance of one's stewardship of life in all aspects. One must be able to profess belief in Jesus Christ to be an acceptable candidate for baptism. Jesus said,

"Go ye into all the world, and preach the gospel to every creature. He that believeth and is baptized shall be saved."

A very comprehensive treatise on this subject is found in the Book of Mormon. The eighth chapter of Moroni is quite clear on this point:

"Behold I say unto you, that this thing shall ye teach, repentance and baptism unto those who are accountable and capable of committing sin; yea, teach parents that they must repent and be baptized, and humble themselves as their little children, and they shall all be saved with their little children: and their little children need no repentance, neither baptism."— Moroni 8:11.

Many have supposed that babies were baptized in New Testa-

193

ment times because of a reference to the baptism of a whole house-hold (Acts 16:15). There is no evidence that there were very young children involved, since the term "household" no doubt referred to all persons connected with the establishment of Lydia, a seller of purple. It would be a mere supposition to assume that children of any age were included in the light of the fact that throughout scripture we have record only of believers being baptized.

184. Should Nurse Baptize

QUESTION

Should a nurse who belongs to this church go through the form of so-called baptizing a dying infant where the child is of a family whose faith requires this on pain of the child's being lost in eternity?

Would it be blasphemy to say "I baptize you in the name of the Father, Son, and Holy Ghost"?

ANSWER

The law of this church provides only one kind of baptism. This is by immersion. The word is strictly not applied to any other kind of ordinance. The church also requires that the candidate be of sufficient age to enter intelligently into the baptismal covenant, and this has been set at a minimum of eight years. We do not believe that infants not baptized are condemned.

Furthermore, according to the law set forth in Doctrine and Cove-nants 17 only members of the Melchisedec priesthood and Aaronic priests have authority to baptize. Though holding priesthood, teachers and deacons are not authorized to perform baptism. In the light of this law, by what right would a member perform baptism?

Because there is but one scriptural mode correctly described as baptism—that is, immersion—to perform such in any other way cannot be of any significance and for one to know this and then to go through such motions would be a mockery of sacred things. To say, "In the name of the Father, Son, and Holy Ghost," knowing that one has no authority to do so, would in my opinion be improper. Blasphemy is a strong word and if the intentions of the person were not meant irreverently this may be too severe a definition. However, such a procedure, in my opinion, is sacrilegious—that is, the use of the sacred by those not entitled to do so.

In any case the ordinance so performed would be valueless. If I were a nurse in such a position I would ask my superiors to have someone who has no reservation of belief or conscience function in like situations when some such service is expected of the hospital. The religious views and convictions of nurses as well as of patients are respected in all good hospitals with which I have been associated.

185. Baptism of John the Baptist

QUESTION

Who baptized John the Baptist?

ANSWER

There is no record of this in scripture, and I do not know of any reliable tradition which would offer a clue. Perhaps you may take it that his credentials were sufficient as Jesus specifically requested to be baptized by him (see Matthew 3:13-15).

186. Baptism for the Dead Origin

QUESTION

Is there conclusive evidence that sections 107, 109, and 110, of our 1955 edition of the Doctrine and Covenants, which contain the doctrine of baptism for the dead, were approved by the leading quorums of the church and a General Conference before they were published in the 1844 edition of the Doctrine and Covenants?

ANSWER

We have no record of any specific resolution which would enable us to answer in the affirmative. However, a study of the preceding and subsequent events connected with these documents, particularly Section 107, is helpful to a better appraisal of the matter.

The doctrine of baptism for the dead is included in the document which deals with the building of the Nauvoo Temple and to trace the beginning of this project is relevant to your question. The first important reference to the building of a temple in Nauvoo was made at a General Conference in Nauvoo on October 3, 1840. The minutes state: "The president then spoke of the necessity of building a 'House of the Lord' in this place."

The resolution was then passed "That the saints build a house for the worship of God." A committee was appointed and further resolution provided that the work be commenced within ten days.

The date of a revelation through Joseph Smith which included instruction on the necessity for this edifice and certain references to "baptism for the dead" is given as January 19, 1841 (now Section 107). This was first printed in part in *Times and Seasons*, Volume 2, pages 424-429, June 1, 1841.

The minutes of a General Conference at Nauvoo on April 7, 1841, however, record the fact that a revelation dealing with several of the matters involved in Section 107 was read from "The Book of the Law of the Lord," and that Joseph Smith explained matters therein. At this conference a standing vote of confidence in members of the First Presidency was given and a commitment to follow their leadership was also made by the same gesture.

Certain other matters of organization involved in this section appear to have taken effect; for example, the call to the First Presidency of William Law. There is no means of ascertaining whether the full text of this section was read either as printed in *Times and Seasons* or in the September, 1844, edition of the Doctrine and Covenants. Both printings include reference to baptism for the dead but the statement read on April 7, 1841, concerning the contents of the revelation does not mention the doctrine. However, it should be stated that baptism for the dead was later discussed by Sidney Rigdon, John C. Bennett, and Joseph Smith at the same conference.

There thus appears to have been acquiescence to the document presented, but in the absence of a formal resolution it cannot be said that there is conclusive evidence of its adoption.

With regard to Doctrine and Covenants 109 and 110, these were first published in *Times and Seasons* under the dates of September 1, 1842, and September 6, 1842, in Volume 3, page 919 and page 934 respectively. Actually the second letter continued discussion of the matters in the first. I have found no record of their adoption by a General Conference or quorum action.

The Reorganization passed a resolution in 1878 which endorsed "the revelations of God contained in the Book of Doctrine and Covenants" (see General Conference Resolution 215). This has been generally taken to be the book then printed, which would be the 1844 edition. This resolution referred to no particular edition. However, the last Doctrine and Covenants approved by General Conference action prior to the 1878 resolution was the 1835 edition.

187. Practice of Baptism for Dead

QUESTION

I would like a full explanation of the position of the Reorganized

Church on "baptism for the dead." Under what conditions would it be proper to practice it, if any?

The official position of the Reorganized Church is found in General Conference Resolution 308, which was the adoption of a report of a committee on several subjects in 1886.

"That 'baptism for the dead' belongs to those local questions of which the body has said by resolution: 'That the commandments of a local character, given to the first organization of the church, are binding on the Reorganization only so far as they are either reiterated or referred to as binding by commandments to this church.' And that principle has neither been reiterated nor referred to as a commandment."

A full discussion would be too lengthy for this column. I suggest you study the brochure *Baptism for the Dead*, by Charles R. Hield and Russell F. Ralston. This may be obtained from Herald House, Independence, Missouri.

After much consideration I am of the opinion that baptism for the dead is not a scriptural principle. Unless it is so defined and illuminated by revelation it should be left just there.

Laying On of Hands

188. Later Than Confirmation

QUESTION

What proof is there that baptism with the Holy Ghost may be at a later date than confirmation?

ANSWER

According to the scriptures (Acts 1:8) the early disciples had been baptized and a number of them ordained to specific ministerial responsibilities. However, they had not received the Holy Spirit, though it was promised. In the second chapter of Acts we find the fulfillment of this promise. Thus in the very first instance of the Holy Spirit being confirmed upon the church members, a time elapsed between baptism and the reception of the Holy Spirit. It should be said that it is for God to bestow the Holy Spirit. Whether it comes in a marked way at the very moment of confirmation or gradually is in his hands. The promise is that it will come if the law is kept. Many bear testimony to this.

189. Candidates Face Altar

QUESTION

Should candidates for the laying on of hands face the altar or Communion table or the audience?

ANSWER

In our churches there is no provision for an altar before which worshipers kneel. Sometimes the words are used at Communion, "Let us kneel facing the altar." This probably arose as a method of gaining respectful and unified procedure in administration of the sacramental emblems.

It seems somewhat disrespectful to turn away from that which is emblematic of the sacrifice of our Lord. The attitude in the heart of the communicant is the important element. Unity of movement and procedure enhances the effectiveness of worship, and we have wisely developed good customs in such matters.

It is recommended that we face the altar or Communion table when partaking of Communion but if there is a Communion table set up when an ordination or confirmation takes place, the preferred position for the candidate is facing the congregation.

There is no official ruling or Conference action on these points, but respectful attitudes and the need for orderliness have resulted in the procedure I have outlined as being the general practice.

It is not wise, unless special circumstances dictate, that the ordinances be combined in one service. Each has a special meaning and intent and should be given its proper setting. This is difficult to do when several are combined in a service. The problem of a candidate's having his back to the Communion table does not arise if the ordinances are attended to in separate services.

190. Blessing before Church Assembly

QUESTION

Does the text which reads, "Every member of the church of Christ having children, is to bring them unto the elders before the church, who are to lay their hands upon them in the name of Jesus Christ, and bless them in his name" (Doctrine and Covenants 17:19) mean that they must be brought before the church assembly?

Is it permissible to bless children in homes, and if so under what circumstances?

ANSWER

One needs to study the purpose and function of the blessing of children to get a clear answer to this question. There is the prophetic element involved in the pronouncement of blessing upon a little child. This is undoubtedly indicated in the scriptures, especially in the Old

199

Testament. The classic example is the blessing by Jacob of his twelve sons. This prophetic element has led to an undue expectancy on the part of some parents, especially when they overlook the part that parents play in the life of the child given into their care. There are other elements involved in this ordinance of the church.

Our experience in the Restoration has led the church to greater understanding of this important experience in the life of the family. It has come to be realized that, in addition to the simple truth that a blessing is imparted, the occasion is one of deep dedication and the acceptance of parental and congregational responsibility.

If this concept be rightly involved in the blessing of children the ideal place is before the congregation. This is so equally from the point of view of the child, the parents, or the congregation. Each is a partner in the fulfilling of God's blessing in the life of the little one. This is what is envisioned in the text, "bring them unto the elders before the church."

We would say, then, that it is most desirable to bring our children publicly for blessing. There may be occasions and circumstances where this is not possible and for quite legitimate reasons; when this is so it may be assumed that presenting the babe for the blessing of the elders is in spirit presenting him before the church.

My opinion is that such circumstances are rare. I personally have not arranged for a private blessing where the alternative is possible, nor where the reason for the request has been lack of cooperation and opposition of one parent as to the desirability of the ordinance. The home should be united at this point and should one of the parents be opposed, the responsibility rests with that one. I mention this because this is one reason I have known advanced for requests for "private" blessings.

Church members should be encouraged to use the church service as the place to present their children for blessing "unto the elders before the church."

191. Tradition in Blessing Baby

QUESTION

Is there anything more than tradition in the use of certain words often used in blessing a baby? The words I refer to are that the child's name is written in the "Lamb's Book of Life."

ANSWER

I know of nothing obligating an elder to state that a child's name is being recorded in the Lamb's Book of Life. The only way I know of this record being made is by one's obeying God's commandments and then continuing to walk with him in his paths to the end of life. I think the practice you refer to is traditional and the words are often tritely used. Though a desirable petition, it is in no way part of the rite. It is a prophetic utterance that one should not lightly make.

192. What Used for Anointing

QUESTION

Matthew 6:18, I.V., states that when we fast we should anoint the head. What should be used for the anointing? Does this mean that the Saints should use consecrated oil?

ANSWER

This text has little literal application to us in our day. The counsel given by Jesus was to Hebrew people and in terms of Hebrew customs; therefore one must look for the principle or basic truth behind the mechanical elements which were involved. Oil had a symbolic meaning to Hebrew religious culture and also appears to have been used in medication. In the text quoted, I see no distinctly symbolic use but simply a counsel not to make a demonstration of fasting so as to be noted for formal piety. The counsel was that when fasting, one should give the appearance of going about normal activity.

Any efficacy in observing a fast is in one's inward and spiritual attitudes, and the Lord's counsel is to give this due attention while not neglecting the normal wholesome customs of toiletry. Christ lifted numerous rituals out of mechanical observance into the realm of the spiritual. Thus, to wear sackcloth and smear one's body with ashes was no longer a necessary symbol of repentance, sorrow, or worthiness. No anointing in the sense implied by this ancient Hebrew custom is required in our culture.

The circumstances of anointing at the time of administration for the sick are in a different category and are retained because of the symbolism of healing and soothing involved. There is no change in efficacy in the physical qualities of olive oil when consecrated.

193. Origin of Consecrating Oil

QUESTION

What is the origin of the practice of consecrating oil for use by the elders in administering to the sick?

I have not been able to discover any specific instruction on the blessing of oil. On the other hand there appears to be no rule or principle which would make this practice improper. It has the support of precedent over the past 130 years at least, and in the light of the fact that there is nothing contrariwise it would seem a good practice.

The setting apart of some physical element or instrument which is to be used only for sacred purposes appears to me to be quite proper and consistent. The danger comes when the consecrating act is interpreted as placing some specific power in the element as such. Our understanding of its use is that it is symbolic and is based on the Hebrew practice of anointing with olive oil for several purposes, one of them being medical.

As with all physical symbols, the virtue is in the spiritual application of the rite and in relation to the performance thereof by the priesthood.

The earliest references available to me indicate that it was practiced in the early days of the church, and of course the Reorganization period shows the continuing practice. The first recorded occasion of consecration in the Restoration seems to be January 19, 1836, when Joseph Smith said:

> "At early candlelight I met with the Presidency at the west schoolroom, in the temple, to attend to the ordinance of anointing our heads with holy oil; also the councils of Kirtland and Zion met in the two adjoining rooms, who waited in prayer while we attended to the ordinance. I took the oil in my left hand, Father Smith being seated before me, and the remainder of the Presidency encircled him round about. We then stretched out right hands towards heaven, and blessed the oil and consecrated it in the name of Jesus Christ.
>
> "We then laid our hands upon our aged Father Smith and invoked the blessings of heaven. I then anointed his head with the consecrated oil and sealed many blessings upon him."
>
> —*Journal of History,*
> Volume 18, page 60

Note that this reference uses the words "blessed," "holy," and "consecrated," and is in connection with the imparting of a special blessing.

The early fathers make reference in their writing to consecrated oil and its uses in sacred rites including ordination, healing, and blessing. I have found no instructions on this particular point in these readings, but the reference there to *consecrated* oil is suggestive of its being a rule of great antiquity.

194. Blessing Olive Oil

QUESTION

Should olive oil used in administering to the sick be blessed in public, in a specially planned service, or in private? Should consecrated oil be used for purposes other than administration?

ANSWER

There is no scriptural authority for the use of consecrated oil in anointing by other than the priesthood. There is no particular virtue in it of itself, other than in its correct medicinal use. It is the prayer of faith through administration that is efficacious. Therefore, the keeping of oil in the home for other reasons than to be used when the elders are called is not necessary and obviates the necessity of bringing of oil in bottles for public consecration.

There is no ruling which would forbid this being done in public but it is usually done in private. Most ministers do not make special occasions for consecrating oil. If they did, it would tend to place the emphasis on the material agent rather than the act of faith involved in calling for administration.

We have grown in our understanding of sacred ordinances. At one time I heard of a request to consecrate a large quantity of oil for distribution; this indicated a complete lack of understanding of the place of this element with regard to healing. Fortunately we understand this more fully today. "The prayer of faith shall save the sick" (James 1:5).

195. How Anoint

QUESTION

After an administration to the sick, I was questioned by an observer on my procedure of moistening my finger from the vial of oil and thus anointing the head of the sick person. His thought was that it takes pouring of the oil to constitute the act of anointing. What is the procedure?

ANSWER

Webster gives the meaning to anoint as "to smear, to rub, to apply, or to pour." This, therefore, does not require a pouring of oil in administration.

Medical knowledge was quite limited in the days when the text found in James 5:14, 15 was formulated, and olive oil was a medication.

In many cases it had a soothing effect. The Good Samaritan "poured wine and oil" into the injured man's wounds (see Luke 10:34). Luke is said to have been a physician, and it is interesting to note that he alone gives this story. In the Christian church it became a symbol of soothing and healing, and it is used in this sense when the ordinance of administration for the sick is performed.

Seeing that the word anointing is used to cover all methods of application, the current procedure of a small quantity of oil being placed upon the forehead with the elder's finger is a good one.

196. Elders before Doctors

QUESTION

When one is ill should he call for the elders before asking advice from a medical practitioner? Should one do all possible for himself before asking for administration?

ANSWER

The decision to ask for administration for sickness is not contrary to calling for the doctor as well. God has given us an intelligence which we should use, and where we can help ourselves it is our duty to do so. Nevertheless, the divine power is available for our need and therefore when we feel the need of this help we are privileged to seek it through administration. This should be done intelligently and not used as a magic formula to receive what we desire in physical revival without effort on our part. We can claim spiritual help in all our affairs of home and business, but one would not think of substituting prayer for action in conducting those affairs. Yet one should pray in the conduct of all affairs while applying practical methods.

On the other hand administration is not to be used only when we are at our wit's end. The knowledge which the medical profession has is part of the total truth of the universe, and in this sense divine. The calling for administration involves getting one's total self in harmony with the divine will. The medical side of the situation involves using what is already given.

To affirm that one should call for the elders first before seeking skilled help would be like having a serious accident on the highway which occasions gross injury and calling for the elders to lay on hands but failing to call for an ambulance and applying first aid. In serious illness why not call the doctor and then the elders to bring the consolation and faith-building benefits of administration? In minor ills where intelligence suffices, we should use it in the spirit of faith.

197. Patriarchal Blessing for Nonmembers

QUESTION

May a nonmember receive a patriarchal blessing? I understand administration is not restricted to members.
If not, in which of the church ordinances may a nonmember participate?

ANSWER

It would seem to me that the preparation, condition, and faith of the one seeking a blessing is a primary factor in this ordinance. A patriarchal blessing is intended as guidance and direction in the tenor of one's life's work and is extended especially to those who have committed themselves through obedience to the initiatory ordinances of the gospel, acceptance of which is evidence of the desire and determination to walk in God's ways.

Because of this, it would be unusual for a nonmember to seek guidance along the lines of the patriarchal blessing if, for reasons within his control, he had not as yet given obedience to the basic commandments of the gospel.

One of the procedures followed by the patriarchal ministers is to encourage preparation to receive blessing in the proper spirit and worthiness. When this approach is taken, the question would naturally arise as to willingness to follow God's commands.

In certain circumstances, which would be exceptional, a member or nonmember may seek a special blessing and counsel, and this may be given under the laying on of hands. Whether this is recorded is at the discretion of the minister so functioning. This, however, is not the blessing generally known as "the patriarchal blessing" but a special privilege of ministry. Administration for sickness would be a seeking for a special blessing in a particular way, though not necessarily through a patriarch, since any elder is authorized to administer. It therefore would not have the same limitations as when one is seeking a patriarchal blessing. Of course, repentance, faith in God and his appointed ministry should be prerequisites to receiving the blessing of healing.

In addition to administration, a nonmember may have the privilege of child blessing by the Melchisedec priesthood. Of course the ministry of the church is available for marriage and burial. The Church of Jesus Christ is a body which serves mankind, and its services are freely available, but the ordinances have significance only when the conditions involved are met and officiating ministers are charged with the responsibility of deciding whether the provisions of the law are complied with.

The Lord's Supper

198. Close Communion

QUESTION

Recently nonmember visitors have been critical of our practice of close Communion. Would you explain why we follow this practice?

ANSWER

The principle upon which our church practice is based is well expressed in the Book of Mormon.

"And when the multitude had eaten and were filled, he said unto the disciples, Behold, there shall one be ordained among you and to him will I give power that he shall break bread, and bless it, and give it unto the people of my church, unto all those who shall believe and be baptized in my name."—III Nephi 8:32.

"And this shall ye always do unto those who repent and are baptized in my name; and ye shall do it in remembrance of my blood, which I have shed for you, that ye may witness unto the Father that ye do always remember me."—III Nephi 8:40.

"And as I have prayed among you, even so shall ye pray in my church, among my people who do repent and are baptized in my name."—III Nephi 8:48.

It will be noted that the instruction to the ordained minister is concerning those "who shall believe and be baptized in my name." These references indicate that those to whom the emblems shall be served are of the church of Christ.

Those of our church have committed themselves to serve Christ in a particular way which involves the obeying of certain commands, including repentance and baptism by ministers of particular authority.

When we partake of the sacrament we do it after the following prayer has been offered for the bread and a similar one for the wine:

"O God, the eternal Father, we ask thee in the name of thy Son Jesus Christ, to bless and sanctify this bread to the souls of all those who partake of it, that they may eat in remembrance of the body of thy Son, and witness unto thee, O God, the eternal Father, that they are willing to take upon them the name of thy Son, and always remember him and keep his commandments which he has given them, that they may always have his Spirit to be with them. Amen."—Doctrine and Covenants 17:22 d, 23 b.

An analysis of this prayer reveals it to be a reaffirmation in the essence of the baptismal covenant which made us members of Christ's body. This reaffirmation involves the concepts and intent of the previous covenant. Therefore it would be meaningless for those who have not been initially obedient, as we understand the scriptures, to go through the motions of sharing.

The ceremonial procedure has no significance without the concepts of what true obedience to Christ means. In partaking, the communicant testifies that he has made the necessary adjustments to God and his fellows. Mere partaking does not make this adjustment but symbolically testifies that one is in this condition of heart and mind.

If one were to partake otherwise it would not be without personal meaning, but there is a collective fellowship involved and that is membership in the organism known as Christ's body. We believe that this means a specific group of obedient members (III Nephi 8:40, 48.) If one has not identified and committed himself in this way there would be reservations in his mind and therefore the true significance of his act would be destroyed.

Our friends seldom feel hurt if there is considerate explanation made, prior to attending the Communion service, that this sacrament has this meaning to us and therefore can be properly administered only in this way. Though friends may regard their ecumenical relationship as sufficient qualification for Communion they will see that with our concept of a specific church organism and the intimate corporate fellowship involved, we could not rightfully include others not of our covenant in the administration thereof.

199. Sharing Communion

QUESTION

Doctrine and Covenants 46:1, 2 states that we should not cast anyone out of our sacrament meetings. Why do we not share Communion with visiting nonmember friends?

ANSWER

The church follows the practice of close communion; that is, only those who have entered into the church by the covenant of baptism and have been confirmed by the laying on of hands by authorized ministers of this church are offered the emblems at a Communion service. While this is true, anyone may attend the Communion service, and we are instructed to exclude none from attendance at these services.

This sacrament, described by President F. M. Smith as "the second great sacrament," is a reaffirmation of the covenant made in baptism; therefore, one who has not made his covenant with God in this way cannot reaffirm it. It is well that a Saint inviting his friends to such meetings inform them of this belief. If this is done prior to the service, embarrassment is avoided.

200. Partaking with Another Church

QUESTION

I would like an opinion as to whether or not a member of our church or a member of the priesthood should partake of the emblems in a sacrament service when visiting another church. Or if there is no branch of our church in the city and members are regularly attending another church, should they partake?

ANSWER

I think I can answer best by repeating a statement made in the editorial column of the *Saints' Herald* some years ago when Joseph Smith III was editor. It was in answer to the question, "Are we close communion?"

"If by this question it is intended to ask, Do you as a church administer to and partake of the sacramental emblems, bread and wine, with other religious bodies, we answer, No.

"Our reason for thus answering, is that we are commanded not to let communicants partake unworthily; this unworthiness in part is the failure to discern in the church the Lord's body; or, in other words, the church acknowledged of Christ as his.

"In this we are not altogether alone. There are other religious bodies who believe it to be improper to permit those not of their way of thinking and worship to partake with them of the sacrificial elements.

"There is much, in our way of thinking, to justify our position in regard to this sort of close communion. Paul wrote, 'Ye are the body of Christ and members in particular.' The commandment, 'As oft as ye do this, do it in remembrance of me,' was given to the disciples, the church. If Jesus and his disciples were justified in being close communion at that time, then the church now existent is justified in being close communion now.

"As a people we are commanded not to cast any one out of our prayer and sacrament meetings; but this does not justify us in giving to them those emblems in the partaking of which we solemnly assure the Lord and each other that we are willing to take upon us the name of Christ, to remember him, to keep his commandments, in order that we may have his Spirit to be with us. Whoever should partake with us in this covenant, by eating and drinking of the bread and wine, would by such act of partaking also be virtually assenting that the church by whose officers the emblems were offered and administered was the church of Christ, and the officers administering were acting in the name of the church and Christ. This acknowledgment we have not the right to demand or permit them to make without the previous baptism which the word of God requires; hence the wisdom of the church in not permitting those not of the faith into which we have been baptized to partake of the sacrament with us; and as a consequence to decline to partake with them in their lovefeasts or sacrament-meetings."—*Saints' Herald,* Volume 53, October 24, 1906, page 1,004.

I have given this statement first because of its clear logic and definite counsel and with the purpose that it may be seen that the converse is true with regard to a member of this church accepting the sacrament from a minister not included in our own special covenant relationship with Christ's church.

Our opinion is that in the light of the principles outlined, one would be advised to abstain from partaking in other churches. This in no way means that fellowship of a social and devotional nature should not be shared.

201. Confirmation Prior to Lord's Supper

QUESTION

Does the church have a definite rule providing that confirmation should be administered prior to our partaking of the Lord's Supper? If so how do we explain "Church History," Volume I, page 77, where at the initial meeting it is recorded that the members partook prior to confirmation?

ANSWER

There is definite provision for the procedure outlined in the first part of your question. This is found in Doctrine and Covenants 17:18. The correct interpretation of this places the ordinance of confirmation as a requisite for full membership. The peculiar difficulty is that the prophet chose to place equal clauses in the order that he did. You will note, however, the italicized preface to Doctrine and Covenants 17. To read this and the full context in *Times and Seasons* (see Volume III, pages 915-917 and 928, etc.) from which it comes is to realize that the charter members and leaders were ignorant at first of many details of the law and of procedure. When the more complete insight into the dual nature of the new birth was had, the present view which requires baptism and confirmation for full membership was followed. Doctrine and Covenants Section 17 is revelation but evidently not one single document originally. It is a composite document and represents growing understanding up to 1835. Paragraph 17 was not in the first printings of the text known as "Articles and Covenants." This paragraph first appeared in the Doctrine and Covenants of 1835.

I do not know of any later incident than the one you quote where confirmation was not required to complete entrance into the church before Communion was administered. The fact of inexperience is the only reasonable explanation I can give. The Saints were using alcoholic wine prior to instruction otherwise. The church organization and procedure has always been an unfolding process. Therefore the preface of Section 17 states: "In this manner did the Lord continue to give instructions from time to time concerning the duties which now devolved upon us."

202. Serving New Member

QUESTION

Is it proper procedure to serve the emblems on the occasion of first Communion to a new member before those at the table have been served?

It is not normal to so do. I have never seen this done, nor have I followed this routine when administering the sacrament. There is no directly stated procedure in scripture, but custom and the place of priesthood at the Communion table would indicate the propriety of administering to the ministers there first. This is established procedure, although it is a friendly gesture for the pastor or presiding officer to serve the new member first, signifying that the church is aware of the presence of the new baby brother or sister.

Scriptural precedents indicate that the ministry were served prior to the gathered Saints. The Book of Mormon account of the serving of the sacraments states:

"And when the disciples had come with bread and wine, he took of the bread, and break and blessed it; and he gave unto the disciples, and commanded that they should eat.

"And when they were eaten, and were filled, he commanded that they should give unto the multitude."—III Nephi 8:30, 31.

It seems fitting that priesthood members should reaffirm their covenant by partaking of the emblems prior to serving them to the people.

203. Serving Immediately after Confirmation

QUESTION

Inasmuch as it is our belief that by partaking of the Lord's Supper we renew our covenant made at baptism, is it proper procedure to serve the emblems to candidates immediately after baptism and confirmation when there has been no time lapse for the covenant to be either kept or broken?

ANSWER

I will quote the statement of Brother Charles Fry (*Question Time,* page 261):

"We know of no scripture which specifically says that partaking of the Communion is a renewing of our covenant with God, though it is often so spoken of in our services. It is not so much a renewal as it is an acknowledgment of the existing covenant and an affirmation that we have done and are willing to continue doing the things our covenant and the law of God require us to

211

do. It is an enacted testimony or a witnessing that we have, since last partaking, either kept ourselves from those faults and sins which would estrange us from our fellowmen and from God or, having fallen into any such sin, we have followed the law of repentance, and have effected reconciliation, leaving our conscience clear and our souls an acceptable offering to God. The requirement that the emblems are to be partaken of in remembrance of Christ undoubtedly involves more than keeping in mind the fact of his crucifixion and death, and includes remembering his commandments at all times and places. In partaking, we are reminded of our covenant to serve him and keep his commandments."

I think your problem arises from a variation of meanings read into the word "renewal" in connection with Communion. It may help if we call other words to our service in an endeavor to explain more fully the function and purpose of this sacrament.

The use of the words "reaffirm" and "acknowledgment of existing covenant" would avoid the difficulty of interpreting "renewal" to mean that there has become necessary another or second covenant because of the lapse of the first.

The adjustments required in the law involving repentance and restitution, which one must exercise before sharing in Communion, restore relationship with God and one's fellows without the specific rite of partaking of the emblems. I know of no scriptural statement which states that to partake of the bread and wine is essential as part of the act of repentance or reconciliation. Of course it is very significant, following these adjustments, and has a vital place in the spiritual life. There are scriptures which do forbid making the sacramental testimony before adjustment is made by repentance. The act of partaking of the emblems is an affirmation or testimony of one's identification with the body of Christ and the purposes and standards thereof. Those who have made their covenants through authoritative baptism are admonished to present themselves at the sacramental table where they bear witness by their partaking and evidence their remembrance of Christ and their obligations to keep his commandments.

There are other aspects of this rite which may be enlarged upon but to read the prayer which is outlined for this occasion (see Doctrine and Covenants 17:22, 23) is to understand the basic witness of oneness with Christ, his church, and with one's fellow Saints, which is signified by partaking. This a person may do at any time after being baptized and confirmed.

The need to partake of the emblems is not wholly dependent upon the fact that one may not have fully kept the baptismal covenant. Where one has not, he should make himself right in all aspects of fellowship and so fit himself to truthfully testify to this relationship. However, it is not necessary to have broken the covenant of baptism to be eligible to share in Communion. If "renewal" is used in this sense, the word is inadequate. President F. M. Smith is often quoted as using this word. It is a question of semantics, and one should avoid reading more into a word than was intended when used by President F. M. Smith. There is definite spiritual renewal in partaking of the Sacrament, but it is not a rebirth which baptism alone signifies. Elbert A. Smith stated in the *Priesthood Journal:*

"At which time we have opportunity to renew the covenant made in baptism; or if we do not actually renew it we at least reaffirm it."—Volume 2, page 23.

204. Serving to Those Not in Room

QUESTION

Is it right to serve the sacramental emblems to members who are not in the room during the service and do not hear the prayer of blessing?

ANSWER

This question must be considered in the light of the spirit and the purpose of Communion. The answer is found in that purpose. If there is room in the sanctuary where the service is in progress, no person should be seated elsewhere unless for special reason. I cannot imagine a person wanting to stay in the foyer and apart from the main worshipers when there is room and still wishing to take Communion. Such an attitude would seem to require the attention of the presiding officers.

Should a mother be outside the main group due to a child's restlessness, or other reason, the meaningfulness of the rite is not in any way destroyed should the priest step outside to include her.

The emblems are blessed "to the souls of all those who partake" of them (Doctrine and Covenants 17:22). The essence of the rite is fellowship with God and his church and a witness to the fact that we are determined to live so as to maintain that fellowship and to always remember the Redeemer, that we "may always have his Spirit" to be with us.

Should a person be ill and unable to attend Communion, he may request the priesthood to bring the emblems to the bedside, and if the prayer of blessing has previously been offered, a second prayer is not obligatory. This also would be the case when one would receive the emblems without hearing the prayer.

205. Requesting Communion for Sick and Shut-ins

QUESTION

Should the Communion be taken to the sick and shut-ins in their homes without request? Do they need to ask for it before it is taken to them?

ANSWER

One cannot state a rule on this. It is obviously the responsibility of the sick or shut-in and those associated with him in the home to make his needs known. Where a person is sick over a period of time, an arrangement should be made if the Communion is desired. It would not be right to expect at all times that priesthood anticipate the desire of absent members and arrive at the home to administer the emblems. On the other hand, good pastoral ministry does not fail to keep aware of the needs of the flock. On a member's occasional absence from Communion, the ministers would not be expected to be aware of his need unless a specific request was made.

Then, too, all should be done through a responsible channel to avoid confusion or duplication of visits. This channel would be the pastor or one specifically designated.

The ministers should recognize that sick people are particularly sensitive and often entertain a feeling of being neglected more than appears justified to the person in good health. Where there are shut-ins I feel it is the responsibility of the pastor to arrange for such ministry as will enable him to be aware of needs, so that the sufferer may have an opportunity to make his needs and desires known.

Our ministers are busy men. Therefore it is unreasonable for a member to lie ill and feel neglected while making no move to ensure that the pastor is aware of his needs and desires. This has often occurred in the case of administration.

206. Withholding Communion

QUESTION

What is the responsibility of the priesthood in administering the

Sacrament where there is known to be unrepented sin or the existence of animosity between brothers and sisters? Would a minister be justified in withholding Communion?

ANSWER

The responsibility of priesthood in the matter of administering Sacrament is clearly set forth in the following Book of Mormon text:

"And now behold, this is the commandment which I give unto you, that ye shall not suffer any one knowingly, to partake of my flesh and blood unworthily, when ye shall minister it, for whoso eateth and drinketh my flesh and blood unworthily, eateth and drinketh damnation to his soul; therefore if ye know that a man is unworthy to eat and drink of my flesh and blood, ye shall forbid him; nevertheless ye shall not cast him out from among you, but ye shall minister unto him, and shall pray for him unto the Father, in my name."—III Nephi 8:60, 61.

This is not to be administered arbitrarily by the minister. The presiding officer of the branch is primarily responsible, and no member of the priesthood should act hastily or without proper consideration being given or upon personal basis. This provision is not a weapon to punish or discipline the hearts and minds of the Saints but one of salvation in that it protects a member from the results of false witnessing.

Thus if one knowingly partakes with animosity and evil desire in his heart he eats and drinks condemnation to himself. This is a spiritual problem and may have many symptoms—socially, spiritually, and even physically.

I would remind you that the responsibility for the sharing in the Sacrament is not only on the minister but upon the offended as well as the offending one. The Master said that our offerings at the altar are not acceptable unless we are right with our brethren. If we know that one has anything against us we are obligated to seek adjustment.

I suggest you study the following extra references upon which my reply is based: Matthew 5:23, 24; Doctrine and Covenants 42:23; I Corinthians 11:27-30.

207. Deciding Worthiness

If the Communion should not be administered to the unworthy, how is worthiness defined? Does the priesthood member presiding have the right to decide?

The scriptures do teach that one should be worthy to rightly partake of the Communion. The matter of worthiness rests basically upon the communicant who alone knows best his inner self. Worthiness should not be interpreted as one's being free from all sin. However, one should not partake without sincere desire and determination to do right, having truly repented of that which has been wrong in his life. It is only in matters of overt or obvious sin that the responsible priesthood officer can apply the instruction which states that he should not allow anyone to partake unworthily. If a person is known to be unrepentant and to have not made the necessary adjustments in himself and/or to others, he should be prevented from involving himself in an insincere covenant. However, this action should be taken in a kindly and tactful way—and no public refusal in normal circumstaces would be acceptable. This does not apply to those who have not been baptized by proper authority, and they of course should not be given the emblems. However, the refusal should not be voiced in a hurtful way. A statement of our position on "close Communion" is often made when nonmembers are present. In the broad sense only those who have made the covenant in baptism and have approached the service in a proper condition are "worthy."

208. Meaning of "Wine"

QUESTION

What is covered by the word "wine" in connection with the Sacrament? Does it mean "fermented" or "unfermented" wine? Where is the authority to serve grape juice in place of wine?

ANSWER

The answer is found in Doctrine and Covenants, Section 26:1, and in Section 119:5. Both of these references give explanations which will help considerably. You will note that in the first reference the Lord said, "Wherefore a commandment I give unto you, that you shall not purchase wine, neither strong drink of your enemies; wherefore ye shall partake of none, except it is made *new* among you." Here a distinction is made between the purchasing of wine and the purchasing of strong drink—which should answer your question. We should use only unfermented wine. The Word of Wisdom gives definite instruction that strong drink is not for human consumption. Therefore there can be no question of a fermented beverage being used in the sacrament of the Lord's Supper. It is our opinion that the word "wine" covers in a normal sense both that with alcoholic content and that juice of the vine which has no alcohol. The instruction is that it be made *new* among us. Wine that has fermented is not *new* in the sense of this instruction.

Then, again, in the second reference, Section 119:5 c, note that it says "clean vessels for the wine, *or the water,* as may be expedient." Again, in Section 119:5 a the instruction is "cease to contend respecting the sacrament." Then follows instruction which indicates that those partaking should be more concerned with the attitude and condition under which they partake rather than the content. Even water may be used. Grape juice would be wine, new wine, and is the "fruit of the vine."

209. Homemade Wine

QUESTION

Should the wine used in Communion be homemade? If not, are the communicants denied a blessing?

ANSWER

The instruction given in Doctrine and Covenants 26:1 is the key to this procedure. If you read the historical data in the italicized paragraph preceding the section, you will note that Joseph Smith, Jr., was on his way to purchase wine for the ceremony when he was told to use wine which was nonalcoholic. Up to this time it is obvious that no distinction had been made between fermented and non-fermented wine. Purchase of nonalcoholic wine appears to have been impossible; therefore, it had to be prepared by the Saints themselves.

There is the added precaution advised of not purchasing from enemies. In the days of the frontier (this instruction is dated August, 1830) temperance was a prominent issue among the religious denominations. The church stand was taken quite early; Section 86 was to follow in February, 1833, outlining by counsel a standard in matters of food and drink. Today pure and unfermented grape juice can be purchased with confidence. Hence, the instruction in the official brochure *Administrative Policies and Procedures* (page 34) states that commercially prepared juice is acceptable. It would be superstitious to suppose that there is any particular virtue in grape juice prepared by the Saints, provided, of course, that the instructions on strong drink are observed. The latter counsel, if not followed, could be fraught with consequences. The fact that other elements may be used as a substitute indicates that the virtue is not in the element but in the attitude of the communicants.

217

210. Commercial Grape Juice

QUESTION

Is it in conflict with Doctrine and Covenants 26 to use commercially prepared grape juice?

ANSWER

In the brochure *Administrative Policies and Procedures,* page 34, the following statement appears:

"The apparent intent of the instruction that wine shall be made rather than purchased (D. and C. 26:1 b) is to avoid the risk of using fermented wine. . . . This does not appear to prohibit the purchase of wine for sacramental use so long as it is clear that this wine is unfermented."

Then follows a quotation of General Conference Resolution No. 702:

"Fermented wine should not be used in the Sacrament services of the church, but either unfermented wine or water should be used and so be in harmony with the spirit of the revelations."— General Conference Resolution 702; Doctrine and Covenants 26:1, 86:1, 119:5.

Note the words, "spirit of the revelations." To understand this, the time and circumstances involved in the giving of Doctrine and Covenants 26 should be considered.

Using the phrase "and not of your enemies" was an endeavor to ensure the provision that unadulterated and unfermented wine should be used. In these days the various national food and drug regulations make unlikely the problem of not being able to obtain a pure product if purchase is required.

211. Communion Cup

QUESTION

We make a particular emphasis upon the importance of maintaining the correct method of baptism as in Christ's day. Are we consistent when we vary the procedure for Communion in that we do not use a common cup now?

ANSWER

You are correct in your appreciation of our insistence on the baptismal mode. This is important because the significance of complete washing, burial, and rising to new life are involved and kept vivid through the practice of immersion. To sprinkle or pour loses this import.

However, it is not a parallel to the Communion cup. The symbolism of the common meal is preserved and the bread is broken and shared; likewise the wine. We break the bread symbolically. Analogy can be carried to extremes and break down. Hygiene requires our present practice. It may be argued that the divine power will override the problems of infection, but I find no authority in scripture for disobeying the rules of health and then claiming immunity.

Christ used the symbolism of a meal to portray unity and fellowship with him in the gospel, and in so doing acted as was the custom. As a church, we insist on the precise prayer to keep the import of the Sacrament in its true significance.

212. Procedure in Serving at Table

QUESTION

I have observed a difference of procedure in administering the sacramental emblems. My question is: Should the presiding elder serve other ministers associated at the table or be first served by another? I think that there should be a definite procedure, and that the pattern set in the New Testament should guide.

ANSWER

There is no direct instruction on this point of which I am aware, and there has been no official ruling which would bind as to procedure. It may be that it comes within the scope of the instruction given on another point which admonished the church to cease to contend over the administering of the Communion (Doctrine and Covenants 119:5). This section lays emphasis upon the spirit of partaking rather than upon time, ritual, or substance used as emblems. If the participants are preoccupied with procedure during this most sacred service, good is lost to their souls.

This having been said as to the attitudes prevailing at the Communion service, it may be observed that the church has given increasing attention to dignity and order in the conduct of the rites and services of the church. One thing that detracts from the value of the Communion service is evidence of uncertainty as to procedure by those in charge or of uncertainty in the congregation. For this reason marked sudden changes in customary routine should not occur. All procedures should flow calmly so that the major significance of the service will stand at the center of the thoughts of the communicants.

Concerning precedent in the New Testament, it is true that the scriptural records of the New Testament and Book of Mormon show that Jesus took bread and broke it and then gave it to the disciples. According to the account in III Nephi 8:30, 31 and 9:40-42, Jesus then commanded that they should give it to the multitude. In Matthew 26, Mark 14, and Luke 22 the same procedure is followed except that there is no attending multitude. On the New Testament occasion Jesus said, "Take this and divide it among yourselves" (Luke 22:17). As this was the first occasion it was necessary for Jesus to personally break and offer the elements. The disciples were new to the whole experience.

There is no precedent in Restoration history which would serve as a guide. The procedure followed at the first Communion service on April 6, 1830, does not indicate who administered the emblems first, but the emphasis is upon sharing.

It would appear that some consistency of practice in a given group may be helpful but—provided the officiating ministers are clearly aware of the procedure prior to the service—either is permissible.

213. Seating Priesthood around Communion Table

QUESTION

What basis is there in the law and doctrine of the church for seating priesthood around a Communion table in preference to the use of an altar centered to the rear of the priesthood?

ANSWER

I know of no rule which prescribes the method of seating at Communion. There is no instruction on the use of altars either.

The basis for the use of a Communion table is in the type and origin of the Lord's Supper. The first Communion was around the table with the Lord. There were only thirteen persons present, thus there was no problem of accommodation. As the church grew to great proportions this exact procedure was not possible.

In this church the custom of using a table has been maintained and would appear to be symbolic of the family of Christ eating together in fellowship as a commemoration of the great event of the Lord's sacrifice.

Doctrine and Covenants 119:5 gives very valuable counsel on the Sacrament, and in this scripture the words "table of the Lord" are used. We have no instruction on the seating of priesthood, but the tradition of sitting behind the table is the normal practice. One should hesitate to institute innovations, as it is so easy to lose the simplicity of the sacraments.

It perhaps should be said that there is no early precedent for the emblems being placed on the altar, although the table has been so referred to. Altars with sacred vessels and so forth seem to have been later introductions in the Christian church until the rituals over-shadowed the basic meaning and the congregations played a minor part in what became pageantry.

214. Priesthood Serving Self

QUESTION

The statement is made that the elder presiding should receive the Communion from a fellow minister. Does this imply that one elder should refrain from participation if he is the only member of the priesthood present with authority to administer Communion? Briefly, should this elder serve himself?

ANSWER

I see no objection to a minister's sharing in this symbol of covenant of fellowship by partaking himself if he is the only minister present with authority to so act.

It is, however, the duty of every member of the priesthood to make as frequent contact with the main body of the church as possible so as to have the larger fellowship. These problems do occur in isolation, but the minister should be alert not only to *take* but to seek every opportunity to receive ministry at the hands of others. By his efforts to do this he witnesses to his group the importance of our interrelation-ship in the body of Christ. It would be a rare situation where lone participation would need to be continued indefinitely.

215. Served While Standing

QUESTION

Should members be served the sacrament of the Lord's Supper while standing? It reminds me of drinking a toast.

ANSWER

Repeatedly it has been necessary to remind ourselves that over-concentration on minor details respecting the serving of the Communion

221

is unwise. We have been counseled that contention concerning the sacrament is unseemly (see Doctrine and Covenants 119:5).

I know of no instruction on the inquiry made, and I am aware only of custom in the matter. I have seen all stand at the table, but I have noted that in most places the ministers sit. I have never seen the whole congregation stand while receiving the emblems, though my experience may not have been wide enough for me to have observed this.

What may be reverent in the United States or in Australia may be irreverent in French Polynesia, Japan, or Europe. To stand in proposing a toast is an act of respect in my native country, and one would be disrespectful to sit. To loll one's tongue out in some Maori tribes is an act of approval, but this is not acceptable in cultured Western society. If another national group uses the tom-tom instead of a pipe organ to express joy in religious faith, is it less acceptable before the Throne? I suspect the original Communion cup was shared while the participants reclined at the low table. I have eaten a Japanese meal at a cultured home sitting cross-legged on the floor.

My point is that customs have only those values with which we invest them, and the same action may have reverse meaning in another culture. As long as we maintain the essential meaning and do those things which in our own different cultures convey respect for the basic truth involved, it matters not whether we sit or stand as long as all is done in order. One of the problems of the Jews of Christ's day was that they paid more attention to the form than to the spiritual content of the law, substituting rules and procedures instead.

216. Dramatic Settings for Lord's Supper

QUESTION

To what extent are dramatic settings for the sacrament of the Lord's Supper justifiable with the objective of making the occasion more impressive?

ANSWER

In my view the essence of the Communion service is in its simplicity, and it should be kept so. One should not be extreme, however. It may be that some procedures do not have more than custom or tradition as their authority, and we should be aware of this when we make judgment as to what should be.

We should consider what is the central thought at a Communion service and remember that the simple ritual of breaking bread and

222

sharing in the wine was the symbolism by which the Master himself chose to embody the significance of Communion. If this is kept in mind the elder planning the service will not allow any single detail to obscure the basic significance.

An analogy between a picture and its frame may be helpful. All have at some time seen a small, delicate picture obscured by a frame of massive proportions in such a way that the frame becomes the object of attention to the consequent loss of the message of the picture itself. On the other hand suitable framing lends emphasis where it belongs. When this concept is held, the place of the necessary elements of worship are sensed. Advisedly I say "sensed" rather than "defined."

Novelty is certainly out of place in such a service, as this is both irritating and distracting to most people. Changes in procedure may occur but by transition rather than by doing violence to custom. In my pastoral experience I have observed strong reactions from worshipers when a symbol foreign to their concepts and traditions has been introduced. Remembering that we are ministering to souls will help us avoid making changes that are not appreciated by those to whom the sacramental occasion should minister.

Obviously our present pattern of the Communion service is different than that even of the early Reorganization. It is certainly different from the early days of the Restoration as shown by a reading of some procedures of those days. However, the central theme and element are the same.

This service is essentially dramatic. However, it depends not on colorful pageantry but upon simplicity and quiet dignity for its appeal. When suitable music, scripture, and the spoken word all draw our souls to the central act of Communion we are ministered to.

217. Uncovering Emblems for Blessing

QUESTION

When we have Communion in our branch, we use a set of trays for the bread which has one above the other. The cover of the upper tray is removed for the blessing but the one beneath is left covered tightly. Should this not also be uncovered?

ANSWER

You will find instruction on the serving of the Sacrament in Doctrine and Covenants 119:5. The emphasis in this passage is upon the spirit of unity prevailing during its administration rather than on contention about the procedures and times of serving. There is also some counsel given as to preparation "to avoid confusion" (paragraph 5 c). Further advice is given in paragraph 5 d as to the time of breaking the bread and pouring of the wine. You will note that it is not arbitrary advice but that alternative procedures are acceptable.

Paragraph 5 e states, "both bread and wine are to be uncovered when presented for the blessing." One must look for the purpose of this uncovering of the emblems. I am of the opinion that this is so that the emblems will be in evidence before the waiting congregation and, therefore, recall all the significance of the broken body and spilled blood of the Savior's sacrificial offering. The symbolism is the thing to consider so that the meaning may remain pure and clear.

In the days (1887) when this counsel was given, there were no double-tier Communion sets, so detailed procedure for all eventualities was not attempted. I see no breaking of the spirit of the instruction in not lifting the set to uncover the second plate. Technically it is not uncovered and, to observe the detail of Doctrine and Covenants 119:5, it should be. However, the main point of the text is to avoid contention; so long as the spiritual intent of the Communion is symbolized, the details of administering are not of primary importance.

I agree with your sentiment that instructions should be followed so that the intent and meaning of ceremonials will not be lost. I do not see that this meaning is being lost in the situation out of which your question arises. Technically, the point could be carried to the last detail. However, I'm sure that we are not saved by ceremonial detail but by the inward spiritual quality of our mutual sharing in kingdom activity.

218. Objects on Communion Table

QUESTION

Should other objects than the Communion utensils and emblems be on the Communion table during the service? I refer to the habit of placing a watch, a book, or notes on the table.

ANSWER

Any clutter on the Communion table distracts from the symbolic nature of the bread and wine. The emblems should always be simply placed so as to focus the attention on the meaning of the service.

I personally do not favor other ornaments or contrivances, or even over-ornate furnishings used in conjunction with the emblems. For the reason stated and for the sake of dignity, there should be no extraneous objects in view of the communicants if it can be avoided.

However, not all Communion tables are constructed in a way to facilitate the placing of books, notes, or even a watch where it will not be visible. The Standard Books are not out of place before our people, but they should not be strewn about. Some units have a shelf a few inches below the tabletop which obviates the placing of objects within sight. Where there is not, what is the minister to do with his aids? There should be no arbitrary ruling, therefore. The table holds no inherent sacredness that would amount to a taboo for other articles than those directly associated with the bread and wine.

No ruling has been given, but the aspects I have referred to should enable a correct judgment and also the necessary preservation of dignity and propriety.

219. Communicants and the Communion Plate

QUESTION

I am concerned when I see communicants other than the ministering priests touch the plate used in the Sacrament service as the bread is administered. Should our people not be more careful about this in the light of the instruction to the Hebrews not to touch the Ark which contained the sacred vessels?

ANSWER

I think we have to distinguish between vessels and their uses. That which is sacred is that which has a special use for holy purposes, but there is nothing intrinsically sacred in a silver or china plate. Beyond the reservation of utensils intended for the dispensing of the emblems for their proper use, I see no reason to be concerned that other than the priesthood should come in contact with them. Where special utensils are possessed I think it proper that they should be so reserved. However, just as impressive spiritual effects in the lives of the Saints have been observed where groups used ordinary plates and glasses as where special equipment has been available.

The power is not in the elements or the vessels but in the attitude of those sharing. It must be realized that the rituals which involved a considerable amount of instruction as to handling, as instituted by Moses for the children of Israel, were for a people of a particular stage when respect for divine things needed to be taught. Often this

225

was through discipline that required strict rules such as not touching the sacred things of the Ark. The people needed to be brought to a realization beyond the artifacts themselves to what they portrayed. This the Christian dispensation exemplified on higher levels. If you read the provisions of the Pentateuch you will realize the impossibility of applying these in detail under the gospel.

The power of the Sacrament is in neither the plate nor the emblems. These remain plain physical objects and definitely no change occurs in them as we either touch to partake or handle in the process thereof.

220. Finger Bowls

QUESTION

Are finger bowls for the cleansing of ministers' hands before breaking the bread in order or necessary?

ANSWER

I know of no authoritative statement either way. I have seen finger bowls used but not to any extent and not in recent years. It always appeared to me that an effort was being made to emphasize the fact that cleanliness was being practiced.

My personal view is that it is unnecessary to make this gesture of washing at the Communion table. Your question prompts a comment on cleanliness in general which no doubt stimulated your concern. Any member of the priesthood who is about to handle the emblems should make sure his hands are hygienically clean. This is a basic obligation out of consideration for feelings of others and the sacredness of the ordinance. This is best attended to immediately before going to the table. It is most distressing to worshipers to note the emblems being touched by grimy fingers or to see unclean hands passing them. Some churches provide a napkin inconspicuously placed with which those breaking bread may wipe perspiration from their hands. This seems a good practice.

Ministers administering Communion should also see that hands are not used to shield a cough. They should have a clean handkerchief available for such emergency. In short, recognition of the refinements of our cultural pattern will guide in this as in all social relations where sensitivity is required. It is assumed that those involved in the preparation of emblems prior to the service will observe the principles involved in this question.

221. Women Handling Communion Utensils

QUESTION

Should women handle the Communion glasses and other utensils either during preparation or after the service?

ANSWER

I think it may be most helpful in answering this question to give an extract from an editorial by President F. M. Smith which can be found in the *Saints' Herald,* Volume 84, page 36, January 9, 1937. In part it reads as follows:

"In the past many questions have been asked concerning the details of procedure in preparing the emblems and I presume that the late President Joseph Smith has answered these questions through the *Herald* in one form or another in the fifty-four years of his presidency of the church, scores of times.

"The customs prevailing when congregations were uniformly small are likely to be quite different from those which will be followed in larger congregations. For example, I well recall that according to my early observations the elders broke the bread before the congregation and the previous preparation consisted only in slicing the bread. What would we do now if we were to undertake to break the bread in this fashion to serve a congregation of 5,000 or more as we have several times in the Auditorium? The preparation of the bread and the wine in its last analysis goes much farther than the slicing of the bread, or the pouring of the wine, and it would involve the making of the bread and the wine both.

"After all, the great thing to be desired is to preserve the true symbolic significance of the rite; and hence if one or two slices are broken at the table by the elders the full significance of the symbolism is preserved and the same is true of the wine. I therefore suggest that the emblems be prepared by the deacons, even assisted by some of the good sisters, if so desired, by having the bread not only sliced but broken, leaving a slice in the case of a small congregation or where only one elder is officiating, or two or three slices where two or three elders are officiating. These then can be broken in the presence of the congregation. I would suggest also that the wine be poured into the individual cups (and these should always be used where practicable) so that with a reserve supply of wine on the table where necessary or wise the emblems can be spread upon the table during the blessing of the emblems.

227

"This method of procedure would be to use the deacons in the preparation of the emblems up to the time they are placed upon the table and the utilization of the priests of the Aaronic priesthood for the passing of the emblems."

Then the writer concludes by saying that others of the Melchisedec priesthood may also administer. The statement concerning the sisters is apropos to both phases of the question.

222. Priesthood Take Oblation

QUESTION

Does the person taking the oblation at the Communion service have to be a priesthood member?

ANSWER

Not necessarily, but where there is a deacon it is proper to respect him. The deacon's function involves a degree of responsibility for temporalities and ministry to those in need. This is the purpose of oblation—to provide the means for help in this area. The deacon is normally associated with the branch treasury, also.

To say that no other person should be permitted to receive the oblation would be an error, but this matter comes within the normal oversight of the deacon under the overall administration of the pastor. This should be properly worked out with the deacons by the pastor and due consideration given to the development of young men in performing services for the congregation.

Probably other services may provide more suitable opportunity from this point of view than the Communion. Normally the deacons will function in the receiving of the oblation.

223. Deacon or Teacher Deliver Message

QUESTION

Can a deacon or teacher deliver a Communion message?

ANSWER

Deacons or teachers are not normally involved in the Communion service beyond the work of preparing the emblems and other necessary appointments (table, vessels, etc.). Their priesthood work is normally within their own branches (see General Conference Resolution No. 449). With members of the Melchisedec and Aaronic priests available, it would not be a usual thing to have a deacon or teacher address the congregation.

The words "administer the sacrament" may possibly be construed in such a way as to exclude the officers concerned. They of course do not administer the emblems personally (this is forbidden), but I can imagine a situation where the pastor might feel that a teacher could be most helpful in the ministry of reconciliation by making the Communion address. In this case he is assisting the elders or other priesthood.

We should not split hairs on fine points but seek to see the various ministries in their primary roles. The spiritual ministry is primarily Melchisedec and will normally be the channel for the ministry you ask about. Doctrine and Covenants, while definite in the statement that the teachers and deacons have no authority to baptize, administer the sacrament, or lay on hands, states also, "They are, however, to warn, expound, exhort, and teach, and invite all to come to Christ" (Doctrine and Covenants 17:11 f).

I feel that this ministry may be inclusive of a Communion message where the officer has prepared himself to give such reconciliatory help. This, in my opinion, would be more likely to involve a teacher than a deacon. Each should use his calling first to perform its specific tasks. This keeps the various ministries in balance.

Fasting and Prayer

224. Nature of Fasting

QUESTION

What is fasting? How does it relate to particular foods? Is fasting before Communion necessary?

ANSWER

Fasting as a religious practice dates so far back that its origin is obscure. Some researchers have thought that it was a ritual observed in refraining from eating and drinking and placing the victuals beside the dead. The living fasted that the dead might eat. Others have thought it had origin in the discovery of primitive man that abstinence from food placed the mind in a fit state to have dreams and visions and thereby made contact with spiritual forces possible. Sometimes it was indulged in for a period before partaking of ceremonial or sacred food as a matter of ritual.

The Bible gives us the basis for fasting as Christian people engage in it, although in various forms and degrees. There is evidence of fasting as an expression of deep sorrow, repentance, or grief. It is found connected with deep and urgent desire being expressed as fasting and prayer.

There were certain fast days set down by the Jews after the exile. Private fasting was a custom in Judaism; evidence of this is shown by the example of Jesus. He followed the custom presumably to prepare himself for taking up his ministry.

Jesus emphasized that fasting was a personal matter and not for public display or parade (Matthew 6:16-18; Luke 18:9-14). It is to be performed with singleness of heart. It is not a means by which one pressures God; rather, it places one in a spiritual condition to receive a blessing and often to see clearly the wisdom of denial.

Fasting is referred to in the early church associated with ordaining officers (Acts 13:2-3; 14:23). The church extended the practice as years passed. The scripture even had references to fasting added which are not found in the older documents. An example of this is the *Textes Receptus,* a version prepared in the sixteenth century and the basis for the King James Version (Matthew 17:25, Mark 9:29, Acts 10:30, I Corinthians 7:5).

Fasting is mentioned about ten times in the Doctrine and Covenants. Two texts are noteworthy at this point. The first reference of Section 131 is a statement that a fast was called for on April 5, 1914. The president "in common with the brotherhood, observed the rule requiring the fast, and spent that day in meditation and prayer. . . ." A revelatory document was presented as following this prayerful observance. The other reference is Doctrine and Covenants 59:3 a, b. After instructions as to how to observe fasting in paragraph 3 a, this appears in paragraph 3 b: "Verily this is fasting and prayer; or, in other words, rejoicing and prayer."

Fasting before Communion is, of course, voluntary, although at times (as on the occasion just mentioned) it may be officially requested. The decision to fast should be made in light of the considerations here given, taking into account the physical condition and the advice of one's physician where necessary.

225. Calling for Prayers and Testimonies

QUESTION

Should the minister in charge of a prayer and testimony meeting call on members to pray or testify without approaching them beforehand?

ANSWER

All activity in a prayer and testimony meeting should be voluntary. I have never heard of a presiding officer making a practice of naming people and expecting them to respond in prayer or testimony spontaneously. Of course in a spirit of giving encouragement to one feeling diffident, the leader of a meeting might use tactful suggestion to get some response, but to put a person on the spot by calling him by name could only embarrass. Persons so peremptorily called on would be most likely to refrain from attending, and so in the long run the aim of the leader, however well intentioned, would be unrealized.

226. Family Altar

QUESTION

How does one proceed to establish a family altar?

ANSWER

The traditional family altar suggests a picture of a family gathered at the dining table with the head of the house presiding. Father or mother would call for the family Bible, select a passage to be read, after which prayer would be offered by one or more as the age and circumstances of the family indicated. This would be at either morning or evening meal. It could be varied so that family worship might be in the living room after meals, but it was usually quite formal.

This was a pattern of home worship adapted to the more placid life of a generation now past. It had much to commend it in principle, and much spiritual stimulation resulted. Children certainly learned appreciation for the words of scripture and the necessity of making thoughts of their heavenly Father part of their day's activity. If conducted in the morning it had the effect of recognizing God at the beginning of one's day.

If the situation of your home and the schedules of the various members of the family permit, there is no reason to discard this time-honored routine. Its advantages are regularity and consistency, among others. But pressure which results in reluctant participation will result negatively.

There are many families who find this type of formal worship impossible in these days of urban and rural change. It is hard to have the family together at a regularly scheduled time, but there is just as vital a need for family devotions and spiritual fellowship today as before.

The parents of the home should be alert for opportunities to bring the family together wholly or in part as often as practicable. There are many phases of homelife that allow for this even if at times the observance is less formal than in years past. Normal home activities can be made worship centered and in the hands of a skillful parent may be led to a devotional climax:

The story hour in winter, outside fellowship in summer, a period of song around the home piano, a conversation around a meal table when the noting of a poem or other literature, a passage of scripture, a news item can all be spiritually directed, and many times may naturally end in prayer. Many families pause for a longer prayer at one meal-time each day and expand the usual short "grace" into a more meaningful event for the family.

At bedtime the parent and family relationship can be spiritually focused, informally perhaps but often quite powerfully. Moses' mother is the classic example of one who used the opportunities thus presented. She possibly had little chance for any but informal worship with her boy, as she would no doubt sing him to sleep with the songs of her God.

If you approach your problem in the manner suggested, you will find almost unlimited opportunities for devotional experiences in the family.

Turn to your *Church Member's Manual,* pages 46 and 47, for an amplification of this answer.

227. Ending of Prayer

QUESTION

Is it correct to end a prayer, "For Jesus' sake, Amen"?

ANSWER

From a dictionary is gleaned the following meaning for the word "sake": in the interest of; out of consideration for; because of; in order to please or honor. "For his name's sake" is explained as: "because he bears the name he does or in the interest of his reputation." From these quotations I gather that to end a prayer with "for Jesus' sake, amen" is simply intended to say, "I ask this prayer because of the interest Jesus Christ has in my life, actions, and desires." In a sense it implies, "not my will but thine," or in another sense, "grant this for the sake of the cause of Christ." When thoughtfully used, it signifies that we do not ask for selfish reasons but are humbly presenting the request in the right spirit.

It is not the form used in a prayer that is important but the heart of the one praying. Of course, habitual use of irrelevant or meaningless phrases may produce departures from effective prayer, so voiced prayers should use expressions of intelligent meaning.

It is still true to say that "prayer is the heart's sincere desire, uttered or unexpressed." I have come to see prayer predominantly as an out-reaching of the heart, mind, and talent for the sake of Jesus Christ's mission to all mankind rather than a "give me" ritual to which we

233

append a formal ascription by which I sometimes feel we hope to enlist Divinity in our cause rather than enlist ourselves in his program.

I would not want my comments to be used to discourage properly worded prayers or to encourage careless and meaningless expressions. What we present in worship by music, word, or other means should be of the highest intelligence and culture possible. In this attitude of understanding I can use with good reason in my prayers, "For Jesus' sake."

Marriage

228. Religious and Civil Ceremonies

QUESTION

Is it proper to have a religious ceremony some time later if a couple have been previously married by civil authority?

ANSWER

I am not aware of any official pronouncement on this. There is no General Conference resolution. I would venture a personal opinion that there would be no reason against a reaffirmation of what has been contracted in a civil sense. The civil contract is legal and binding whether a religious ceremony takes place or not. Whether it would be the thing to do rests with the parties concerned, including the minister in a primary counseling role. It may be better to have a religious service of this nature in more intimate circumstances rather than a public church service. The couple would be acting quite properly in seeking to reaffirm their vows before God as well as in a purely legal way. In short, I would advise against ostentation but see no basic objection in church law. It would definitely carry no legal marriage status but would be a reaffirmation of vows already made. Those involved would have to be guided by the civil authority of the particular state as to the nature of the formalities.

Marriage laws differ from state to state in the United States and from country to country. For instance, Australia has recently made marriage laws uniform throughout all its states. This is not yet so in the United States of America where the questioner resides. In some countries where the religious ceremony is not considered legal, the civil ceremony is followed by the religious service, but the civil action is the legally recognized covenant. These circumstances make the service in a church not only proper but desirable.

Of course the whole problem is handled better if before marriage we realize the place of God in our marriage and plan to take this into consideration and, therefore, are married by the proper authorities within the fellowship of the church.

229. Marriage between Races

QUESTION

What does the church teach in regard to marriage between races of different color? Is there anything in the Three Books concerning this?

ANSWER

There is no direct statement forbidding or endorsing intermarriage of colored and white people. There are a number of texts which make clear the principle of the equal value in the sight of God of all peoples. To these principles all true Christians should adhere. The church upholds the principle of divine love enunciated in scripture.

There has been no legislative action by the church to clear the matter further. Certain states have laws on marriage between certain races, and these laws we are obliged to obey. Where no law of the state forbids, there is no rule of the church that would forbid.

The advice and counsel of the church is offered in general principle through its ministry to all who plan to marry. This counsel suggests that they consider well the degree of compatibility in religion, race, color, family, and other social relationships. It is true that what may be a successful marriage in one situation would be unwise in another. Not only should the immediate personal and social relationships be taken into account, but the future children should also be taken into account and the effect of a mixed parentage on their lives.

There is no biological objection to mixed-color marriages. According to modern science there is no question of "lower" qualities of either color dominating in such marriages. Much has been attributed to mixture of race which is purely the result of social influences.

At this stage of development of social understanding those of mixed color friendships would do well to examine their desires in the light of practical situations. They will be guided by their assessment of the value or lack of value of their union in the light of its contribution to the kingdom.

230. Marrying out of Church

QUESTION

What is the meaning of the statement in Doctrine and Covenants 111:1 that those marrying out of the church are weak in the faith?

ANSWER

First, it should be noted that this section is not a revelation. In the explanatory preface it is described as an article on marriage. It was accepted as the rule and standard of the church and became binding by action of a Conference at Kirtland, August 17, 1835. At this assembly the Doctrine and Covenants was approved in the form prepared by a committee and the section on marriage was included.

Now with regard to your special point as to "marrying out of the church" I would say that there are two points of view as to the meaning.

The more general and traditional approach has been to regard this phrase as referring to marriage with nonmembers. There is no disposition of the writer to minimize the wise counsel given concerning the necessity for religious unity in the family. Experience has shown this to be basic to happy marriage and certainly to be a vital factor in the nurture of children. I suggest that the last paragraph in this answer be given serious attention before making final conclusions.

However, a close analysis of paragraph 1 will indicate that there is a primary emphasis intended which is the authority of the priesthood functioning through the restored church. The principle of an authoritative ministry is at the heart of the Restoration movement.

The restoration of priesthood authority was the primary action of God in the organization of this church. It was undoubtedly intended that Section 111, paragraph 1, emphasize this authority, though as stated there it is not proper to "prohibit" those determined to marry by "other authority" from so doing. The paragraph begins with a statement that this section is concerned with marriage "in this Church of Christ of Latter Day Saints," and the phrase "out of the church" must be considered in relation to this. In my opinion the word "prohibit" ties the "authority" references to "out of the church." The whole of the context is concerned with "authority."

The historical setting of this section gives some help in making the right emphasis. At the time it was written, it was important that the identity of the church be clearly marked as one having authority. In 1835 it was particularly important that this definition be clear. One marrying out of the church—that is by other authority—was to be considered weak in that his very action would indicate that he did not hold the authority of the church of primary importance.

The rites of the church by which authority one marries are basic in the intent of the contract. One marrying according to Mohammedan rites, for instance, would be able to marry polygamously; and for one marrying according to Jewish rites certain other concepts are assumed.

Marrying by other authority also exposed people to the danger of the aberrations of many sects at the time Section 111 was documented insofar, as we have just said, that the concept of the minister performing the ceremony and the conditions attached thereto put meaning of a specific nature into the covenant. For instance, those sects not holding the ideals of monogamous marriage could not perform marriages involving this concept. Other groups were experimenting with so-called spiritual wifery and "free love," and so forth. There is evidence in my personal research that members of some of these sects moved into early church communities and therefore confused the popular image of the church. This was a probable reason for Section 111 being affirmed as our standard in Kirtland in 1835.

To be married "in the church" was some assurance that the right principles were being recognized. A careful reading of the paragraphs which follow in the section under review makes the terms and conditions of the marriage covenant clear.

The question of the inadvisability of marrying nonmembers rests upon other premises than this section provides and the factors involved in making decision to marry those not of the faith need careful consideration. It may be that the Latter Day Saint partner feels such strength of faith that he or she will be able to bring the realization of the true church to the other partner. I personally would not class one so marrying as weak in the faith, but after many years as a minister I would strongly counsel that one examine his motivations and reasoning as objectively as possible because of the hazards of unequal yoking in marriage.

To make this emphasis upon what I feel is the primary point in paragraph 1—that is, authority—in no way does violence to the caution required in nonmember partnerships. If the other view is taken it simply implies weakness and is not illegal or prohibited.

My reconsideration of this section was made because of my observations that those who had married nonmembers often did so after much deep concern and a decision that they could bear strong witness to the partner. Many of these have proved that they were far from weak in the faith. This did not seem to harmonize with the traditional interpretation—and so my modified opinion.

238

231. For Time and Eternity

QUESTION

Does our church believe in marriage for time and eternity as it is taught by the Utah church?

ANSWER

The Reorganized Church does not believe in marriage "for time and eternity." We believe in marriage for time. This is a lifetime contract only and is binding as long as both parties live. Should one partner die or the marriage be dissolved for just cause as set out in the rules endorsed by World Conference of the church, one is free to remarry. This contract also remains in force during life only.

The Utah practice is to seal men and women in marriage for eternity. This philosophy and practice has led to many aberrations, including polygamy, in the Utah Mormon church. The Reorganization early repudiated these doctrines as false, and they have no part in our belief.

No scripture gives any indication of the Mormon doctrine of marriage for eternity. Our church rejects the Utah claim that Joseph Smith ever presented a revelation to the church proclaiming the Utah doctrine of marriage. This is why we brand Section 132 of the Utah Doctrine and Covenants (on the eternity of the marriage covenant and polygamy) spurious.

We say again, we do not believe in marriage for eternity.

232. Doctrine and Covenants Revelation

QUESTION

Is Doctrine and Covenants, Section 111, a revelation?

ANSWER

This section is not a revelation as a reading of the introductory paragraph will show. The word was used rather loosely in the answer, as the sections of the Doctrine and Covenants are often referred to as "the revelations." This section is a statement on marriage read and adopted at a General Assembly, August 17, 1835.

While on the subject of the basic policy I would observe that this article coming so early in the definition of beliefs of the early church makes our position very clear as to the Christian standard of monogamy being fundamental. The document was an advanced one for its time.

233. Qualifying Churches

QUESTION

Do all religious organizations have to meet certain specifications to qualify as functioning churches according to the law of the land (United States of America)? If so, how could a church with unorthodox views on marriage be recognized as such?

ANSWER

One of the basic freedoms sought and obtained by the founding fathers of the United States of America was the right to worship according to one's own desires and conscience and therefore to be free not to worship in a certain way also.

I would be surprised to learn of any law, either federal or state, that would prevent people from functioning as a church regardless of their beliefs. A person may believe what he wishes, or he may choose not to believe. He may organize with those of sufficiently similar ideas and thus belong to an association or church.

Individual states have certain regulations which govern the activities of church ministers in performing marriages, but this is because marriage involves an established unit of society at large.

Probably you are confused with such procedures as incorporation which has a legal status with certain advantages in the method of holding property and in acting corporately in other ways. A group does not have to become incorporated to function as a religious body. Such incorporations as have been effected are purely for convenience of doing business and not with regard to belief.

The RLDS Church is incorporated in Australia and New Zealand, Canada, and in the states of Illinois, Iowa, and Missouri. Incidentally, Graceland College and the Independence Sanitarium and Hospital are also incorporated (see *Rules and Resolutions*, pages 194-220). There is no restriction on an association provided it does not plan subversion. Naturally any subversion would receive the attention of the government. Even the Communist society has not been declared illegal, although certain requirements to register as such have been made on its members by the federal government. I understand this has been more honored in the breech than the observance. In the light of the foregoing what a church believes about marriage is not significant at this point. However, the law of the land makes the practice of polygamy illegal, and any such bigamous actions as this implies are subject thereto. Action has been taken from time to time in Utah and Arizona. It is the overt act with which the law is mainly concerned. The RLDS movement is not involved in this question.

240

Polygamy

234. Accusation of Polygamy before 1835

QUESTION

Upon what grounds was the accusation that the church believed in polygamy made before 1835? The document on marriage, Doctrine and Covenants 111, is the cause of my inquiry.

ANSWER

Doctrine and Covenants 111:4 b states:

> "Inasmuch as this Church of Christ has been reproached with the crime of fornication, and polygamy: we declare that we believe that one man should have one wife; and one woman but one husband, except in case of death, when either is at liberty to marry again."

I have never heard of any specific accusation concerning any particular case of this nature in the period preceding the first publication of the statement on marriage. It is a fact, however, that there were many social experiments in the first part of the nineteenth century, and a great number of them centered in the northeastern area of the United States. A number of these communal societies included experiments in love and marriage relationships, ranging from celibacy on the one hand to polygamy on the other. Because of this, any community organization was likely to be interpreted at times as being involved in these aberrations, and the fact that as early as 1830 the church became concerned with the establishment of a Zionic community would place it in question. A number of people living in a society which was sponsored by Sidney Rigdon and known as "the family" (prior to his baptism into the early Restoration) also joined the church and this may have prompted the statement with which we are concerned.

It is known, too, that Orson Hyde preached during a missionary tour to a number of families which, his diary states, believed in a doctrine of spiritual wifery. They were called Cochranites. He observed that it was in his opinion a family relationship more accurately termed polygamy. He did not use the word, but his comments indicate that this was what it was. We have no record of any Cochranites joining the church but any contact with these people could have led to the charge. The early leaders, therefore, felt the necessity to disclaim the doctrine, and it is fortunate that they stated the church's position as early as they did.

A book which discusses the social experiments of the time may be available in city libraries. It is entitled *Social Ferment in Vermont, 1791-1850,* by David Ludlum, published by the Vermont Historical Society. A more comprehensive text is *The Communistic Societies of the United States* by Charles Nordhoff, published by Hilary House Publishers, New York.

235. Joseph Smith and Document on Polygamy

QUESTION

Did Joseph the Martyr ever receive a document on spiritual wifery or polygamy? If so, what happened to it?

ANSWER

The answer is "No." I give this answer after many years of close examination of the statements of those who claim to the contrary, and more recently several years as church historian have given me opportunity for more thorough perusal of the so-called evidence which has resulted in confirming the results of previous studies.

There is no need for a true follower of the Restoration movement to be reluctant to view the facts. Novelists have found the erroneous claim more suitable to their purposes than the truth and so perpetuate the myth of Joseph Smith as a polygamist, but evidence of a credible nature is completely lacking.

No authentic document pronouncing these doctrines has ever been produced from the pen of Joseph Smith or copied from his dictation and bearing his signature. All the statements of Joseph Smith published in his lifetime speak against these doctrines. The only two claims concerning documents which seem to require refuting bear no evidence that Joseph Smith was responsible for the doctrine of polygamy being taught or practiced.

242

The most famous is the document presented by Brigham Young in 1852 to his church in Utah. This has received the consideration of competent judicial minds and has not been accepted as authentic. Actually the document was not in the handwriting of Joseph Smith and was not signed by him. Witnesses called to establish it as genuine have differed and made statements as to length and source, and other aspects, which conflict with fact. It is amazing how pseudo-historians use documents in their writings and accept statements as valid which would not be admitted in a court as evidence. This Utah document is one of the greatest untruths of the last century.

The other document not so generally known but of sufficient importance to require consideration was a notarized statement by Austin Cowles in the *Nauvoo Expositor* of June 7, 1844. This paper had only a single issue. The Municipal Council of Nauvoo ordered the *Expositor* press destroyed because of libelous statements in that newspaper; therefore there were no subsequent issues. It was this action of the Municipal Council which precipitated unlawful mob action resulting in the assassination of Joseph and Hyrum Smith at Carthage, Illinois.

In the *Expositor* Austin Cowles claimed that he heard a document read by the prophet's brother Hyrum in a Nauvoo High Council meeting. He quoted what he said he remembered hearing. No doubt Cowles heard some kind of document read, but his testimony was admittedly from having heard something read and his memory thereof. The document has never been presented to the world by the Utah church. If Cowles' statement was accurate Brigham Young failed to use it to establish authenticity for his 1852 presentation. The only reason I can see for his not using Cowles as a witness is that two weeks later in the *Nauvoo Neighbor* (June 19, 1844) Joseph Smith denied the correctness of the statement made by Cowles. This, of course, contradicts Young's claims concerning Joseph Smith's being the author of Young's presentation in 1852.

In his statement to the Nauvoo City Council Joseph Smith explained his position concerning the Cowles allegation and concerning a discussion on marriage. This was reported as follows:

"Mayor said he had never preached the revelation in private as he had in public—had not taught it to the anointed of the church in private, which statement many present confirmed, that on enquiring concerning the passage in the resurrection concerning "they neither marry nor are given in marriage," etc. [Matthew 22:29, 30] he received for answer, men in this life must marry in view of eternity, otherwise they must remain as angels, or be single in heaven, which was the amount of the revelation referred to, and the Mayor spoke at considerable length in explanation of the principle. . . ."

It is reported in the same column:

"Councilor H. Smith proceeded to show the falsity of Austin Cowles in the *Expositor* in relation to the revelation referred to, that it was in reference to *former* days, and not the present time as related by Cowles."

It is reported of Joseph Smith on the same occasion:

". . . they make a criminality for a man to have a wife on earth, while he has one in heaven, according to the keys of the Holy Priesthood—and he then read a statement of William Law's from the *Expositor* where the truth of God was transformed into a lie concerning this thing."—*Nauvoo Neighbor,* June 9, 1844.

Certainly no document was ever presented to the church that would make spiritual wifery, celestial marriage, or polygamy a teaching of the original church. That certain people were engaged in teaching the doctrines of spiritual wifery and polygamy in Nauvoo is a matter of historical fact. It is also on record that Joseph Smith said it was "an accursed doctrine" and asked the president of Nauvoo Stake, William Marks, to take official action to deal with those teaching or practicing this heresy. (See *True Latter Day Saints' Herald,* Vol. 1, p. 22.)

Most important is the fact that any document expounding the doctrine of polygamy would be contrary to accepted scripture. (See Book of Mormon, Jacob 2:28-32; Doctrine and Covenants of Reorganized Church, Section 111; Doctrine and Covenants, 1835 edition, Section 101.) The principle of monogamous marriage is still found in all editions of the Book of Mormon and was retained in the Doctrine and Covenants of the Utah church until 1876 when the original section on marriage was removed and replaced by the unauthentic document of 1852. (See Doctrine and Covenants of Utah church, Section 132.) All Reorganized Church editions have continued to carry the original statement as in 1835.

Joseph Smith III, son of the martyr, spent a long life in research to get the facts on the allegations which endeavored to connect his father with polygamy. This involved visits to Utah and personal interviews with alleged plural wives and with those reported to have evidence. He stated that as the years passed, his confidence in his father's innocence increased.

236. Revelation on Polygamy

QUESTION

In reading Orson Pratt's introduction of the so-called revelation on polygamy in Utah in 1852, I do not find that he stated that it came through Joseph Smith. Nor did Brigham Young appear to say so at that time. Where is the reference that states that they did?

ANSWER

It is a fact that both Orson Pratt and Young did so state giving Joseph Smith as the one who received it.

In the introductory address of Orson Pratt to which you refer we find the following words:

"This was the word of the Lord to His servant Joseph the Prophet himself."
—*Millennial Star* Supplement, 1853, Volume 15, page 26.
Reprint from *Deseret News* Extra of September 14, 1852.

At the 2:00 P.M. meeting the same day (August 29, 1852), Brigham Young said:

"You heard Brother Pratt state, this morning, that a Revelation would be read this afternoon, which was given previous to Joseph's death. It contains a doctrine, a small portion of the world is opposed to; but I can deliver a prophecy upon it. Though that doctrine has not been practiced by the Elders, this people have believed in it for years."
—*Millennial Star* Supplement, 1853, Volume 15, page 31.
Reprint from *Deseret News* Extra of September 14, 1852.

On the page following this statement is found: "Elder Thomas Bullock then read the following. . . ." Then is printed the false document that is now Section 132 in the Doctrine and Covenants of the Utah church.

Later, in 1862, Young reiterated this slanderous statement about Joseph Smith, Jr. In an address reported by G. D. Watt and published in the Utah *Journal of Discourses,* Volume 9, page 322, he said:

"Why do we believe in and practice polygamy? Because the Lord introduced it to his servants in a revelation given to Joseph Smith, and the Lord's servants have always practiced it."

These statements are mostly generalized affirmations and not documentary proofs. These assertions have not been backed by evidence acceptable in a court of justice. Considering all the guns that have been trained on Joseph Smith in an endeavor to hit the target of his sponsorship of this practice, none have scored a hit. If there were any real evidence, one hundred and twenty-five years of vigorous research should have brought it to light. The verdict on the evidence is "not guilty."

237. Statements of William Marks

QUESTION

William Marks seems to have written several letters which are interpreted by those opposed to the Reorganization to implicate Joseph Smith in polygamy. I refer to statements in the "True Latter Day Saints' Herald" and in "The Return." These are repeatedly used to argue that a prominent leader of the early Reorganization knew this to be a fact, but we do not care to admit complicity. Please explain.

ANSWER

You are right in saying that certain statements concerning the situation in Nauvoo as to Joseph Smith and polygamy just before the martyrdom were made by William Marks in the 1860's and later. The wording varies slightly from one statement to another. From these comments it is often inferred that he was saying he believed Joseph was implicated. It is not correct to assume that Marks ever made statements intended to admit this. There is record of Marks being asked what he meant, and fortunately he had the opportunity to explain further. This is raised so often in letters and conversation that I will here quote at some length from an article by a man whose word we can accept. I quote from *Saints' Herald*, Volume 50, pages 363, 364, April 22, 1903. Edmund C. Briggs stated therein that he asked William Marks certain questions and gives the following account:

" 'Did you, when you had that conversation with Brother Joseph, think he had been in any way mixed up in polygamy, or had favored it?' He replied, 'No. I had more confidence in him at that time than I ever had in all my life before, and was satisfied that he was pure from that gross crime. I had been troubled over the condition of the church for some time, and been fearful that Joseph did not bring the pressure against some men in the church that he should have done. You see from John C. Bennett's time there had been so many rumors going the rounds, I was fearful that there might be something in the stories afloat that might implicate Joseph. But Joseph was so free and positive in his denunciation of polygamy in every form, that I took courage; and I could see Joseph was in earnest and felt just as I did about it. . . .'

"I then said, 'Brother Marks, did you ever see the revelation on polygamy before it was published in 1852 by Mr. Pratt?' Marks emphatically replied, 'No, never.' 'You were president of the stake at Nauvoo, and if Joseph had such a revelation, would you not have been privileged, according to custom, to have seen it, or heard of it?' He replied, 'Yes, without a doubt. There was no such revelation in existence during Joseph's life. . . . Brigham Young would have showed it to me when I opposed his measures. But he never pretended to any such thing to me, that there was such a revelation on the subject from Joseph.' "

William Marks, it is said, indicated that Joseph Smith "had been deceived." E. C. Briggs gives Mark's explanation of this reference in these words, "But I thought he [Joseph] had been deceived in some of the men and elders of the church, and had too much confidence in some of them." This later comment by Marks himself disposes of any contention that Joseph Smith confessed to being deceived in receiving a revelation of the nature of which he has been accused. I hope this is helpful in settling the question as to William Marks's alleged implication of the prophet in this unchristian doctrine. That there was a document on marriage in existence in Nauvoo is indicated by statements of Joseph and Hyrum Smith in the *Nauvoo Press* of the time. This, however, does not admit of the contention that a revelation favoring polygamy was ever given. The statements of these men prove the prophet's opposition to this doctrine of plurality of wives. Joseph called the accusation a lie.

238. Word of Consolation and Polygamy

QUESTION

Does the Word of Consolation written by John Taylor, Willard Richards, and W. W. Phelps and published in "Times and Seasons" (Volume 5, Number 12), condemn polygamy?

ANSWER

There is a communication over the signature of W. W. Phelps, W. Richards, and John Taylor in *Times and Seasons*, Volume 5, Number

12, page 568 (July 1, 1844), in which the following is found in connection with the murder of Joseph and Hyrum Smith: ". . . we have considered the occasion demanded of us a word of consolation."

This reference has no doubt been the basis of the term "Word of Consolation" being applied to this letter by you. I do not know if others have referred to it in this way. It does not mention polygamy.

Another document, and one which the Reorganization captioned "A Word of Consolation to the Scattered Saints," is a pamphlet authorized by the reorganizing branches at a conference held October 6, 1852. This was printed along with additional observations by the committee appointed at the June conference of that year: J. W. Briggs, Z. H. Gurley, and J. Harrington.

The *Times and Seasons* letter does not deal with polygamy nor does the "Word of Consolation" authorized by the conference of scattered Saints in 1852. However, following the signatures of the committee members referred to, this later document continues: "We cannot forego this opportunity to raise our voice against an evil which has well nigh completed the overthrow of the church." Then follows a denunciation of the doctrines of polygamy.

It seems that you may have confused these two documents of 1844 and 1852. The publication date of the second document was February, 1853, at Beloit, Wisconsin.

239. Section 111 in Utah Doctrine and Covenants

QUESTION

Was the document on marriage, now Section 111 of Doctrine and Covenants (Reorganized Church edition), ever included in the editions of the Doctrine and Covenants published by the Utah church?

ANSWER

Doctrine and Covenants Section 111 (Reorganized Church edition) states the principle of monogamous marriage and is exactly as first printed in 1835 by the early church. This, along with the rest of the Doctrine and Covenants of 1835, was endorsed by the church and has remained the only rule of marriage of the true continuation, the Reorganized Church.

Those supervising the English mission at the time of the Brigham Young departure encouraged the English Saints to follow his leadership, which many did. Publications in England after 1844 were made under the leadership of those who joined the Utah group. Among these were John Taylor, S. W. Richards, and Orson Pratt. All editions of the Doctrine and Covenants published in England included the original statement and rule of monogamy. These followed the text of the last (1845) Nauvoo edition and were printed in 1845, 1847, and all editions through 1869.

This section enjoining monogamy was deleted by the Utah church in 1876, and the spurious document on polygamy known as Section 132 was inserted in its place. The 1876 edition was the first printing by the Utah church on its press in Salt Lake City, all previous editions after 1845 being published in England.

The Reorganization has followed the 1835 edition authorized by the early church in all its publications.

240. Statement in II Samuel

QUESTION

In II Samuel, Chapter 12, we find that the Lord sent the prophet Nathan to King David with a message, stating that God had been very gracious in giving David his master's wives. Due to the king's injustice to Uriah, the Lord would give all of these plural wives to a neighbor! The Inspired Version and others are identical, but something appears misleading here. Could you clarify this?

ANSWER

Polygamy undoubtedly was socially respectable in the Israelite culture in the period with which this text is concerned. This statement does not imply in the least degree that is was divinely instituted or approved. Samuel, after whom the Old Testament book was named, was himself the son of a polygamous family. At the risk of repeating over and over again, may I say that a fundamental principle of scriptural interpretation is to see an incident, a practice, or a belief against the backdrop of the time or era.

Prophets certainly spoke as they were moved upon. At times they spoke from a very limited setting socially and educationally. Whoever wrote the record (if perchance we were to agree the words recorded were actually used in the original which has long since disappeared) they still must rest on the basis that the recorder himself made this deduction, ascribing it to Divinity. In the primitive religious development of Israel, every happening was either an act of God or of evil—hence the statement that God gave David's plural wives to someone else.

249

I have often used the illustration that these early men, as do primitives today, lived so close to nature and its source that they spoke of every phenomenon in direct relation to the supernatural. An example may help. An eminent theologian was on his way to give a lecture on prophecy at Oxford, England. As he rode his bicycle, he was giving undue attention to his speech, and was unexpectedly thrown from his seat because of contact with a stone in the road. As he felt his bruises, the thought flashed through his mind, "How would Isaiah have described this incident?" Quickly came the answer, "And lo and behold, the Lord, he did take my wheel from under me!"

He could have voiced a scientific answer in terms of gravity and force, but he saw the ancient prophet taking the direct route to the ultimate, ascribing responsibility for the incident directly to God.

So the writer of the text in II Samuel assumed that that which had happened was a retribution of God. This was not actually so, as we know that God would not command acts not in harmony with high principle. The highest marriage relationship is that of monogamy. God does not command lower standards.

Joseph Smith did not complete a full revision of scripture in the Inspired Version. This text is one taken directly from the Authorized Version.

241. Document to U. S. Government on Polygamy

QUESTION

Did William Smith and Isaac Sheen send a document to the United States government in which they blamed Brigham Young for polygamy?

ANSWER

This is correct. There is a photostat of the original document in the church archives. It is an interesting document from several points of view. First, its date is of interest. It was filed in the United States Senate on December 31, 1849, two years at least before the practice of polygamy was admitted by the Utah Mormons.

In 1852 when presenting the doctrine, Brigham Young stated, "This people have believed in it [polygamy] for years," but he is faced with many statements during that period of years when Utah leaders denied its belief.

The document of William Smith and Isaac Sheen contains the following (page 2, beginning in the third line):

"The rulers of the Salt Lake church hypocritically pretend to venerate the name and character of the Prophet Joseph Smith that they may retain their popularity among the people who believe that he was a true Prophet. These rulers are apostates from the true church of Jesus Christ of Latter Day Saints, which church Joseph Smith was president of. These rulers teach and practice polygamy."

Note that it describes Utah leaders as "apostates from the true church . . . which Joseph Smith was president of. These rulers teach and practice polygamy."

This statement by William Smith and Isaac Sheen is significant in view of the fact that the Utah church often endeavors to make Sheen a witness to the allegation that Joseph Smith, Jr., practiced polygamy. To do so they use statements out of context making Sheen recorded in the *True Latter Day Saints' Herald* to admit Joseph Smith's involvement. They state that Sheen said Joseph Smith "repented" of the doctrine.

This must be interpreted in the light of all the evidence. In the petition to the Senate, Sheen signs his name to the document which accuses Brigham Young of apostasy and gives as a chief example the Utah rulers' teaching and practicing polygamy. Sheen was obviously Joseph Smith's champion.

Sheen was not in Nauvoo at the period of Smith's alleged connection with the doctrine of polygamy and could only have been a hearsay witness of events at best, but obviously some other explanation than that Sheen regards Joseph Smith as a sponsor of polygamous doctrines is required by the statements in the petition under review. The extract from this petition of 1849 makes his stand quite clear.

242. Uncorrected Statements

QUESTION

Why does not the church have the matter of the authorship of Mormon polygamy cleared at the sources from which so many incorrect and mostly derogatory statements originate? It seems that so often they go uncorrected. A recent series in a nationally distributed magazine contains gross untruth, even listing names of alleged plural wives. This has embarrassed me as a member because I know these are false.

ANSWER

The church officially and through letters by many private members makes constant representation to the publishers and authors of these erroneous statements. Occasionally an author or publisher who has made a statement unwittingly in error is willing to make correction. However, those peddling the stories which reflect upon the prophet Joseph Smith's moral standards are mostly motivated by the profit motive. While having no personal desire to injure his memory or his true followers, they find that this kind of journalism has a ready market while the truth is not sensational.

The old journalistic cliché is applicable here. If a dog bites a man that is not news, but if a man bites a dog that is news. Stories of righteousness fail to get attention but crime and sensational allegations, true or false, make headlines.

After the publication is distributed there is little that can be done, and even a correction in a small corner of a publication fails to catch up with the error.

It is likewise impossible to anticipate where these unfortunate statements will show up.

One remedy may be to have a competent documentary text placed on every shelf where those who publish magazines and encyclopedia and other publishers may go for the comparative information. However, I am not too confident that this would achieve our purpose fully. One of the largest and most popular encyclopedia publishers recently referred us to one of the most scurrilous of pseudohistorical works in refutation of our point of view.

It seems we can take the matter up only from time to time and hope that eventually more may realize the facts. We are constantly giving this attention.

243. "Men to Match My Mountains"

QUESTION

I am currently reading the book, "Men to Match My Mountains," by Irving Stone. In the chapter on the Utah church he says the following:

"In 1843 Brigham Young married Augusta Adams, who was probably one of the wives of Joseph Smith. In 1845 Brigham Young married Olive Frost, another of Joseph Smith's wives, and in 1846 he married Maria Lawrence, who was also one of the wives of Joseph Smith."

Could you tell me what information Mr. Stone might possibly use to make such a damaging claim regarding Joseph Smith?

The author has no solid ground for his statement. Many statements of this kind have been made by novelists, but they rarely attempt documentation. Mr. Stone's statements are in this category. If these marriages were actually made, they (according to the Mormon sponsors of the polygamous cult) would have been official marriages, and records, therefore, would have been kept. Affidavits in abundance have been offered by women with the unhealthy urge to bask in the light of this unpleasant aura. None stand the test of legal scrutiny, and no authentic records have been produced by the church sponsoring this archaic and now heathen practice, though repeated attempts have been made to have any such records reviewed. Posthumous marriages seem to have been many, but a man can hardly be implicated in the acts of females who gain peculiar satisfaction in attachment to a dead man.

Accusations concerning this doctrine have been frequent both before and after 1844, and though no informed person would deny that the speculative theology of Nauvoo involved moral principles which true Saints have always renounced, no evidence of a specific case involving Joseph Smith in polygamy that could be accepted in a court of law has been produced.

The situation is simple. If the statements referred to by such authors as Stone and Brodie are true, Joseph Smith must be impeached. If he were involved as a participant in a polygamous marriage, he bore false testimony in public too many times to be ignored. To say that he bore testimony knowing it to be false is to discredit him utterly. On this basis he would necessarily be regarded not only as weak but wicked. The issues are clear at this point and, to my mind, irreconcilable. I personally still have to see corroborated documentary evidence. One can understand how a person as superficially informed as Mr. Stone appears to be would accept statements made by members of the Utah church. Therefore, we should be on guard against undue hostility on our part to such uninformed acceptance of inadequate data.

Since there was such a regrettable period in the life of many church members, we must endeavor to be more objective and to view the Nauvoo period in perspective. The early leaders of the Reorganization did this from the beginning, disclaiming belief in a number of doctrines being taught and stating their strong position for righteousness. Joseph Smith III also did this. It is perhaps fortunate that he was only twelve years old when the tragedy of 1844 struck. There is, therefore, no question of his involvement or about his stated stand that if any person whatsoever was guilty personally of such a moral aberration, this was not a part of true Latter Day Saintism. It was to maintain the true church doctrine that the Reorganization was effected.

253

Physical and Moral Issues

244. Bearing Arms Viewpoint

QUESTION

Would you please explain the church's position as to supporting a person who desires not to bear arms in the protection of his country? My understanding of the "Report on Peace, War, and the Use of Force" is that the church supports an individual who is thoroughly conscientious in his objection.

After reading an article by President Israel A. Smith in the "Saints' Herald" for January 1, 1951, entitled "Our Attitude on Military Service," I would like to have the matter explained further.

ANSWER

This is as difficult a question for Christian people today as it has always been. The church through its leaders has stated:

(1) War is deplorable.

(2) We should seek peace.

(3) A nation has a right to defend itself.

(4) Should war eventuate and the nation demand service, it acts according to its rights.

(5) If a citizen is drafted, the nation accepts moral responsibility for acts required by its orders.

The document on "Peace, War, and the Use of Force," adopted by the 1960 World Conference, was formulated by a World Conference committee after mature consideration of past statements. Paragraph three adds a statement concerning the rights of conscience, affirming the right of the individual to have his conscientious objection to "bearing arms" respected. This paragraph also states, "The church supports such individuals in thoroughly conscientious objection, asking that they be allowed to serve if possible in noncombatant positions."

The procedure indicated is that the conscientious objector should file a statement with the president of the church. The Presidency, if satisfied that the conscientious objection is genuine, will support the citizen's request to be relieved of the obligation to bear arms and ask that noncombatant service be substituted.

It should be made clear that one is not entitled to use his church affiliation to be exempted from national service, but one may ask for respect of his conscience. The substitute form of service may not be less dangerous but may be more dangerous.

The conscientious objector is entitled to ask the church for the necessary documents to support his claim for consideration before such national authority as may require it.

245. Command to Kill or Not Kill

QUESTION

How can we explain to children the Ten Commandments law, "Thou shalt not kill," when we read in I Samuel 15 a command stated as of the Lord to kill Amalek and spare none—men, women, or infants?

ANSWER

The understanding of this apparent paradox is to be found in a correct understanding of what scripture really is. The statement, "Thou shalt not kill," has a basic commendation of truth borne out by the experience of the human race even from the beginning of history. The second reference in I Samuel 15 is a reflection of the barbaric culture of that period before Christ. Because this action fails to harmonize with deeper revelation of the love of God for mankind throughout scripture, I can only believe that whatever impelled the prophet Samuel to give the instruction to be so brutal was misinterpreted, and that he assumed it was the Spirit of God when it was the spirit of revenge, which is not godlike.

Then again it may be that the editors who later brought the book of I Samuel to us in its present form misinterpreted history and represented Samuel's command as the "voice of the words of the Lord." The books of Samuel are a historic synthesis and went through a number of editorial hands. We cannot assume that God evolved or progressed in his understanding, so the weakness must lie in the human channels of transmission and interpretation of phenomena.

In interpreting scripture, it is just as valid to test what was stated to be in the name of the Lord in past ages with his actions today as it is to test the present by the past. It would be a peculiar type of reasoning for one to assert that God would command genocide today or that God is inconsistent at this point.

As to teaching children the story of I Samuel 15, I personally would refrain from dealing with it until they are old enough to comprehend an explanation in harmony with the deeper principles I have referred to. There are more lofty sentiments in the overview of scripture than the wholesale killing of opposing tribes of primitive days. The Inspired Version does not help at this point; verse 3 is the same as in the Authorized Version.

246. Kill in Self-defense

QUESTION

Doctrine and Covenants 42:6 states, "Thou shalt not kill." This is clear, but in Section 95:5-7 it is indicated that after a number of attacks, action in self-defense is not condemned even though life be taken. Is this not contradictory?

ANSWER

Not necessarily. The first is a statement of general principle that murder is a violation of divine law. There is no doubt about the definiteness of the commandment and the serious result of disobedience thereto.

There is no prohibition of self-defense in the first statement. This is clearly a rule against aggression. Section 95 also clearly states the basis and degree of restraint required when aggression is made against a people. I know of no commandment which denies in a final sense the right of self-defense. If in the course of necessary defense a person is killed, the responsibility is not on the defender.

It is required that one "sue for peace," that is, seek peaceable means of settling difficulties. Doctrine and Covenants 95:6 should be read in a qualifying sense and not as an opposing statement.

After much study of the laws of God as given in scripture in relation to the problem of war, World Conference has considered that genuine defensive action is legitimate. The results would be the responsibility of those precipitating the conflict.

247. RLDS Ministers in World War II

QUESTION

Why were there no Reorganized Church ministers in the front line divisions during World War II in Europe? I looked for them when I was there and there were none; therefore I had to attend Protestant churches. Please answer.

ANSWER

We had no full-time chaplains in World War II at all. The reason for this lack was partly due to the requirement of Army authorities which approved chaplains according to the number of members of a denomination who would be likely to be ministered to by a chaplain of their own faith. In proportion our numbers were considerably less than most others and not sufficient for approval of a chaplain according to the rule.

A second limiting factor was that to be accredited as a chaplain in the United States Army, a minister must have a bachelor's degree plus three years of formal theological training in an approved seminary, or an equivalent in pastoral duty which would require over eight years in addition to the degree. With these restrictions it was not possible for us to have chaplains.

There were a number of assistant chaplains, but these were soldiers already in the regular services who acted in certain duties under the supervision of a chaplain. All of our ordained men in the service gave ministry to our members where possible.

248. Building Shelters

QUESTION

When and where the Civil Defense Authorities advise the building of shelters for protection from a nuclear attack, would it be a lack of faith to so proceed as members of God's church or should we wait for commandment?

ANSWER

When the civil authorities give definite instruction as to the advisability of taking any precautionary measure for the protection of those within their jurisdiction, it is our duty to comply insofar as we are able. It is not necessary to wait for specific instruction of a divine nature on such problems, but to use the native capacity for judgment and the intelligence which God has already given us.

God expects us to use our intelligence and does not move in areas where a man is capable of moving for himself. One might as well argue that because God allows the rain to fall and the sun to shine we would expect him also to give us protection from the elements; therefore we need not build a house to shelter us. We are born without clothing, and yet we take steps to protect ourselves from extreme heat and cold by using clothing. Of course you might say that God does not drop the nuclear bomb. However, forces out of our own personal control operate and the same principle applies. In recent tidal waves in the Hawaiian Islands, members of the church suffered along with those who were not members of the church. It would be uncharitable even to suggest that those who suffered were lacking in faith. Our experience in contact with these people has indicated that they are most faithful. They were probably unable to make moves for self-protection because of the rapidity with which the disaster occurred.

Paul's teaching that faith without works is dead is to the point. A typical example of this is found in the book of Nehemiah: "Nevertheless we made our prayer unto our God, and set a watch against them day and night, because of them" (Nehemiah 4:9). Read the whole chapter from which this text is taken.

249. "Avoid" and "Addicted"

QUESTION

Section 119:3 d of Doctrine and Covenants tells us, "Avoid the use of tobacco and be not addicted to strong drink in any form." The word "avoid" indicates total abstinence and refers to the use of tobacco while the phrase "be not addicted to" concerns strong drink. Does this mean that we have not been admonished to abstain from strong drink? Can one properly construe the wording to mean that the occasional social drink is permitted as long as one does not become addicted?

ANSWER

To avoid means to keep away from, to shun, to abstain from, and is used in this text with this definite meaning. Because the word "avoid" is not repeated in the same sentence but instead "be not addicted" is used, this in no way weakens the stricture placed upon the partaking of strong drink.

Because the word "addicted" may be construed as meaning "habitually under the control of" rather than of periodic use is no argument for moderate drinking. There is no doubt about the intent of the word of the Lord to the church or of the understanding of the Restoration church throughout its history.

The earliest modern scriptural reference we have by way of instruction on strong drink is in Doctrine and Covenants 26:1 d:

"Wherefore a commandment I give unto you, that you shall not purchase wine, neither strong drink of your enemies; wherefore ye shall partake of none, except it is made new among you; yea, in this my Father's kingdom which shall be built up on the earth."

I suggest you read the italicized preface to this section for the historic setting. It appears that because of prevailing custom it had not occurred to Joseph Smith, Jr., to question the use of fermented wine until this time. On receiving light on the matter, he forthwith gave the instruction and followed it.

In Doctrine and Covenants 86:1 we have the following principle expressed:

"That inasmuch as any man drinketh wine or strong drink among you, behold, it is not good."

The word "addicted" cannot be isolated from the context and liberally interpreted to allow social drinking. Now I am not saying that one cigarette or one drink will send a person to eternal punishment, but it surely may start him on the downward path. The church cannot, therefore, uphold members and particularly members of the priesthood who by their actions lead others to believe that alcoholic drinking is a harmless social activity. There is only one stand for all Saints to take in this matter, and that is total abstinence. Alcohol is a factor in such a large percentage of crime that any discerning person cannot dissociate the two. The answer is in a definite "no" to the first drink. Therein only does safety from addiction lie.

According to the *Nauvoo Neighbor* (January 24, 1844, page 3) an ordinance was passed that liquor was to be sold in Nauvoo only for medicinal purposes. Those who were to vend it were licensed. This purpose had not always been so clearly understood by the Saints, but growing understanding brought about the action referred to until today our membership standards demand strict adherence to the rule of abstinence from intoxicating liquor as a beverage. Every adult member has a sacred duty to witness to this and so teach our young people, because the problem has become acute. This is not the opinion

of the narrow-minded but a deep concern of national authorities who
have no particular religious ax to grind.

250. Original Wording

*Does the document known as the Word of Wisdom as published
today contain the exact wording of the original? I have been told
that the original used the words "tea and coffee" instead of hot drinks.
Would you state the facts?*

ANSWER

The section to which you refer is Doctrine and Covenants 86. This
was first published as Section 80 of Doctrine and Covenants in the
Kirtland 1835 edition. It did not appear in print in any of the church
periodicals prior to this. It bears the date of February 27, 1833.
The church does not possess the original manuscript for this section.

The wording of the revelation has never been changed in any
authorized publication since its first printing, and as the committee
involved in its first publication included Joseph Smith, we can be
assured that it appeared with his approval in the 1835 edition of the
Doctrine and Covenants.

251. Official Position of the Church

QUESTION

*Does the church have an official position on the Word of Wisdom?
Is obedience to this necessary for eternal salvation?*

ANSWER

The answers to both these questions are found in the document
itself and particularly in the preface by Joseph Smith. In Doctrine
and Covenants, page 209, Section 86, is found this editorial statement
introducing the document:

"An inspired message to the church received by Joseph Smith,
Jr., prophet and seer to the church, February 27, 1833. Joseph
prefaces this revelation known as the 'Word of Wisdom' by this
statement:"

Then follows this statement in italics:

"A word of wisdom for the benefit of the council of high priests,

260

assembled in Kirtland, and church; and also, the Saints in Zion. To be sent greeting, not by commandment or constraint, but by revelation and the word of wisdom; showing forth the order and will of God in the temporal salvation of all Saints in the last days. Given for a principle, with promise; adapted to the capacity of the weak, and the weakest of all Saints, who are or can be called Saints."

Difficulty of interpretation appears to have occurred from the early days. However, in consideration of the explanatory paragraph which introduced the revelation, one finds that it was intended as wisdom for our temporal salvation but not by way of commandment or constraint. On this basis it would seem improper to make this counsel a standard for fellowship or a matter of judgment of our fellows. This is contrary to the spirit of the document.

The word "constraint" means coercion, compulsion, or binding obligation, and this the document clearly states it is not.

The greatest values of this counsel accrue to the people of the church as they accept it and abide by it as a statement of principle designed generally to augment in a temporal way their observance of all commandments of God (Section 86:3 c).

252. Serving of Tea and Coffee

QUESTION

At General Conference I noticed the serving of tea and coffee by the Laurel Club. Is this not contrary to the church rule?

ANSWER

I know of no General Conference rule which would allow me to state that it is contrary to church law. Some controversy over the exact meaning of "hot drinks" mentioned in Doctrine and Covenants 86 has been had over the years and probably will continue while persons continue to place major emphasis on minor considerations. Actually tea and coffee are not mentioned in any of the revelations or resolutions approved by General Conference.

President Israel A. Smith gave his opinion (see *Saints' Herald,* Volume 96, page 150, February 12, 1949) that temperature was the point made. This has scientific backing.

The content of any beverage is another question. Certain constituents such as caffeine (in coffee, tea, cocoa, and colas) are known to be deleterious to health if taken in excessive quantities. The stewardship of the individual is involved in this and would cover also the unwise use of chilled beverages as far as deleterious contents are concerned. Personal agency was left by the section referred to in that the preamble states "not by commandment or constraint." It is a "word of wisdom." The temperature at which the beverage is imbibed is the primary point. This is not so regarding alcoholic beverages of course.

The availability of tea and coffee at church activities is not a question of church law but one of personal decision and stewardship. Personally, my opinion is that the appraisal of President Israel Smith is sound.

253. Mild Drink

QUESTION

It is stated in Doctrine and Covenants 86 ". . . and barley for all useful animals, and for mild drinks, and also other grain." What is a mild drink? Is there a recipe you could give?

ANSWER

A mild drink, according to my view, is the opposite to a strong drink. As strong drink obviously means alcoholic beverage, a mild drink would be a nonalcoholic beverage. There are various mild drinks based on the grains mentioned in the text. Some, in my opinion, are more palatable than others, so I refrain from offering a recipe.

254. Leviticus and the Word of Wisdom

QUESTION

I would like light on Leviticus 11 which deals with what we should not eat, etc. The word of wisdom (Doctrine and Covenants 86) does not distinguish between different meats. I am particularly concerned about the meat of swine.

ANSWER

Most counsel and instruction which comes (or has come) to the people of God (either now or back in the days when the Mosaic laws were given) is related directly to the time, place, and circumstances. If we endeavor to apply what is loosely called "the unchangeability of God" in a narrow sense, we come up against unlimited problems and much confusion.

That God is consistent in quality and action is, of course, obvious from an overall point of view. What we call laws are simple verbal distillations of his mode of working. Thus we have developed (and often under inspiration) codes by which we apply God's will. It is clear that circumstances alter the application of so-called rules. People seeking counsel in the Arctic regions will have different food provisions than those in the intense heat of the tropics. Likewise people, in a day when hygiene was not understood and animals were kept in unsanitary conditions and fed disease-carrying offal, needed education to survive. As civilization develops slowly, so temporary rules must be followed until the need for them no longer applies.

If Moses were instructing people today who had refrigerated foods available, I have no doubt he would include some sound scientific counsel on the danger of misuse of frozen meals.

The Israelites came out of a state of degradation in Egypt and needed the elementary rules he laid down so wisely to these liberated slaves. Moses, with his insight, wrote even better than he himself knew (as all truly inspired leaders do) and thus has been termed "the father of modern hygiene." This does not mean that all the rules for primitive desert camp life now apply in this age of scientific advancement.

The Word of Wisdom is what its caption implies, counsel. The people of western New York were very interested in the problems of temperance and food. The counsel given by Joseph Smith, Jr., was applicable to a certain era and climate. Research into the era demonstrates this. If the situation had been as it was in the times of the Exodus, no doubt some of the details of those rules would have been included.

This is not meant in any way to disregard the good counsel in Doctrine and Covenants 86 as it applies to life today. When we distinguish between rules and basic principles we find no conflict. When we understand and act on the basis of the principles of life, we do not need to have detailed rules spelled out to the point of minutiae. This concept is involved in the difference between what has been called the "law of carnal commandments" and the "law of liberty" or of the spirit.

255. Alcohol and Cooking

QUESTION

Has the church taken a position on the use of alcohol in cooking?

Is the fact that there is evaporation during cooking justification for the use of this ingredient?

This is rather a fine point and from the nature of your second question would appear to be a matter of argument. The basic principle as set down in Doctrine and Covenants 86 is that alcohol is not for internal consumption. This is usually taken to refer to alcoholic beverages.

Alcohol in some form or other is involved in the preparation of many food products. For instance, many people use essence of vanilla and other flavorings without thought of the alcoholic base. I think Paul's admonition, "Let every man be persuaded in his own mind," must apply to your question, but be sure you take into account the basic disapproval of alcohol as a beverage. The fact of evaporation you mention would suggest that alcohol is not present after cooking, so one would not be overtly offending.

As a matter of a standard in our own home we have made it a practice not to have alcoholic beverages in stock for cooking purposes. This was a practical gesture to our family lest tolerance to the idea of alcohol be developed in our children.

Again, should medical doctors prescribe *spiritus frumenti,* it would come within quite a different category.

256. Cards and Dancing

QUESTION

In view of the General Conference resolution in 1958 which rescinded a former General Conference resolution condemning dancing and card playing, on the condition that church duties are not neglected would there be any harm in our group participating in card games and dancing? We have an Over-Forty adult fun club and recreation hall.

ANSWER

First, your concept of the 1958 resolution is in error. It is true that the Conference passed a resolution endeavoring to deal constructively with the problem of these amusements. To do so, it was felt necessary to first remove resolutions 317 (1886), 377 (1893), and 671 (1912). The reason given for these being rescinded was that resolutions 813 and 924 dealt more affirmatively with the problems than those being rescinded. The three paragraphs that follow give no reason for the deduction that the church intended to remove its previous counsel concerning the undesirability of these pastimes. To the contrary, it continues to discourage the practices that you are concerned with as those likely to lead to temptation and away from Christ and his church.

Because the church is not opposed to the happy life, the resolution embodies the previous counsel toward constructive activity and the responsibility of every good steward for developing his program of recreation, so that the result is not only pastime but really creative. I am including here the pertinent paragraphs of the 1958 resolution. Please note that there is no statement about rescinding the resolution "on the condition that church duties are not neglected."

"*Resolved,* That General Conference Resolutions 317, 377, and 671 be rescinded, and that General Conference Resolutions 813 and 924 stand as the more mature judgment of the church, and be it further

"*Resolved,* That it is the belief and experience of this church that the repeated practice of social dancing by church members should be discouraged as likely to lead them toward temptation and away from Christ and his church, and from the higher spiritual life of his kingdom, and be it further

"*Resolved,* That it is the considered conviction of the church that as stewards over time and talent, it is incumbent on each church member to make his leisure time activities contribute to his own mental and spiritual development, the service of his fellow man, and the building of the kingdom, and

"That as a means to this end, the church should encourage and help to train all age groups among our membership in an appreciation of the best in art, drama, literature, music, painting, sculpture, and all allied cultural, artistic, scientific, educational, and recreational fields, in order that they may make wise, informed, and spiritually sound choices of activities for leisure time."

After reading the foregoing, you will see that there is no justification for drawing the conclusion that the church has removed its previous discouragement of the practices under consideration, nor that the last resolution would make one feel free to engage in them as a church group. The denouncing of conduct not immoral in itself is not likely to reap a constructive result. The Mosaic Law said, "Thou shalt not." The more positive and Christian approach is to lead men to do those things which are for their salvation. Whatever our personal opinion may be on the matter, the church passed this resolution as I have presented it and it is incumbent on us all to carry it out in the spirit in which it was placed upon our statute books.

265

257. Church's Stand on Bowling

QUESTION

What is the church's stand on bowling as recreation? Can we justify our use of money and time in this activity?

ANSWER

This is one question concerning the quality and standards of recreation which must be considered along with many others. One must be a steward of his own time and energy and decide his priorities for himself. To issue rules for individual activity (other than those of basic moral importance) would be a task beyond the capacity of the rule book to contain.

Bowling, *per se,* is a healthful recreation. There is nothing immoral about it. In some areas, church groups sponsor teams and engage in healthy competition.

As in other recreational activity, Saints should be selective in the choice of company. Here it is important that local church leaders be constantly aware of the needs of young people for recreation. Physical recreation is essential. Where pastoral awareness is adequate, guidance is provided, not only when problems arise but by wise channeling of group activities into constructive channels. The same stewardship principles should guide in the amount of money spent in any recreational activity.

You ask me to draw a line, and that I personally cannot do. The church has not drawn arbitrary lines but has chosen rather to encourage individual and group decisions on the basis of constructive activity.

258. Stand of Church on Birth Control

QUESTION

Has the church taken an official stand on the subject of birth control? If so, what is it, and what is the basis for it?

ANSWER

The church has not, to my knowledge, made a specific pronouncement on birth control, nor have I been able to discover any direct instruction or rule in scripture. However, if we look for principles rather than for rules in the scriptures, we do have a guide by which we should exercise the stewardship of our powers of procreation.

I therefore answer your question from the point of view of offering some guidance that will enable you to exercise this stewardship in good conscience.

It is not good stewardship to assume more responsibility than one can handle, nor should a couple avoid the normal and reasonable responsibilities of their marriage. Marriage certainly has among its responsibilities the bearing of children.

The commandment to our first parents to multiply is clear and therefore may be taken as a duty for all healthy married couples. This is certainly a most personal stewardship, although there are other social and Christian implications which cannot be disregarded.

The kingdom of God needs saintly families. The nation needs righteous families. President F. M. Smith stated, "The church should never fail to appreciate the social and religious significance of marriage and its divine institution. The family is a basic factor in national or social stability" (*Saints' Herald,* Volume 74, page 245).

The selfish application of family limitation is a failure in stewardship. Many factors must enter into a couple's decision in this matter, such as finance, health, and heredity. We are not mere animals to be guided solely by instinctive tendencies, but we have been given powers to use with intelligence and restraint. Each must answer to God for this use.

The primary biological purpose of marriage is to have children, but there are other purposes. There is of course no spiritual joy comparable to that of parents in a home with children growing in Zionic expression toward the kingdom.

Most differences among Christians on the question of birth control center in the methods used and not in the principle. This aspect is a question of medical science rather than moral principle. It should be remembered, of course, that the termination of a human life once begun is a sin.

259. Stand of Church on Members Joining Lodges

QUESTION

What is the stand of the church on members joining lodges, such as Odd Fellows and Masons?

ANSWER

This church does not attempt to control the lawful private lives of its members. To what extent they affiliate with other organizations and associations is a matter of agency.

The church, however, gives guidance to its members concerning the quality of their activities and urges them to give primary attention and energy to those activities which are more directly kingdom building.

General Conference has expressed itself in two resolutions. The first has a statement of our position on individual liberty:

"That in the opinion of this body, this church has no right to subvert the liberties of its members by prohibiting their membership with what is known as a 'secret society,' unless such society shall first be condemned by either a decision of the General Assembly of the church, or by the law of the land."—General Conference Resolution 175, adopted April 10, 1875.

The second is more specifically pointed to what are known as secret societies:

"That we discourage members of the Reorganized Church of Jesus Christ of Latter Day Saints from holding membership in any society or order which requires the taking of oaths or the entering into covenant or obligation to guard the secrets, purposes, or doings of its organization."—General Conference Resolution 593, adopted April 16, 1907.

One must make up his own mind in relation to his total stewardship. Joseph Smith III expressed his opinion in *Church History,* Volume 3, page 677, as follows:

"All we wish to write about them is this. We know of nothing in the gospel making them necessary; nor do we know of any authorized by the church. There is nothing enjoined in any of them that is noble, kind, and good, that is not enjoined in the gospel covenant."

260. Preoccupation with Past

QUESTION

I would like to know how to overcome a constant preoccupation with my past. This brings a persistent sense of guilt. What can I do to rid myself of this trouble? I have prayed constantly to be free from this.

ANSWER

You must first realize that you are not alone in your feelings of regret for past sins. This brings you close in fellowship to your fellow beings. The scriptures express it this way: "All have sinned, and come short of the glory of God" (Romans 3:23).

Though one should not find satisfaction with the thought that there are others with like guilt, it does remove that sense of undue accusation of one's own sinfulness. You, as all other humans, are enfolded in the love of God for his children. Do not exclude yourself from his circle of mercy and forgiveness, for he has not excluded you.

Your prayers have served to further deepen the groove of your memory rather than relieve you. Having asked forgiveness, and having done all that is humanly possible under the circumstances surrounding you, and that in the spirit of repentance, you should deliberately refuse to keep mentioning these sins in your prayers. You may need to cultivate a technique of deliberately ejecting the recurring thoughts of an accusing nature. When the temptation to be morbid comes, you might deliberately repeat in your mind certain truths from scripture and so replace the negative thoughts. Remember the story in the Bible of the man's house which was cleaned of devils, but because he failed to invite wholesome guests, more devils than were ejected came and took up abode there (Matthew 12:44). There is no room for evil if we fill our minds with the good.

Some constructive suggestions worth memorizing for use in the way I have mentioned are found in the following scripture:

"In quietness and in confidence shall be your strength."—Isaiah 30:15.

"I can do all things through Christ which strengtheneth me."—Philippians 4:13.

Others are Psalms 23; 37:23, 24; and John 3:16.

Keep praying but not negatively. When a child has confessed his wrong and evidenced sincere repentance, we do not ask him to keep telling us of his mistake.

261. Dating Nonmembers

QUESTION

Since there are no boys in my Zion's League whom I care to date, and since my League's program is insufficient to consume my leisure time and interest, am I justified in keeping company with nonmember young men and women who smoke, drink, and dance, even though I do not engage in these practices? If I don't widen my social circle, what chance do I have of ever having a home and family?

Questions similar to this are being asked by young people throughout the church. Especially do we find this to be true in areas where there is an imbalance between girls and boys active in local League activities or where our numbers are very few.

There is no simple "yes" or "no" answer to your question as to whether you are right in persisting in your habit of associating with young people who do not share the beliefs and standards of our church with respect to the wise use of leisure time.

There is a basic truth about people generally: we all do just about what we genuinely *want* to do. No one can dictate to us specific courses of action regarding how we shall use our own time. We choose a given course, and in pursuing it we seek to justify ourselves in areas where others question either the actions we take or the motives underlying them. This is universally true of all people everywhere.

The World Church at the Conferences of 1934 and 1956 set commendable standards for the use of leisure time which our membership of all ages would do well to use. The 1934 Conference resolved that the church marshal its priestly authority and administrative channels "to direct and nurture, in home and church the Saints in more creative educational and spiritual use of leisure time."

In the same document, G.C.R. No. 939, the church resolved that pastors, priesthood, and especially parents

"having direction of the activities of the Saints reaffirm their belief in the wisdom of restraining our activities so as to exclude *any* and *all* forms of amusements and *uses of leisure time* which *in any way* tend to break down our moral standards or which would *hinder our spiritual development* and that we further . . . give special attention to *developing creative interests and abilities* which will lead to the realization of ideals of the church in the daily lives of its members." (Italics are mine.)

The General Conference of 1956, equally concerned that the membership make the best use of leisure time, resolved that

"It is the considered conviction of the church that as stewards over time and talent, it is incumbent on each church member to make his leisure time activities contribute *to his own mental and spiritual development, the service of his fellow man, and the building of the kingdom* . . . and that the church should encourage and help to train all age groups among our membership in appre-

270

ciation of the best in art, drama, literature, music, painting, sculpture, and all allied cultural, artistic, scientific, educational, and recreational fields, in order *that they may make wise, informed, and spiritually sound choices of activities for leisure time.*" (Italics are mine.)

No amount of legislation can achieve the goals of Zion, but the fulfillment of them awaits the disciplined and unselfish obedience of all the membership to the Zionic ideals.

The primary function of the church and of its members is that of declaring a witness of Zionic living to the world. Whenever one of our members travels with a circle of friends who do not share this commission, not much lasting good will issue from such association unless and until the member tries with all his heart and skill to cause his nonmember friends increasingly to travel closer to the fellowship of the Saints—to win them for the Christ's sake.

The main goal of our church youth, instead of being primarily concerned with finding an "ideal" mate for marriage, should be centered in creating in the home and church a vital, wholesome, and enthusiastic fellowship that will draw nonmembers toward it and bring their lives, together with ours, into closer harmony with the Zionic standard. Any other basis for one's conduct or choice of associations is likely to be disastrous.

One may find a mate, but it is doubtful if he will establish a truly Latter Day Saint home. I suggest that you read the story known as the parable of the prodigal son (Luke 15:11-32).

262. Raising Money for Local Churches

QUESTION

Is it proper to raise money for local church activity by procedures like "parcel post sales"? I recently received a card through the mail which appeared to have been widely distributed asking for a parcel worth twenty-five cents to be sent for sale at a certain function. The parcel was to be unopened, and the buyer would pay twenty-five cents not knowing what was in the parcel.

ANSWER

The question as to whether certain procedures for the raising of church finances are permissible or not arises frequently. In many instances a clear directive cannot be given. It is particularly important

271

that branches as well as individuals keep the principles of conduct in mind as a basis for decision in these matters. Many people want ready-made rules. This does not make for the type of conduct which is character building. It requires a minimum of decision and effort to follow a rule. Agency is the foundation of good stewardship.

The first question I would raise in this particular situation is this, "Has the appeal been made to those not responsible for a local project?" It is not desirable that local branches ask for financial help from people outside of the group responsible for the financing of a local program. This is definitely wrong. If there is a legitimate reason why others than the local group should share in a responsibility, the matter should be presented by the administrative officers to the Bishopric. There should be no direct appeal through the mails or any other avenue to those of other places. Each area has its responsibilities also, and if every group acted as the question implies, the situation would be impossible—in fact, absurd.

The finances necessary for the operation and extension of the church should be in accordance with the law which plainly places our obligations in this order: tithes, offerings, surplus.

There is some advantage in carrying forward activity projects, which require working together to raise money for local purposes. This personal and collective effort has its values by helping in development of good social relationships, character, and abilities toward Zionic quality. Thus a group may work to make an offering in this way. Of course, methods involving any degree of chance or speculation are not approved by the church. Zion must be built according to the laws of the celestial kingdom.

If the question is examined in the light of the foregoing, it will be seen that a "parcel post sale" is an endeavor to use a shortcut. It will be realized, too, that it shifts the responsibility from one's realm to others'. Efforts to build up the kingdom are important. The Lord could raise up donors which could relieve the church of all responsibility, but He has not chosen to do this. He has said in the scripture, "Gather my saints together unto me; those that have made a covenant with me by sacrifice."

It is my opinion that the method referred to is of doubtful spiritual value. It asks for the expenditure of time and money in purchasing and mailing an article, then it offers the article for less than the total expenditure for sale at a local function. The donor has spent time, money, and postage. The buyer then "takes a chance" of getting an unusable or unnecessary article. It seems to me that it would be more sensible to apply the plan of direct giving in the first instance.

263. Christians Charging Interest

QUESTION

Should a Christian charge his brother usury (interest)?

ANSWER

There are only two references in the New Testament where the word usury is found. It is found in the parable of the talents (Matthew 25:27; Luke 19:23) and both references are to the same situation.

It is not used in a condemnatory sense and it seems to be taken for granted that money should be put to use rather than be hoarded.

The Mosaic restrictions do not always carry over into the Christian code of ethics as was demonstrated on occasions by Jesus' own actions which were interpreted by some to be against the law. Christ appealed to the spirit of the law and in this spirit our stewardship of money should be exercised.

The ancient use of the word is not precisely that of today. If it were literally applied it would prevent the acceptance of rent on property. In modern times usury is descriptive of unconscionable and extortionate interest.

In modern society the prohibition of interest would be paralyzing. The church both pays and receives interest in our day. The case for interest may be argued on the basis of cost of handling and also of payment for service. Interest charges are ethical, provided they are not excessive or used to take unfair advantage of a brother's need. Actually in the Old Testament this was what was aimed at.

264. Church's Position on Buying Stock

QUESTION

What is the church's position in regard to buying stock in the stock market?

ANSWER

I have no knowledge of any ruling against the practice of dealing in stocks. Buying stock in a company is quite a legitimate business activity.

There are dishonest practices engaged in by many businesses, and the stock market is no exception. Sharp practices are not to the credit of Christians, and one's stewardship always involves integrity.

We have been warned concerning the spirit of speculation (Doctrine and Covenants 127:7) which can be ruinous financially as well as involving the temptation to exploit the unfortunate. The steward must ultimately decide his own actions. There is scriptural argument for interest on one's investments. This should not be of a usurious nature, usury being understood at this point to mean exorbitant and unjust charges. The scriptures report Jesus as using the principle of investment as a basis for one of his parables (see Matthew 25:27; Luke 19:23). In these texts the Revised Standard Version uses the word "interest."

265. Church Members Filing for Bankruptcy

QUESTION

How does our church feel about members who file for bankruptcy?

ANSWER

I find no specific instruction in either scripture or Conference resolution which I can quote as a succinct statement to help you, but I can give some help in principle.

The provisions for bankruptcy seem to have been made by civil legislative bodies to protect persons who cannot meet debts from being harshly treated by creditors. When a case comes before the judge for consideration as to whether the bankruptcy provisions may be applied, all the facts involved in the situation are considered and relief given according to the circumstances.

Bankruptcy laws were not enacted to give a way out for people who act dishonestly or knowingly incur indebtedness irresponsibly. There are other laws which deal with such cases. Relief in bankruptcy is made possible because even people with the best of intentions can fail in business and find themselves unable to meet obligations.

The law may give relief either of total obligation or in part, but one has a moral obligation apart from any legal consideration to pay what one owes. I feel that when these difficult situations arise one is entitled to seek the relief which the law allows but that while accepting this, the obligation to honor one's legitimate debts remains. The legal obligation is quite separate in my opinion.

We have been counseled against indulging in the spirit of speculation (Doctrine and Covenants 127:7), and also General Conference Resolution 120 states:

"That the members of the Church of Jesus Christ of Latter Day Saints shall not be counted in good standing who will contract debts without a fair prospect of being able to pay the same."

—April 8, 1871

274

Reference to the *Concordance to the Doctrine and Covenants* under the word "debts" will offer numerous texts which affirm the responsibility for the payment of just debts.

266. Chain Letters

QUESTION

Are chain letters of any nature acceptable as a fund-raising method?

ANSWER

Definitely no! Furthermore this practice is quite illegal. It is a serious federal offense as defined by United States Postal Regulation 124.5, and upon conviction a person or organization is liable to heavy penalty. This law defines such a practice as a lottery.

267. Church View on Willing Body

QUESTION

Has the church expressed a view on the propriety of willing one's body for posthumous medical research? Are there any scriptures applicable?

ANSWER

The church has given no expression of opinion on this nor do I know of any scripture that could be in any way helpful.

Where one desires to contribute to medical science in this way I am of the opinion that it is quite proper for him to so do. Sentiment often tends to present objections but provided that the body is handled in a respectful way (which medical schools are obligated to do), there appears to be no principle that would prohibit such a disposition of one's mortal remains.

One should remember that the body is but the tabernacle of the real person and that at death the spirit has returned to the care of the Almighty.

Much medical knowledge has been gained by research through such action as your question involves. I would nevertheless not attempt to advise what any person should do in such a matter. It is highly personal.

268. Scriptural Prohibition of Blood Transfusion

QUESTION

Is there any prohibition of blood transfusion found in scripture?

275

Genesis 9:4 and Acts 15:20, 28 are used by a friend to support objection to this medical practice.

I know of no prohibition in any scripture whatsoever that applies to the modern medical technique of blood transfusion. The advice in Acts 15 is a broad admonition to abstain from pagan practices, including the custom of eating strangled animals which still contained blood. This was particularly abhorrent to the Jews. Another possible explanation has been offered, that certain heathens featured blood in their rituals.

It would appear that the main idea was to counsel avoidance of contamination by participation in pagan ritual. Such contact also would involve failure to witness of the different way of life as well as the danger of drifting from the true principles contained in the gospel.

269. Scriptural Obligation of Burial

QUESTION

Is there scriptural obligation of burial as opposed to other methods of final disposal such as cremation?

ANSWER

The earliest scriptural references where burial is referred to indicate that this word was used in its original Hebraic form to describe more than one procedure. At times it appears to have referred to a place rather than a method. It is often used in connection with a tomb as contrasted with placing in a grave dug in the earth. In Genesis 23:17 there is recorded the "burial" of Sarah in the cave of Machpelah, and in Genesis 25:9 Abraham is stated to have been interred there. Many archaeological investigations have discovered skeletons in caves around the Dead Sea. These have often been used as group sepulchers. Cemeteries of single graves where earth burials have taken place similar to the Qumran Cemetery, where 1,200 persons received individual separate allotments, indicate this Hebrew variant also. Jesus was "buried" in a new tomb "where no one had ever been laid" thus indicating that it was also a custom to use tombs for a number of interments. This could be successive over a period of time, the previous relics being set on one side to make room for the present need.

Where bodily destruction by fire is actually mentioned in the

Old Testament it is used as a sign of vengeance. To the Hebrews this practice was a heathen one.

Lacking any instruction which reveals revelatory insight it would seem that cremation was not practiced by the Hebrews because of its association with heathen groups. Many practices in themselves not involving principles were eschewed because of the need to keep Israel free from the taints of heathen neighbors. This seems to be one of them.

Cremation cannot be supported or rejected on scriptural grounds. It means little ultimately whether the elements are returned to their source by slow disintegration in the earth or by being more quickly resolved by intense heat.

It is always wise to remember that on such occasions we are dealing with a tabernacle of clay and not with the recent spiritual occupant.

270. Church Attitude on Politics

QUESTION

What is the attitude of the church as to politics at the city, county, state, and national levels?

ANSWER

The attitude of the church with respect to politics is that every member should be concerned with the good and efficient government of the country and lend his weight as a Christian citizen to having persons elected to office at all levels who will ensure this. This is without respect to political parties provided the party is not committed to antichristian activity.

The Reorganized Church as an organization has not aligned itself with any particular group. When it has spoken as a body or through its representatives, it has done so only on points of principle and every member is left free to exercise his democratic privilege according to the dictates of his own conscience. Members should keep themselves free from acrimonious involvement detrimental to Christian fellowship and saintly unity.

Doctrine and Covenants 112 is still basic and should be read as a broad statement of RLDS philosophy.

271. Origin of Christmas Tree

QUESTION

What is the origin of the traditional Christmas tree? Is it at all Christian?

277

The custom of decorating a Christmas tree seems to have had its origin in Germany somewhere about the eighth century.

The pagan worship of Odin involved sacrifices being offered to the sacred oak. It is said that Boniface, an English missionary, in an endeavor to remove this paganism, replaced the oak with a fir tree which was decorated in honor of the child Jesus.

It is also claimed, according to the *Encyclopaedia Britannica,* that Martin Luther introduced the tree lighted with candles. It is also said that on the marriage of the German Prince Albert to Queen Victoria the custom of the decorated Christmas tree became popular in England. It later spread to the United States and to most parts of the world where German immigrants were to be found.

Although the pagan background of the Christmas tree might be emphasized, like many other traditions it has been redeemed from pagan meaning. It is now used to signify the joyousness occasioning the birth of our Lord. It is neither good nor evil in itself. The significance of Christmas is of value accordingly as we invest the materials involved with symbolism of greater or lesser meaning. We feast at Christmas, often unwisely, but this does not make the traditional meal undesirable. The Lord took the symbol of the common meal and made it into a great sacramental occasion of his church, which we commemorate each month.

The Christmas tree is not involved in any way in Christian ritual as affecting life and salvation, but it is a delightful symbol of joy. For this reason I have no antipathy to its having a proper place in social life at the Christmas season.

272. Christian Rest Day

QUESTION

What is the correct Christian rest day? It would appear from some literature recently given to me that Sunday is wrong and Saturday is the seventh day as commanded in Genesis.

ANSWER

Certain religious sects have promulgated the idea that God gave the seventh day commandment in the beginning when he finished the creation of the world. Most of these people believe that God performed this vast work in seven days of twenty-four hours and that he hallowed the seventh to be a day of rest.

Genesis 2:2, 3 (Authorized Version) states:

"And on the seventh day God ended his work which he had made; and he rested on the seventh day from all his work which he had made.

"And God blessed the seventh day, and sanctified it: because that in it he had rested from all his work which God created and made."

It must be remembered that this was not written down at the creation of the world and that even the earliest writings were lost long before the five books of Moses became a literary entity. Moses, the chief figure of the Hebrew exodus from Egypt, states that the Lord made a covenant with the children of Israel in Horeb (Deuteronomy 5:2) and then continues to emphasize the fact that their fathers were not among those with whom the covenant was made. The text states:

"The Lord made not this covenant with our fathers, but with us, even us, who are all of us here alive this day."— Deuteronomy 5:3, A.V.

Then follows the detail of the covenant referred to which includes the Ten Commandments, one of which is the instruction on keeping the Sabbath day. Not only is the commandment on the Sabbath day listed but also the reason for its institution is given. This is made clear in these words:

"And remember that thou wast a servant in the land of Egypt, and that the Lord thy God brought thee out thence through a mighty hand and by a stretched out arm: therefore the Lord thy God commanded thee to keep the sabbath day."—Deuteronomy 5:15.

It is apparent that keeping the Sabbath was in commemoration of the deliverance of the Israelites from Egypt.

Why then is the reference to the Sabbath found in Genesis 2? Moses was writing proleptically, that is, with the knowledge of the present when writing of past events. The present understanding was injected into the record as an explanation.

Another factor which needs to be taken into consideration in the light of Deuteronomy 5:15, indicating this was a national commemoration only, is that it is impossible to have a particular day kept simultaneously all over the world. It would take a period of forty-eight hours to do this. For instance, I cite Samoa and Fiji. Ordinarily these islands would be only half an hour in time apart. But when it is 12:00 noon Sunday in Fiji it is 12:30 P.M. Saturday in Samoa. The reason is the intervening International Date Line which follows (approximately) the 180 degree meridian. One often spends two Sundays (or Saturdays) with no intervening days between on the journey from Australia or New Zealand to the United States and may completely miss one of these days when returning.

Therefore we reason that to make a point of salvation out of the keeping of a specific period is not logical nor is it possible to apply the law of Moses at this point. Who are keeping the Sabbath, the Samoans or the Fijians?

However, from New Testament times Christians have kept the first day of the week as a memorial of the Savior's resurrection. They are not concerned with a time period but with the significance. As Latter Day Saints we are instructed to keep the Sabbath for the purpose of rest and worship. This is important in the preservation of divine standards of life.

Apostasy, Reformation, and Restoration

273. Reformers and Restoration

QUESTION

What is the basis for the claim our people often make that Luther and other Reformers realized that their reform was not sufficient—that something more was needed (interpreted by us as the Restoration)?

ANSWER

Many of the Reformers were concerned with the correction of doctrine and institutional procedure and form of the dominant church of their times. They made brave efforts to correct what they severally felt were specifics needing this. That some of them felt they were performing works which were part of an ongoing trend toward the emancipation of religious thought and to the implementation of greater truth is undoubted.

That Luther believed specifically he was a forerunner of what we call the Restoration is not demonstrable in my opinion. He did make a statement that he had wondered if he was perhaps Melancthon's forerunner. This, however, cannot be construed as some have done. Melancthon was Luther's mentor, and he most likely meant that he was breaking ground for the greater theologian. Luther is probably better known than his teacher.

There are several statements which indicate that earlier religious thinkers felt "God himself would in his own time erect for himself a new church, free from every blemish and impurity; and that he would raise up certain persons, and fill them with heavenly light for the accomplishment of this great object" (Mosheim, *Ecclesiastical History,* Vol. 4, pp. 200, 201).

281

Men like Roger Williams are credited with statements of the impending movement of God in this direction in this era. Undoubtedly many were looking for what we call a restoration. The followers of Alexander Campbell were among these. John Wesley's statement in his seventy-first sermon speaks of signs of "the glorious day that is approaching" which, he felt, "if not begun are nigh, even at the very door." He also said in the same sermon, "What could God have done which he hath not done to convince you that the day is coming, that the time is at hand when he will fulfill this glorious promise, and will arise to maintain his own cause, and set up his kingdom?"

John Wesley's brother, Charles, wrote a hymn (now No. 285 in *The Hymnal*) to which you might refer. This has been quoted as evidence of his expectancy of a restoration. Though centered in the idea of the restoration of Israel, this hymn does indicate an expectancy of a new apostolic church.

Those often quoted might not be happy to be used in support of our specific movement could they speak today. Perhaps all we can say, with due respect to facts, is that they were expecting God to move to fulfill his purposes. That God did so move is the witness of the Restoration.

274. Separation between Eastern and Western Churches

QUESTION

When was the separation between the Eastern and Western churches effected?

As in all great movements toward division, there is no specific date on which separation actually took place. Seeds of difference between what eventually became the Roman Catholic or Western Church and the Eastern Orthodox Church (Greek Orthodox) began quite early in Christian history. A study of the various councils reveals the differing positions progressively.

It is commonly believed that complete dissociation was in effect by A.D. 1054. This date is named because of the fact that at this time there was a difference of opinion on the nature of the bread used in Communion. Pope Leo IX attempted to excommunicate Michael Cerularius, Patriarch of Constantinople, and his followers. This was resisted, resulting in the disassociation between Rome and Constantinople, the latter becoming the seat of the Eastern Church (Greek Orthodox).

Apostasy or separation of viewpoints can never be dated to the year but is a process more or less observable as time moves on. The two churches, however, were regarded as separate communions from the eleventh century.

275. Catholic

QUESTION

What is the origin and meaning of the word catholic?

ANSWER

The English word "catholic" comes from the Greek *katholikos* which literally means "general." It was used quite early in the Christian church to mean the total body of the church throughout the world as distinguished from a local congregation. It was also applied to the teachings applicable to all parts of the church in the sense of their universality.

Some epistles therefore were called catholic epistles—that is, written for the general body as compared with some written to meet a specific local situation. Thus we have the general epistles of James; I and II Peter; I, II, and III John; and Jude. Paul's epistles on the other hand were not originally intended to be catholic, being written to Corinth, Rome, and so forth. However, they involved general principles.

Later the word catholic was used to distinguish between the main body of the church and heretical factions which split off as dissenters. This is a theological connotation.

276. Contradiction in Scriptures

QUESTION

I am confused by the apparent contradiction in scripture concerning the church. I Nephi 3:220-222 states that there are only two churches, one of God and the other of the devil, yet III Nephi 12:19-23 speaks of a church built upon the works of men. Is this consistent?

ANSWER

The word "church" is generally used to define the specific organization instituted by Jesus Christ, and as used by Latter Day Saints includes only those who have entered into the specific fellowship under conditions and procedures which the Saints believe are authoritative. The church in this sense is exclusive. The word "church" is used to describe a particular denomination of Christendom. The title "Church of Jesus Christ" is one which distinguishes it from those churches which are not organized in accordance with the authority and teachings of Jesus Christ.

In the scripture we find reference to "church of Christ" (Mosiah 9:49; III Nephi 13:36), to "churches of men" (III Nephi 12:19-23), and to "church of the Devil" (Doctrine and Covenants 16:4 d).

There is, however, a sense in which the Church of Jesus Christ is not defined as consisting of those who are formally enrolled following submission to the ordinances of baptism and confirmation but are his church as they qualify by lives of Christlike righteousness. To spend time identifying the degrees of righteousness from the "church of the Devil" through so-named "churches of men" and thus drawing an arbitrary line between classifications is not a very profitable exercise. In my opinion the emphasis in I Nephi 3:220-222 is upon being identified with Christ and his church by obedience to his way of life. Thus it is stated, "Behold there are save two churches only." Ultimately men's works will classify them as of one or the other accordingly as they are for God or against him. The conclusion of the matter is found in Doctrine and Covenants 3:16:

> "Whosoever repenteth and cometh unto me, the same is my church; whosoever declareth more or less than this, the same is not of me, but is against me, therefore, he is not of my church."

It profits us little to approach this question negatively by defining the church of the devil and the churches of men, but it is most profitable for us to identify ourselves with the Church of Jesus Christ by positive obedience in our lives. The fine justice of God will reward all men accordingly. (See Doctrine and Covenants 76.)

I believe that the scriptures indicate the existence of a specific fellowship, an organized body of professing disciples through which man is ministered to toward perfection. However, we must not rest upon mere membership, for in the finality our classification is one of quality.

277. Angel Who Used Words of Revelation

QUESTION

Was there an angel who appeared to anyone of the Restoration movement who used the words of Revelation 14:6, 7? If not, is it not possible that it is misapplied to the Restoration?

I know of no claim by anyone that these actual words of Revelation 14:6, 7 were used by an angelic messenger, though I have frequently heard them quoted as containing the essential proclamation of the latter-day work.

Students of prophecy have differed as to the actual time to which the predictions of this complicated book of scripture refer. It is generally conceded that Babylon mentioned in verse 8 referred to Rome. The great persecutions of the Christians no doubt centered here and were in the mind of John. That Rome should and did fall because of her wickedness is a prophetic and historic fact.

Therefore, in principle this angel's message applies to the call to righteousness in the latter days. I, like you, would question a literal and actual fulfillment predicted upon the relation of Revelation 14:6, 7 to a particular historic incident involving the actual words.

278. Woman in Revelation; Church of the Devil

QUESTION

To whom, or what, does the woman of Revelation 17 refer?
Please explain the reference to the church of the devil in the Book of Mormon, I Nephi 3:221.

ANSWER

There is no doubt that consideration of both questions at one time is required.

Opinions have varied on the interpretation of these passages, and some see an apparent contradiction. The consensus of opinion among the elders of the Restoration has been that reference was made here to a specific organization which has been seen as the organization which succeeded or supplanted the original church of Jesus Christ. In this connection the "woman" of Revelation 17 is seen as the usurper in the place of the true church represented in Revelation 12. Much of the detail in these chapters seems to parallel the subsequent historical record.

The passages themselves give some of the interpretation of the writer. The seven hills, the kings of the earth, the waters as peoples, etc., are explained in the text itself (Revelation 17).

It must be conceded that in the mind of the Book of Mormon writer there was the basic idea of an ecclesiastical movement which without doubt evidences the same characteristics of the "woman" in

Revelation 17. One finds it difficult to avoid the conclusion as to the identical figures. I Nephi 3:139-144 must be read in conjunction with verses 220-236 of the same chapter.

Doctrine and Covenants 16:4 states, "Contend against no church, save it be the church of the Devil." This implies that there are other classifications than the two, of God or of the devil. The reference "above all other churches" (I Nephi 3:140) also indicates plurality to some extent. I Nephi 7:50, 51 classifies as of the devil all churches that are built up to get gain, etc. This implies that there may be some not so motivated. In II Nephi 11:24; 12:34 we have further amplification of this matter.

One should consider all this in the light of the following: "There are save [but] two churches only: . . . Whoso belongeth not to the church of the Lamb of God belongeth to that great church, which is the mother of abominations" (I Nephi 3:220, 221). It would be illogical to interpret this text to mean that all who do not belong to the church of God belong to the Roman Catholic denomination.

Obviously, there are two emphases in scripture. The first concerns those organizations that qualify for inclusion in the groups indicated in I Nephi 7:50, 51 as being of evil. This group may be headed by a different organization as the instrument of antichrist at different periods and in different locations. Undoubtedly, the Roman Apostasy has played and still plays a part. Communism qualifies in other respects. Many non-Catholic or non-Communistic organizations have also engaged in persecution of truth and righteousness. Some non-Christian religions could be included also.

This lends to consideration of the second emphasis—that in the ultimate we are in one of two categories, for God or not. Doctrine and Covenants 3:16 states clearly, "Whosoever repenteth and cometh unto me, the same is my church." Those who do not are not of his church. This principle places the issue above mere denominational membership. We are not necessarily "in the church of God" by any ordinance or by enrollment, but in fact only according to our true repentance and obedience to Christ and the resultant quality of life.

This must not be construed to mean that the church of God is not a specific organization to which men must come in order to achieve God's purposes. Doctrine and Covenants 1:5 e states that this is the only church upon the earth of which He approves. Note the qualification "speaking collectively and not individually"—in other words, the only church organized according to His plan, will, and authority to accomplish the kingdom task. There are many other forces at work for good also.

It should be stated here that many students do not agree as to any specific denomination being meant at all and thus feel that the broad interpretation, which classifies those who are for God on the one hand and those who are opposed, is sufficient explanation. There is no official interpretation other than the texts in the scriptures.

279. Alexander Campbell and Restoration Movement

QUESTION

A recent newspaper article carried the statement that Alexander Campbell laid the foundation for and launched the "Restoration Movement." This description has always been applied to the Latter Day Saints in my church experience. Is the newspaper statement correct?

ANSWER

The Campbells came from a strong Presbyterian background. Thomas and his son, Alexander, became concerned over the differences between the catechism and the Bible. Thomas had preached for the Seceder congregations in Ireland and migrated to the United States of America after a period of time in Scotland, where young Alexander had engaged in intense religious studies. The family arrived in North America in 1809, two years after Thomas came. Withdrawing from the Seceders on the grounds of failure to follow the Bible, Thomas proposed a Christian union upon the basis of the scriptures. At first the movement was vague with no formal understanding of common belief except "the Bible." The "Disciples" proclaimed "where the Scripture speaks we speak; where the Scriptures are silent we are silent."

The work of the Campbells, and Alexander in particular, was defined by the latter as a ministry to bring about a union of believers on the basis of a restoration of the Bible as the rule. As early as 1835 Alexander published a book in Bethany, Virginia, with the cover title *Christianity Restored.* On the title page are found these words as part of the subtitle: "Capital Positions sustained in an attempt to restore the original gospel and order of things."

In another book, *The Christian System,* written by A. Campbell, this statement appears:

"Finally while endeavoring to abolish the old sects, let us be careful that we form not a new one. . . . Our platform must be as long and as broad as the New Testament."—Page 103.

Other writers among the Disciples use the word "reformation" freely and apparently interchangeably for their concept of "The Restoration."

287

In the book referred to, *Christianity Restored*, Campbell included a chapter entitled "The Regeneration of the Church." On page 281 he says:

"Should any one imagine that the state of things to which we have attained, is the sole, or ultimate object of our aspirations, or our efforts, he would do us the greatest injury. Societies, indeed, may be found amongst us, far in advance of others, in their progress towards the ancient order of things; but we know of none that has fully attained to that model. It is, however, most acceptable to see so many societies formed and forming, under the banners of reformation, with the determination to move onwards in conformity to the sacred oracles, till they stand perfect and complete in all the will of God."

This brief outline of the movement and its aims will help you understand the Disciples' use of the word "restoration," which without doubt is in their early literature.

The Latter Day Saint usage involves the concept of the bringing back to earth of a divinely commissioned priesthood, contemporary revelation, and a church organization as well as doctrinal principles. It would be difficult to decide who used the term first. The earliest reference using the word "restoration" in our movement is Doctrine and Covenants 26:2—"the restoration of all things."

Sidney Rigdon was associated with the Disciples before joining our church and no doubt contributed to the expansion of the meaning of the word to include the fuller concept found in the Latter Day Saint movement. It became a matter of usage and an explanation of our role in the last days.

Where the Disciples used it they did so with particular reference to the belief in scripture and not in the specific sense we do. This is shown in the quote from their writings given herein.

280. Reorganization Original Church

QUESTION

Is the Reorganization the same church organized on April 6, 1830, or another church following the loss of the original?

ANSWER

In a critical consideration of the first issue of the *True Latter Day Saints' Herald*, Elder E. C. Briggs makes the following comment:

288

"Another mistake I noticed in this *Herald*. New organization! I never heard that name before applied to the Reorganization. The word *new* contradicts the idea that has always been understood by the church. The term *reorganization* conveys the idea that the church has been disorganized and is now again being established as it was before; but not another thing or system that had never been before."—*Saints' Herald*, Vol. 50, p. 364.

This is how the early members of the church viewed the movement which culminated in the coming of Joseph Smith III to the leadership. The conference of 1852 passed a resolution which stated that those reorganizing regarded the Church of Jesus Christ as in existence wherever six members were, according to the pattern given when the church was restored. To contend that the difficulties of 1844 through 1852 or until later, when permanent leadership was again established, constituted a total loss of the church as a body is not good reasoning. For this to have occurred the church would have had to regress beyond the required minimum organization which was effected April 6, 1830. It is true that whole quorums became disorganized and branches also, but the essentials of priesthood authority and basic organization remained. Judicial references to this have been made when various matters have been considered by the courts and the terms "successor" and "continuation" have both been used. The Reorganization is definitely a continuing church from 1830 to the present. There is no apostasy either in doctrine or principle.

281. Church Rejected after Death of Joseph Smith

QUESTION

If the church was rejected after the death of Joseph Smith, when was it accepted again—or has it been?

ANSWER

It all depends on what you mean by rejection. If you mean final casting off by God, I do not believe that this was done. The Reorganization claims to be a continuation of the original church, and this opinion has been given by judges who have had to consider this question in an endeavor to arrive at proper judgments on other matters such as property rights. There was undoubtedly rejection of the conduct and procedures of many of the early church members including some quorums such as the Council of Twelve, but unless the church regressed to a situation less than that of April 6, 1830, it continued to exist as the church. The church needed reorganization because of the degree of failure evidenced by the disasters of Nauvoo. While members of the Melchisedec priesthood and an organization of at least six members remained faithful to their covenants, the authority for carrying the Restoration forward remained and the church was in existence.

282. Prophecy of Lutius Gratianus

QUESTION

Are you in a position to state whether a prophecy attributed to Lutius Gratianus, allegedly published in his work, "Hope of Zion," is authentic? I have been informed that this can be seen in the Library of Basel, Switzerland.

ANSWER

As far as one can be positive of something, I will answer and say, "It is not authentic." This question has frequently come under notice and as recently as April, 1959, request was made by church officers to the library at Basel, Switzerland. On each occasion of inquiry the chief librarian of the University at Basel answered by enclosing a mimeographed sheet. It appears that they are asked this question often and to avoid repetition of work used a copying machine to deal with the volume of demand. I am printing the purported prophecy and the reply from Basel.

"The old time gospel and the gifts thereof are lost. False doctrines prevail in all the churches on the face of the earth. All we can do is to exhort the people to be just, fear God and shun evil, and pray. Prayer and purity may cause an angel to visit a deep and distressed soul, but I will tell you, God will have spoken within one hundred years.

"He will restore the old church again. I see a little band of people led by a prophet and a faithful leader. They are persecuted and burned out and murdered. From every nation shall true believers be gathered by speedy messengers, and then shall the Almighty God speak to the disobedient nations with thunder, lightning, and destruction such as men have never known before."

Herewith is the librarian's answer:

"Memorandum on 'Hoffnung Zions' (Zion's Hope) by the Swiss Divine, Samuel Lutz.

"In 1893 there appeared, in two periodicals published by 'The Church of Jesus Christ of Latter-Day Saints', vis the 'Juvenile Instructor' and 'Der Stern,' an article in English and one in German respectively, notifying that in 1739 a book had been published in Basel, written by one Lutius Gratianus, & bearing the title: 'Die Hoffnung Zions' (Zion's Hope), in which the genesis of the 'Church of Jesus Christ of Latter-Day Saints' was clearly prophesied.

"As the University Library of Basel often receives queries concerning this would-be prophecy, this memorandum is intended for briefly stating the facts.

"In 1732 the leader of Swiss Pietism, the clergyman Samuel Lutz (Lucius, Lutius), published, in Bern, under the disguise of 'Christophilus Gratianus', a book, 'Die Hoffnung Zions', of which a second and third edition appeared in Basel, in 1737 and 1756 respectively, forming part of a collection of Lutz's writing, entitled 'Ein neuer Strauss von schonen und gesunden Himmelsblumen' (A new bunch of beautiful and wholesome heavenly flowers). The 'Hoffnung Zions' proves to be a free exegesis of Jes. 60 and interprets this tremendous prophecy both as an imminent period of salvation for the church within the world's history, and as the coming of the final Kingdom of God; it must, however, be admitted, that the author does not sufficiently distinguish the two eras of salvation. Yet in no case do we find any hints at the 'Church of Jesus Christ of Latter-Day Saints'.

"Despite all our searching, a Basel edition of 1739, as mentioned in the articles in 'Juvenile Instructor' and in 'Stern', has not yet been found. And even if it should exist, it would be, considering Samuel Lutz's mode of viewing things, very unlikely, nay as good as impossible, that it should contain the alleged reference to the Church of Jesus Christ of Latter-Day Saints.

"Thus the articles in 'Juvenile Instructor' and in 'Stern' seem to rest upon some misunderstanding."

The "prophecy" has been alleged to be a "Mormon fabrication." Whether this is justifiable or not, someone with more wishful thinking than basis of evidence has fallen for flimsy support in an endeavor to substantiate a case. "Der Stern" was a Utah German publication in Zurich, Switzerland, about 1870-1871.

Authority and Priesthood

283. Emphasis on Priesthood

QUESTION

Why does the RLDS Church lay such emphasis upon priesthood?

ANSWER

To hold priesthood simply means to hold the responsibilities of a priest, The word priest has its origin in antiquity, and in the Hebrew the word was *kohen*. This denoted being able "to divine." To divine in this sense was to have a familiar spirit on intimate terms with the supernatural, good or evil, and thus tell what was going on in the unseen world. Thus *kohen* or *priest* came to mean one who could tell what the will of God is, because he is on intimate terms with God. It is thus also prophetic in the wider sense. Because of the wrongful emphasis upon the authority of priesthood as coercive rather than prophetic, many groups have rejected the idea of priesthood authority residing in an individual. They have broadened the concept into what is known as the "priesthood of all believers."

This is not totally wrong, for all believers have a responsibility to make God known to others; but this church believes that God calls men to specific witness and to act for him in the gospel ordinances.

This authority was expressed at its highest point of priestly function in Jesus Christ. This does not mean that it was concluded with Christ, but that he was the perfect personal revelation of the nature of God, serving, loving, and giving for man's fulfillment. This is the sense in which priesthood is important to the church. That Christ endorsed this function of priesthood is indicated in Paul's letter to the Ephesians (4:13, 14).

284. Two Priesthoods

QUESTION

Can the idea of two priesthoods be supported by the King James Version and later editions of the Bible?

ANSWER

The answer to this depends on how you interpret the various texts of scripture. Undoubtedly there is mention of priests after the order of Melchisedec (See Genesis 14:18; Psalm 110:4; Hebrews 5:6, 10; 6:20; 7:17, 21).

Also, Exodus 28:1-4 describes the appointment of Aaron and his associates to the priest's office. The fact that only some of Moses' honor was placed on Aaron has been interpreted to indicate a lesser priesthood than Moses held. Another order was that of the Levites who ministered in the physical matters of the tabernacle (See Deuteronomy 10:8, 9).

The mentioning of high priests in Hebrews 5 certainly indicates that the Melchisedec and Aaronic ordinations were familiar to those who were being written to. Personally I question whether this chapter in the King James Version can be used alone to sustain conclusively that the writer of Hebrews is doing anything more than using the Hebrews' knowledge of the priesthood to explain the functions of Jesus Christ as a mediator.

However, the Doctrine and Covenants gives an explanation of priesthood in Section 104 which, being accepted by the church as a revelatory document, makes these priesthoods part of the church organization. In the form in which scripture has survived, we lack many pieces of information we desire. The concept of restoration postulates that revelation is necessary at this point and the Doctrine and Covenants provides this, we believe.

285. Origin of Melchisedec Priesthood

QUESTION

When did the Melchisedec priesthood begin on earth?

293

The following is found in Doctrine and Covenants 83:2 c-g:

"And the sons of Moses, according to the holy priesthood, which he received under the hand of his father-in-law, Jethro; and Jethro received it under the hand of Caleb; and Caleb received it under the hand of Elihu;

"and Elihu under the hand of Jeremy; and Jeremy under the hand of Gad; and Gad under the hand of Esaias; and Esaias received it under the hand of God;

"Esaias also lived in the days of Abraham who was blessed of him, which Abraham received the priesthood from Melchisedec; who received it through the lineage of his fathers, even till Noah;

"and from Noah till Enoch, through the lineage of their fathers; and from Enoch to Abel, who was slain by the conspiracy of his brother; who received the priesthood by the commandments of God, by the hand of his father Adam, who was the first man;

"which priesthood continueth in the church of God in all generations, and is without beginning of days or end of years."

286. Authority of Melchisedec Priesthood

QUESTION

If the ordination by John the Baptist under the direction of Peter, James, and John was necessary for the first ordination of Joseph Smith, Jr., and Oliver Cowdery, could officers of the Melchisedec priesthood function in the case of Joseph Smith III without a new dispensation of authority?

ANSWER

Yes. The authority of the high priesthood had not disappeared. The incident evidently referred to in your question is recorded in *Times and Seasons*, Volume 1, page 34. This, of course, refers to the Aaronic ordinations of Joseph Smith and Oliver Cowdery. They were also told that the Melchisedec priesthood was to be restored, but that the ordinations should be delayed until an expression of consent by their brethren should be had. This occurred at the formal organization meeting, April 6, 1830.

Marks and Gurley held this latter (Melchisedec) priesthood from the lifetime of Joseph Smith, Jr., and the others who participated in the ordination of Joseph Smith III held their priesthood through the line of those with similar authority. This dates back in an unbroken line from the early restoration of priesthood, May 15, 1829.

At the first ordination of a man to the Aaronic priesthood the prophecy was given that it was never to be taken again from the earth until the fulfillment of God's purposes. It has not been, as the authority of both priesthoods has continued to this day and is exercised in the Reorganization.

287. Authority to Presidency

QUESTION

It has been stated to me in discussion that Brigham Young assumed the Presidency by right as president of the Twelve after Joseph Smith, Jr., died. Doctrine and Covenants 104:11 (107:24, Utah edition) was quoted as authority. Please explain our reason for believing to the contrary.

ANSWER

There is no reference in this passage to succession in the Presidency. All that is given here is information about the relative authority of quorums, particularly the Presidency, the Twelve, and the Seventy. Under certain cricumstances, they are equal in authority. We are not entitled to assume from this that the president of the Twelve automatically becomes president of the church.

When Joseph Smith was assassinated, the Twelve had a place to fill, and we have no record that they were in any other way sustained than in their calling, which was certainly not to preside over the church as a First Presidency.

The law was clear (see Doctrine and Covenants 43:2 and 99:6). This gives authority to the prophet to appoint his successor through revelation.

288. Priesthood Authority after Death of Joseph Smith

QUESTION

Since God restored priesthood authority to Joseph Smith, where was that authority between his death and the selection of his son to lead the Reorganization?

While men of the priesthood remained true to their covenant by continuing in righteousness their authority was not abrogated. The first elders of the church ordained each other to the Melchisedec priesthood by commandment, and later Joseph was ordained to the presidency of the high priesthood. This high priesthood remained in the charge of good men during the interim to which you refer; these men acted within their calling in organizing the scattered Saints toward effective functioning church life again. The leaders of the reorganizing movemet found they could not follow claimants to leadership when such leaders deviated by sponsoring erroneous teachings, some of which had their origin in Nauvoo. As I have stated in this column before, as long as at least the simple status of April 6, 1830, existed, neither the church nor the priesthood was lost. It remained for these men to respond to divine leading in the rehabilitation of the work. This they did.

The conference held at Beloit, Wisconsin, in 1852 stated this position in the following words:

> "Resolved, that we believe that the Church of Christ, organized on the 6th day of April, A.D. 1830, exists as on that day wherever six or more Saints are organized according to the pattern in the Book of Doctrine and Covenants."—Pages 3 and 4 of original minutes of the June, 1852, conference.

289. Joseph Smith III Designated by Father

QUESTION

A recent issue of the "Saints' Herald" contains the statement, "When Joseph Smith III appeared before the Amboy Conference of the Reorganization to accept the presidency, for which he had been designated by his father, and by revelation . . ."

Please give references that indicate the correctness of this statement.

ANSWER

If eyewitness testimony can establish fact, it is certain that Joseph III was designated by his father to succeed him as the leader of the church.

Joseph Smith III stated at various times that he was designated. To be specific, we give the verbatim sworn testimony he gave in what is known as the Temple Lot Suit.

296

"About my selection by my father to be his successor in office, I remember of being called in his office or in a room adjoining his office, and receiving the laying on of hands, and a prophetic blessing or setting apart, whatever it may be called. I remember that, and also remember that just before his departure to Carthage, with a number of others, I was called into a room in the Mansion House, and there again received the laying on of hands, and the blessing. I was also present at a meeting in a grove near the temple, and I remember my father laying his hands on my head, and saying to the people that this was his successor or was to be his successor. I remember some of the parties that were on the stand, a few of them I remember, but do not remember all of them. William Marks, George J. Adams, and I think Willard Richards were on the stand."—Abstract of Evidence, page 40, paragraph 52.

Furthermore, James Whitehead, personal secretary to Joseph Smith, Jr., until his death, is on record in the same case. In sworn testimony he said,

"The church did take action as a body on the question of the ordination of young Joseph as his father's successor. The church consented to it . . . at a meeting held in a grove at the east end of the temple . . . Joseph Smith had been preaching that day, and at the close of the sermon made the announcement to the congregation, that his young son, Joseph, had been appointed as his successor."—Abstract of Evidence, pages 27, 28, and 33.

Another witness, John Carter, also bore the following sworn testimony:

"Joseph Smith came on the stand leading his son, young Joseph, and they sat him down on a bench at the prophet's right hand, and Joseph got up and began to preach and talk to the people, and the question he said was asked by somebody, 'If Joseph Smith should be killed or die, who would be his successor?' And he turned around and said, pointing to his son, 'There is the successor,' and he went on and said, 'My work is pretty nearly done,' and that is about all he said in regard to his son . . . and he pointed to his son, young Joseph, who was sitting at his side, and said he, 'There is your leader.'"—Abstract of Evidence, page 180, paragraph 377.

Lyman Wight, who with Joseph Smith, Jr., was in jail at Liberty, Missouri, in 1839, bore testimony on one occasion of designation by

297

blessing. In a letter to the editor of the *Northern Islander*, July 1855, is found the following,

> "Now, Mr. Editor, if you had been present when Joseph Smith called on me shortly after [we] came out of jail to lay hands with him on the head of a youth and heard him cry aloud 'You are my successor when I depart,' and heard the blessing poured on his head. I say had you heard all this, and seen the tears streaming from his eyes, you would not have been led by blind fanaticism or a zeal without knowledge."—See *History of Reorganized Church*, pages 789-791.

The previously given testimonies evidence that the spirit of revelation vouchsafed the call to those present. Joseph III stated, "In Liberty Jail, the promise and blessing of a life of usefulness to the cause of truth was pronounced upon our head . . . and by the Spirit confirmed through attesting witnesses" (*Saints' Herald*, Volume 14, page 105).

In 1868 Jason W. Briggs said,

> "In 1851 certain intelligence was communicated by the Holy Spirit respecting the purpose to redeem the Latter Day Saints from the thralldom of false guides and false practices, growing out of false doctrines . . . at which time the scattered Saints, like sheep without a shepherd, were seeking unto the God of Israel— who is a God of revelation—to raise up the one mighty and strong to set in order the house of God [the church], according to His promise.

> "Had the Lord a right to answer those prayers? Or have we a right to believe He has, seeing there was no accredited prophet, seer, revelator, etc.?

> "Having received the answer, the Saints in conference, with the instruction in that answer, in A.D. 1853, did begin to organize the quorums, by commandment to prepare the way for the chosen prophet, who should perfect the same, and preside in the stead of him who had been taken."—*Saints' Herald*, Volume 14, No. 3. pages 33, 34.

290. Joseph Smith III Selected as President

QUESTION

How was Joseph Smith III selected as president of the church?

Doctrine and Covenants, Section 43, paragraph 2, states that the designation of a successor to the prophet was the responsibility of the incumbent leader. Young Joseph testified, as did others a number of times, of his "blessing" which was bestowed by his father and which designated him as successor. This has been contradicted by some of those who were ambitious for leadership, but the evidence shows it to be factual. Upon this basis Joseph Smith III was accepted by common consent at the conference of the Reorganization in 1860. The provision had been made according to the law given, and fulfillment only awaited the designated one's readiness. Evidence of specific spiritual guidance at the time of the implementation of the calling is abundant.

291. Ordination of Joseph Smith III

QUESTION

By what authority did those officiating in ordination of Joseph Smith III act?

ANSWER

Joseph III was ordained president of the church at Amboy, Illinois, on April 6, 1860. In the *History of the Reorganized Church*, Volume 3, page 251, it is stated that those acting were Zenas H. Gurley, Sr., and William Marks.

Another reference in the *Autobiography of William W. Blair*, a contemporary in the early days of the Reorganization, states that Samuel Powers, Z. H. Gurley, W. W. Blair, and William Marks were participants. These two references are not in conflict as those named in the first statement are included in the second. It would be natural to assume the statement of W. W. Blair to be a more complete account as he was present and testified to participation.

The minutes of the Amboy Conference in 1860 did not record who was the spokesman.

The officiating ministers ordained Joseph III by authority of their office in the Melchisedec priesthood. It should be noted that both William Marks and Z. H. Gurley, Sr., were members of the Melchisedec priesthood in the days of Joseph the Martyr.

Z. H. Gurley, Sr., was ordained an elder in June, 1838, and later a seventy at Far West. Our *Church History,* Volume 3, page 744, makes reference to a reported ordination to the President of Seventy at Nauvoo but comments that there is no existent record of the event. That he held the Melchisedec priesthood in the early church is indisputable.

William Marks was a high priest in the early church and at the time of the death of Joseph Smith was president of the Nauvoo Stake and of the High Council there.

The remaining two—though not ordained, according to our information, in the days of Joseph, Jr.—received their ordination through those who were. The Reorganized Church has taken the stand that those who were affiliated with the factions in the days of uncertainty and confusion after the apostasy of Young and others did not necessarily invalidate priesthood legitimately conferred. If there is no evidence of violation of principles of conduct or of priesthood, ordination remains valid. Ordinations by those with authority would therefore be legitimate (General Conference Resolution 72; conference minutes of 1906, pages 919, 920).

It is of interest to note that those who did not depart in principle or practice were still of the Church of Jesus Christ. The original movement was not completely lost and, though partially disorganized, was again set in order and continues in the Reorganization. The conference at Beloit, Wisconsin, in 1852, was definitely of this opinion, and this is so stated in the minutes of the day:

> "Resolved, That we believe that the Church of Christ organized on the 6th of April, A.D. 1830, exists as on that day wherever six or more Saints are organized according to the pattern in the Book of Doctrine and Covenants."—Pages 3 and 4 of original minutes of the June, 1852, conference.

292. Nephite Priesthood

QUESTION

What was the priesthood of the Nephite leaders? Specifically is there any evidence of the Melchisedec priesthood in the Book of Mormon?

ANSWER

This has been a puzzling question to many, and, therefore, I am sure will be of general interest to our readers. Some have felt that the stated loss of the Melchisedec priesthood at the death of Moses and what has been regarded as a restoration of this authority at the time of Christ must apply also to the ancient American church. If the Book of Mormon migrations left a people who were without the Melchisedec priesthood in the period around 600 B.C., Moses having died many centuries before, they consequently could take only the Aaronic priesthood with them to the new world. This view holds that Christ restored the Melchisedec priesthood to the Nephites when he visited this continent. (See also Mormon 4:87; Moroni 2:2; III Nephi 8:71-73.)

One point is made for this view—that III Nephi 8:71-73 tells of Christ's giving authority to lay on hands for the conferral of the Holy Spirit. It is reasoned that if that authority (the Melchisedec priesthood) was already held, why the special dispensation? No laying on of hands for confirmation is mentioned in the Book of Mormon before Christ.

The other point of view is that there is indication of the Melchisedec priesthood earlier, and particularly after 100 B.C. in the time of Alma. To support this Alma 2:28 is quoted:

"And thus in the commencement of the ninth year of the reign of the Judges over the people of Nephi, Alma delivered up the judgment seat to Nephihah, and confined himself wholly to the high priesthood of the holy order of God, to the testimony of the word, according to the spirit of revelation and prophecy."

If Alma 9:69-73 is read in conjunction with this, the "priesthood of the holy order of God" will be seen to be the priesthood of Melchisedec. There are many references to this "holy order" in Alma and also in Ether 5:11 which should be read in this connection.

A missing factor in this interpretation is the fact that nowhere is there found a record of the manner in which the Melchisedec priesthood was restored before Christ, nor am I aware of any specific time being indicated.

This statement of the two points of view takes into account the fact that Doctrine and Covenants 83:4 c states that the holy priesthood ceased with Moses, though "the lesser priesthood continued." If the statement in Doctrine and Covenants is taken as inclusive or universal, we have an anomaly. If we choose to interpret it as referring only to the old world, we have no anomaly. Frankly, I do not know what justification there is for this latter deduction. I simply leave the case for the reader's meditation.

293. Aaronic and Levitical Priesthoods

QUESTION

Is there distinction between the Aaronic and Levitical priesthoods?

ANSWER

The key to your question is found in Numbers, chapters 3 and 18, which I suggest you read in this connection.

Aaron, a son of Levi, was chosen to minister in the priest's office (Exodus 28). Chosen with him were his four sons, but two were unfaithful, following after strange gods in the wilderness of Sinai.

Therefore we are told Moses revealed the will of God as touching the ministry still necessary to be performed. The tribe of Levi was called to assist Aaron and his sons in certain matters. The Aaronic priests were to continue to minister in the priest's office before the altar, but the sons of Levi were to assist in the temporal duties associated with the tabernacle. We must remember that the tabernacle had to be carried from place to place and erected and set in order in each location. To Aaron and his sons and successors fell the responsibility of supervising the temporal side of the tabernacle ministry and of performing certain significant rites under the general leadership of Moses. The Levites had a responsibility attached to the particular sanctuary. They had the care of the treasury and of the sacred vessels, and other such things.

We depend on modern revelation for a more complete understanding of these ministries. According to Doctrine and Covenants 17:10 the Aaronic priest is to assist the Melchisedec priesthood in its spiritual functions as well as minister before the congregation in certain rites. As the Aaronic priest is to the high priesthood so is the Levitical to the Aaronic. This is explained in Doctrine and Covenants as follows:

"And again, the office of elder and bishop are necessary appendages belonging unto the high priesthood.

"And again, the offices of teachers and deacons are necessary appendages belonging to the lesser priesthood, which priesthood was confirmed upon Aaron and his sons."—Doctrine and Covenants 83:5 a, b.

Because of the general supervision of the temporal ministries being under the Aaronic order both Aaronic and Levitical offices are often grouped under the title Aaronic.

It remained for the concept of priesthood to be deepened in the later revelation of Jesus Christ, and, though in Old Testament times the functions of certain ministers were more mechanical, we realize today that all functions are spiritually directed. Whether the ministry is by temporal or spiritual procedures the function of all priestly activity is to make God known to men.

294. New Testament and Aaronic Order

QUESTION

If we believe that our priesthood is patterned after the priesthood of the New Testament, where in the New Testament does it give reference to the Aaronic order of priests as continuing?

ANSWER

There is no specific text in the New Testament which you may say makes a complete statement to that effect. However, this conclusion is arrived at by studying the New Testament books.

It is not correct to hold that the record of the complete organization is outlined in the New Testament, although there is sufficient for us to be confident of the organization patterned by Christ for the fulfillment of his purpose.

It has remained for revelation in this Restoration era to supply the understanding necessary for the functioning of priesthood organization. Upon this we depend for our church polity.

The writers in the New Testament take the priesthood function for granted, and this may account for the lack of the specific statement you seek.

The Hebrew letter certainly reflects the accepted understanding of priesthood status in the New Testament when it records "And no man taketh this honor unto himself, but he that is called of God, as was Aaron" (Hebrews 5:4).

295. "Some" in Ephesians 4:11

QUESTION

Please explain the word "some" in the following text of Ephesians 4:11: "And he gave some, apostles; and some, prophets; and some . . ."

ANSWER

The problem here is one of expressing in English a meaning that is clearer in the original languages. Consequently it is helpful to turn to other translations that have been made. The Inspired Version has no additional help here as the text is identical.

The English revised version inserts "to be" after the word "some," thus giving the meaning more clearly. It reads, "And he gave some to be apostles." Moffatt and Weymouth and others follow this translation.

The Peshitta, which is the Authorized Bible of the "Church in the East" and which uses the ancient Syriac as its source, renders the verse in question, "And he has assigned some as apostles and some as prophets. . . ." The English translation (1957) from which I quote is by George M. Lamsa, an Asyrian scholar. By the way, he translates the Lord's Prayer (Matthew 6:14, I.V.) as "and do not let us enter into temptation."

The New English New Testament (1961) gives the passage, "And these were his gifts: some to be apostles, some prophets. . . ."

The emphasis in Ephesians 4, as in I Corinthians 12, is on God's gifts rather than the definition of priesthood. Paul is concerned with the concept of the unity of Christ's body and the fact that God gave to the church various gifts, including those of the various officers, which all work to one end. It is a narrower interpretation to limit arbitrarily the word "gifts" to the first nine enumerated. The emphasis, then, is upon God's giving some "as apostles," and so forth, to the church.

296. Deacon Defined

QUESTION

Is there any clear definition of the office of deacon in the Bible? I know the Doctrine and Covenants mentions deacons but I am unable to find scriptural outline of their duties.

ANSWER

There is very little definition of any particular office in the New Testament. The function of some can be seen in a broad way, for instance, the twelve and seventy. The type and quality of the ministers of the gospel is spelled out in several places, but in most cases even this has to be gleaned from the various pieces of counsel and instruction to the saints and ministry in general.

The word "deacon" occurs in only two chapters in the Bible: in Philippians 1:1 and I Timothy 3:8-12. In the latter text it appears four times and is concerned with the character necessary in one holding this office.

It is noteworthy that these passages are also the only references to the office of bishop in the New Testament. Christ is called the "Shepherd and Bishop of your souls" (I Peter 2:25).

The office of deacon is commonly associated with the incident recorded in Acts 6:1-6 where seven men are chosen to assist the twelve by relieving them of "serving tables." However, these men were not called deacons in the text. One of the seven (Philip) is later called an evangelist (Acts 21:8).

References are numerous in the various writings after the New Testament period. A study of the early writings suggests that the deacon is an assistant to the bishop. In this setting he is pictured as serving him in both liturgical and pastoral responsibilities. Doctrine and Covenants 104:8 makes the office of bishop associated with the presidency of the Aaronic priesthood. The post-New Testament records would bear this assistant relationship out, as Doctrine and Covenants 17:11 d places the deacons as an appendage to the Aaronic order.

However, the historical presentation of the later writings indicates the deacon as a more senior minister than the concept that Doctrine and Covenants provides. Their ranking after the first century appears as third in line—that is, bishops, elders, and deacons.

So you see there is no clear picture of the deacon's duties in any scripture. The Book of Mormon fails to mention the office at all.

Then how do we define their duty today? Based on the principles already referred to and their place in priesthood orders as set out in Doctrine and Covenants (sections 17, 83, 85, 104, 118, 120, and 122) the various functions now associated have gradually become definitized as comprising the deacon's duties.

Out of experience and light coming to the leaders and the church the General Conference of April, 1900, formally adopted Resolution No. 471 as official. This is the basis of present functioning.

297. Basis of Ordinations

QUESTION

Would it be lawful for a presiding officer to ordain his son to the priesthood on the grounds that the priesthood descends from father to son?

ANSWER

No. This is not in harmony with the laws and procedures of the church. The scriptural basis is that no man may take or be given the honor of priesthood without being called of God "as was Aaron" (Hebrews 5:4).

There are a number of scriptural references which indicate that lineal descent of priesthood is both a historical fact and a logical expectancy. Characteristics, physical and mental, are undoubtedly transmitted, and it seems that one's heredity and background may well be factors in the spiritual matters, such as priesthood capacity. For instance, Doctrine and Covenants 130:9 states that "the sons of the leading officers of the church are called and may be chosen to the respective offices to which the spirit may direct."

Two factors are here to be noted—namely, calling and choosing by direction of the Spirit. In this connection the words of Jesus are helpful: "for many be called, but few chosen" (Matthew 20:16).

The calling may be considered as one's potential. The choosing depends on a number of factors—preparation, quality of life, needs of the Saints, maturity. Those charged with the responsibility of voicing calls should be constantly aware of the need for the movement of the Holy Spirit in direction as to when a call to priesthood should be voiced and implemented.

Many times in my experience as an administrative officer, I have been made aware by inspiration of the calling of a man to an office. I have made it a practice not to act on this until further light and inspiration have been granted as to the time of ordination. This has often resulted in rich confirmation and effective service in the one ordained.

The law also provides for approval of calls by higher administrative officers, and my experience here again indicates the wisdom of this procedure. This does not necessarily question the validity of a man's calling, but it does offer opportunity to be assured that the necessary standards have been obtained. Spiritual guidance is available and experienced at this level as well as at the branch level.

298. Ordaining Negroes

QUESTION

Doctrine and Covenants 116:4 states, "Be not hasty in ordaining men of the Negro race." Is this not opposed to the fact that we believe God calls men to ministry?

ANSWER

This was given in 1865 at the end of the American Civil War. To minister effectively one must be accepted socially. Hasty action at that time would not have changed the attitude of those who held deep racial prejudice, and the ordinations would have been fruitless.

There is more than one factor involved in the call and ordination of men to priesthood. First, God does not place men in ministerial authority without the acceptance of those to whom they must minister (see Doctrine and Covenants 17:16 a). The acceptability of a minister is vital to his successful work. Where race prejudice is high, conditions may nullify the good a minister may achieve.

Responsibility is placed upon those voicing calls not only to be sure of the aptitude and basic ministerial call of the potential minister but also to seek divine light so that the call may be implemented at such a time and under such conditions that he may become effective.

It is conceivable to me that in a reverse situation where a member of the Caucasian race would be ill-received as a minister of the gospel among members of another race his call would be subject to the same counsel of caution as in Section 116. When people of all groups realize in their hearts that they are children of the one Father, undesirable barriers will automatically be dissolved and freed from prejudice, and the caution of the nature suggested in the text will not be required.

299. Standing Ministers

QUESTION

Following an admonition in Doctrine and Covenants, Section 83, paragraph 21, that every man should stand in his own office, and labor in his own calling, paragraph 22 states that "the high priests should travel, and also the elders, and also the lesser priests; but the deacons and teachers should be appointed to watch over the church, to be standing ministers unto the church." What is the extent of the calling of deacons and teachers as standing ministers? Would they be overstepping the boundary of their calling to preach in another branch at the invitation of its pastor?

ANSWER

Deacons and teachers are primarily ministers of the local branch. General Conference Resolution 449 reads:

"Resolved, That in our judgment teachers and deacons are authorized by the law to labor as preachers within branches to which they belong, when they are presidents thereof, or with the advice and consent of the chief presiding officer."

The preamble of the resolution quoted states: "Whereas, In Section

83, paragraph 22, teachers and deacons are limited in their duties to local service . . ."

This is self-explanatory, but it still must be understood in the spirit of the law. If applied too strictly and purely to branch activity, no deacon could function in his office at district or World Conference. This was surely not intended.

The intent of the law is that the deacon's services are specifically related to his branch. He should not forget this in attempting the work to which others are called, nor should he normally be asked to function in spheres not covered by the preceding rules.

Actually, invitations to work out of one's designated office or assignment should be accepted only if and when cleared by one's administrative officer. This, according to recent counsel from the First Presidency, is the principle by which those who have General Church assignments also function. It is a reasonable provision, and both rule and courtesy would suggest this at all times.

300. Ministering

QUESTION

If a member of the priesthood does not succeed in ministering to a particular individual, is the failure to respond always the fault of the individual?

ANSWER

Many factors enter into the reasons for any degree of unsuccessful ministry. Personalities are complex, and the relating of lives to each other requires much skill as well as the prerequisite of a sincere love and mutual respect.

Being ordained to an office is no guarantee of perfect skill in the carrying out of the various responsibilities as they affect the lives of people. Where a member of the priesthood has not magnified his office by study of the necessary skills in human relations, to this extent he is unable to reach the objective of gaining response from those he seeks to help.

On the other hand, one cannot be ministered to in a given situation if he is unwilling to receive. A closed mind or heart prevents the receiving of many blessings which God may desire to bestow through the ministry.

Even Christ did not have success in reaching some hard hearts and prejudiced minds, but he promised through John the Revelator:

308

"Behold, I stand at the door, and knock; if any man hear my voice, and open the door, I will come in to him, and will sup with him, and he with me."—Revelation 3:20.

It may be that one minister will succeed in being of help where another may not, and no particular blame would be attached to the one who fails. Notwithstanding what I have said, I do not feel that a minister should give himself any easy alibi; he should make diligent preparation, both broadly and specifically, to meet the need of the moment.

A minister has many aids in doing this, and the prayerful approach will be of the greatest value in producing in him such a loving attitude to those who need him that this will be felt and resistance melted. The intended recipient is always and must remain free to respond or not to do so.

301. Preaching and Priesthood

QUESTION

Do all who are called to the priesthood have to preach, or are there other gifts which may qualify men for ministry, though they are unable to be preachers?

ANSWER

The functions of priesthood as given in the Doctrine and Covenants, particularly Section 17, include preaching as an important medium of ministry. General Conference Resolution 449 has interpreted the intent of the law to include teachers and deacons in their branches, with the advice and consent of the presiding officer.

We should not minimize the value of preaching as a means of grace to those in need of the gospel message. Today we are learning to use many modern vehicles for the message and as aids to ministry, but preaching has that which no substitute has equaled in moving people to respond in heart and mind.

Having recognized the importance of this calling to preach, we must observe that to preach is only one of a number of duties of priesthood. To be "slow of speech" as Moses was is not a shame. It may be that one's ability to teach, counsel, minister in the home or in the temporal areas of the church life may be one's primary gift.

I recall men whom I have never known to preach a formal sermon but whose ministry of a personal but less obvious nature has been unsurpassed. Where branches have an adequate number of standing

309

ministers who are qualified in the ministry of preaching it might well be that some others may never so function. However, it is important to be able to preach, and a minister should seek to qualify to the best of his ability. Preaching will never be outdated.

302. Tobacco and Priesthood

QUESTION

Has the General Church made a definite ruling in regard to men holding the priesthood and the use of tobacco? Is it permissible to ordain a man to any office in either the Aaronic or Melchisedec priesthood if he is addicted to the use of tobacco?

ANSWER

The church has spoken on the use of tobacco on several occasions. Three World Conference references indicate the general principle by which the church counsels its members and priesthood as to their stewardship in this connection. They are as follows:

"That this conference deprecates the use of intoxicating drinks (as beverages), and the use of tobacco, and recommends, to all officers of the church, total abstinence."—General Conference Resolution 92. Adopted April 9, 1868.

"That this body declares that the use of tobacco is expensive, injurious and filthy, and that it should be discouraged by the ministry."—General Conference Resolution 217. Adopted September 13, 1878.

"Whereas, The Lord has spoken against the use of tobacco and strong drink on different occasions; and

"Whereas, In all our appointments we ought to show respect unto said counsel. Therefore

"Resolved, That henceforth we recommend no man for General Conference appointment whom we know to be addicted to either of the above evils."—General Conference Resolution 463. Adopted April 16, 1898.

Since these resolutions have been passed a growing understanding of the obligation of the priesthood to be good stewards and examples in the various areas of life has brought the realization that one who has not measured up in this respect cannot effectively stand in priesthood relationship to the members.

A person who is addicted to the use of tobacco is not ordained today

310

to any office in the priesthood. Though this has not been affirmed as law in so many words, it is our practice growing out of a study of the counsel given to us in the revelations and the voice of the church as to the detrimental nature of the habit.

"Men of God, who bear the vessels of the Lord, be ye clean in your bodies and in your clothing; let your garments be of a sober character and free from excess of ornamentation.

"Avoid the use of tobacco and be not addicted to strong drink in any form, that your counsel to be temperate may be made effectual by your example."--Doctrine and Covenants 119:3 c, d.

It is now a well-attested fact that tobacco smoking is a contributing cause to lung cancer and a number of debilitating diseases, and though tobacco interests are reluctant to admit the connection for obvious reasons, the most recent statements of the American Cancer Society warn of the dangers involved.

In consideration of all the factors of personal hygiene, economic waste, and detrimental effect on the body, administrative officers do not endorse the ordination of users of tobacco. It is a standard of stewardship we quite rightly expect of ordained men with respect to their personal and spiritual obligations.

On this basis approval for ordination of users of tobacco should not be given.

303. Priesthood Calls

QUESTION

It is stated that "high priests within the stakes are approved by these high councils. Ordinations of others are dealt with by the high council of the seat of the presidency." Does this mean that elders and the Aaronic priesthood calls are to be processed only through the Standing High Council?

ANSWER

No, those referred to are high priests who do not come within the jurisdiction of a stake. These would be calls to the high priesthood of those resident in districts, in branches, in unorganized territory, and men under Conference appointment.

304. Administrative Positions

QUESTION

I desire to know if positions in the various departments of the church may be held by other than priesthood members. I have noticed that

311

those in administrative responsibilities at headquarters are ministers. Is this a rule?

ANSWER

The church is governed through priesthood, and definite responsibilities are vested in the priesthood offices. The general administrative guidance is naturally the responsibility of ordained men and therefore in the overall sense by the First Presidency. All quorums and members have access to the World Conferences through defined channels, but the administrative responsibilities rest in the presiding officers.

Members of the First Presidency may call to their aid in the departments those who by aptitude, training, and skill are best fitted to assist. The Doctrine and Covenants gives preaching, teaching, expounding, and exhortation as functions of ministry. Ministers also have in addition the right to administer ordinances according to their office. As, for instance, teaching is a primary duty of ministering, it is logical that priesthood be given primary consideration in this connection. This is not to say that others may not teach. Those not of the priesthood may supervise the work of the church school, the women's department, youth, children, etc., but it must be noted that these officers work under the direction of the pastor, district, stake, or area administrator who must be of the priesthood and in all but branch presidency must be of the Melchisedec order. Some of those who assist in the work of departments are elected, and some (as in the case of class teachers) are appointed.

On the General Church level it is logical that where the work is in line with priesthood responsibility ordained men be so used. There are exceptions here, too: in the case of the General Women's Council (of which there is a chairman) and in the case of girls' work, women must be chosen, but they work in close contact with the Presidency.

305. Reinstatement Status

QUESTION

If a member of our church holding the priesthood withdraws and joins another church, what is his status as to priesthood if he realizes his error and is granted reinstatement as a member?

ANSWER

When a person relinquishes his status as a member of the church, provided there is no cause for official action because of some offense, and should he request reinstatement and this is granted, he is as a minister under silence. This means that his priesthood may later be restored by administrative action. This obviously would depend on evidence being shown of a commitment to the work of the church to justify such restoration of ministerial privilege. No new call or ordination is necessary under these circumstances.

This is not true of expulsion which requires rebaptism to reenter the church, and such a reentry does not carry with it any priesthood status.

306. Wife of Priesthood Member

QUESTION

In what relation does the wife of a member of the priesthood stand? Is she also called to his ministry?

ANSWER

Behind almost every devoted member of the priesthood stands a devoted woman. Mothers, wives, and sisters have places of undying respect in the history of the church in all ages. When a man enters the priesthood, his successful ministry depends greatly upon the quality of his homelife and the devotion of his partner to the cause of Christ. In this respect she shares his calling, and fortunate is the man whose partner realizes her role in this part of her husband's life. She may be invaluable as a wise personal counselor to him.

However, it would not be correct to say that she is called to his ministry. Ordination holds certain responsibilities and functional duties to which the man alone is called and in which he as an individual is authorized to minister. A wife is not called to bear the burden of responsibility in these respects. It would not be valid for her to attempt to do so directly or indirectly.

On the other hand the confidence that exists between man and wife cannot be dictated, and this is that part of his stewardship in matters of church concern. Some wives have felt a lack of trust where the minister-husband has not shared confidences, but this would be unjustified. While there are no "vows of secrecy" in the church of Jesus Christ there are many factors that enter into the discreet exercise of redemptive ministry. Others' standing and individual rights are involved in many aspects of priesthood service. The minister must respect the inalienable rights of every soul.

Where complete confidence is the basis of marriage there should be no tendency to feel distrust when either party acts in the light of his personal stewardship. One partner may not share certain confidences

313

in the interest of the other. Ministers' wives have a right to meet their fellows without the problems that face their partners rising in social contact. If the wife were considered as sharing the official priesthood office this could not be so.

A statement that has often helped me may be to the point. It is, "Confidence does not necessarily involve confidences."

There are roles for which men are by nature and endowment constituted. There are similarly roles for which women are by nature and endowment constituted. It is no disrespect to the other for each to fulfill his own role. In fact to endeavor to do otherwise is often disastrous.

307. Authority to Conduct Service

QUESTION

Does a deacon or teacher have authority to conduct a prayer service if no elder or priest is present? If an elder or priest is present can the meeting be conducted by the deacon or teacher?

ANSWER

Yes. Naturally, all members of the priesthood of a branch work under the supervision of the presiding elder. There are some limitations on the teacher and deacon as to their functioning in wider areas than the branch to which they belong, but within the spirit of the instruction that a deacon or teacher's ministry is primarily localized, there seems to be no reason to prevent his so functioning in a prayer meeting under proper circumstances.

See General Conference Resolution 449.

308. Women Leading Worship

QUESTION

Doctrine and Covenants 17 states that the elder is to take the lead of all meetings, but I have often observed women leading worship services in the church school and from the pulpit. Is this not out of order?

ANSWER

No. There are many situations that cannot be provided for by written laws. This is the difference between the Mosaic and Christian eras. The legalistic approach brings many difficulties in its train and not the least the problem of providing every detail in formulated rules. When this is attempted the law binds rather than serves. All formulated laws must be viewed in the light of the historic circumstances surrounding their formulation.

When Doctrine and Covenants 17 was formulated and published in the *Evening and Morning Star* at Independence in 1832, the relative status of priesthood and women was not involved but rather of the relationship of the various priesthood officers. The idea of women functioning in the departments as they do today was not under consideration, and the social status of women was not what it is today in society. In fact the rules governing the establishment of societies in New York state in 1830 provided only for males to be recognized in the organizational meeting. (There must be present "not less than three and not more than nine male members.")

Our movement was one of the early societies to show ·a growing realization of the place of women and to provide for their expression in the church. This was indicated by the commission to Emma Smith to prepare a hymnbook for worship (1830) and her selection as president of the Ladies Relief Society in Nauvoo in 1842.

At the beginning of the church there was very little understanding of the orderly pattern of church government, and a number of specifics had to be laid down as a result of that need. To this end Doctrine and Covenants 17 was compiled. It is not a single revelation but a compilation of rules, explanations, and inspiration for the setting in order of the infant church.

I am sure it was not in the spirit of the Christian church to exclude women from all functions of leadership and participation in meetings when the principle of authoritative priesthood was affirmed and duties were outlined. Departments had not taken their place when Section 17 was edited; therefore the position of women and departments naturally would not be considered in relation to leadership in meetings. It is true that, in the broad sense, priesthood presides over the meetings of the church even if one not of the priesthood is taking a leading part or is at the pulpit or stand.

There is no statement upon which one may postulate a case for ordination of women to the priesthood, but there are incidents where women have been set apart for special duties (Doctrine and Covenants 24:2 c). Reference to this will indicate that Emma Smith was to expound and teach. Some claim that deaconesses were ordained to church responsibility in the New Testament, but whether a deaconess was the wife of a deacon or an officer herself is disputable.

I am not advocating the ordination of women to priesthood (I believe they have their special callings), but I mention the foregoing facts

315

to encourage a wider view than your question would indicate. Paul would not suffer a woman to speak in the church. This attitude was a reflection of his background in society. If we follow a narrow interpretation of scripture we certainly meet problems. No one considers applying Paul's Hebrew or Hellenistic concepts of women's place to these times. I think women can quite rightfully share in the worship functions of the church as they do in the RLDS church today. They do not perform rites because they have not been called and ordained to priestly functions of that nature, but they do bring distinctive services to the body and among them is an enrichment of ministry of worship and of teaching.

309. Quorum Organization

QUESTION

Are high priests, bishops, and patriarchs organized as quorums or groups such as elders, priests, teachers, and deacons? If so, how many are so grouped? What of the seventy?

ANSWER

According to Doctrine and Covenants 104, quorums of elders have 96, priests 48, teachers 24, and deacons 12 members.

All high priests in the church are members of the quorum of high priests unless they belong to other quorums or orders. There is no definite number, and there is only one quorum.

Bishops and patriarchs belong to the high priesthood, but when ordained to their special office they have place in their own order, the order of bishops or the order of evangelists. Both these orders have a presiding officer—the Presiding Bishop and the Presiding Patriarch. Both these men have special place in the church. If a bishop or evangelist ceases to remain in his order he retains the calling of high priest, provided he is in good standing.

The First Presidency, the twelve apostles, the bishops, and evangelists are all of the high priesthood, and the presidency of the high priesthood is the presidency of the church. This office is not the same as the president of the quorum of high priests which is composed of those high priests not functioning in other orders or quorums.

The seventy are chosen from the elders and are not high priests. Provision is made in the law for quorums of seventy elders specially ordained to be missionary ministers, hence the title. There is provision also for seven quorums of seventy and also for seven presidents of seventy who form a council. Each quorum has a president, and the council of seven has a senior president who gives leadership to the council.

310. Quorum Equality

QUESTION

In an "extended apostleship" would not the quorums stated to be "equal in authority" (Doctrine and Covenants 104:11) be placed off balance?

ANSWER

The answer to this is implied in the explanation given to the question as to how the office of one of the Twelve became extended in presidency. This extension of one of the Twelve into the presidency does not imply that he still holds the position in the first named council. A reading of Doctrine and Covenants 145 and 146 will show that the Quorum of Twelve was completely filled in 1960, thus closing the vacancies caused by the ordination of one apostle to the presidency and the release of three others.

311. Patriarchal Functions

QUESTION

I have observed that some patriarchs emphasize revival preaching while others appear to function in the giving of blessings. Why the difference of approach?

ANSWER

Although men are called to a specific priesthood office it is obvious that all are not gifted in exactly the same way. This is evidenced in all the callings whether high priests, elders, priests, teachers, or deacons. There are high priests and elders who rarely preach but exercise their pastoral and administrative gifts in a marked way to the consequent sustaining of the individual members in the faith and therefore of the church as a body. There are undoubtedly very definitely marked lines of office function which indicate the area of ministry, but within these areas there are naturally less clearly defined lines marking differences of ability.

A revelation given to the church through President W. Wallace Smith in October, 1958, explains this in principle. It is as follows:

"While there is but one office in the patriarchal order, there are multiple functions. All my servants who have been called to this office will not be equally proficient in each of the separate functions."—Doctrine and Covenants 145:6 a.

317

The revelation goes on to specify the particular gifts of two of the brethren who had served most faithfully in the Council of Twelve. The statement points out that one had special ability in the areas of giving counsel and advice and was to give blessings. The other was directed to use to the full his marked gift of preaching. Both these brethren, because of their long experience in the leading councils, are qualified in each of the several areas referred to. The direction of the Spirit no doubt was also to meet the needs of souls by pointing the especial gifts of each man toward supplying them. The total function of this order of ministers is evangelical.

312. Origin and Function of Seventy

QUESTION

Please explain the origin and function of the office of seventy in the restored church.

ANSWER

The designation "seventy" is based upon the statement in the New Testament which speaks of Jesus having "appointed other seventy also, and sent them two by two before his face, into every city and place where he himself would come" (Luke 10:1).

The first scriptural reference to the office of seventy in the Restoration is found in Doctrine and Covenants 104:11 e. This does not mean that there was no knowledge of the office prior to that date of this revelation (March 12, 1835). In fact it appears that this revelation, insofar as it pertains to the seventy, was prefaced by divine instruction through Joseph Smith at a meeting of certain church leaders at Kirtland on February 8, 1835. At this meeting Elder Joseph Young was designated as a president of the seventies.

In keeping with this and other subsequent instructions, the church met in council at Kirtland on February 28, 1835, to consider the selection and ordination of presidents and members of the seventy. Forty-five men were chosen at this time. This happened just fourteen days after the first organization of the quorum of apostles which occurred on February 14, 1835. A second quorum of seventies was organized in January, 1836. We have no evidence that there were more than two quorums at the time of the death of Joseph Smith in 1844. The first seventies of the Reorganization were chosen on April 6, 1853.

The function of the seventy is to be special witnesses to the unconverted in all the world (Doctrine and Covenants 104:11 e). Their work is primarily an extension of the missionary function of the apostles. They are members of the Melchisedec priesthood and thus share the basic responsibilities of all of those of this priesthood, but as other officers of this order have specific callings, so the seventies have their primary function of taking the gospel into all the world.

313. Difference between High Priests and Seventies

QUESTION

A discussion arose recently in church school class on the difference in the offices of high priests and seventies. Some thought all seventies were high priests. Will you please clarify?

ANSWER

Seventies are not high priests, and high priests are not seventies. They both hold distinct offices. In the very early days of the church, this was not fully realized, but later the distinction was clearly made and high priests and seventies were placed in their proper quorums.

A seventy is an elder with a specific missionary function. He is ordained from the elders, but this does not make him a high priest.

On the other hand the high priest is ordained to his specific office which has particular functions also. He may travel as a missionary when this is required, but the majority of high priests function primarily as standing ministers. The twelve apostles are high priests ordained to the special responsibility of missionary supervision and as a second presidency. When relieved of apostolic responsibility they remain high priests. Thus they differ at this point from the seventy in that the seventy, if released from the office of seventy, is an elder. Evangelists and bishops are also high priests with one exception (see Doctrine and Covenants 104:32 a and b). All members of the Melchisedec priesthood are described as elders (Doctrine and Covenants 17: 8 b; 104; 122:7, 8, 9).

314. Order of Bishops

QUESTION

What is meant by the Order of Bishops as distinct from a quorum?

ANSWER

A General Conference Resolution of 1918 states:

"Resolved, that the term 'Bishopric,' as used in Doctrine and Covenants 129:8, has reference to the men holding the office of

319

bishop under a presiding head and that these should constitute the Order of Bishops."

Reference to Doctrine and Covenants Section 104:38-44 makes clear the organization of certain priesthood officers into quorums under presidents. The number of priesthood members constituting a quorum is fixed by this section. The size of the select groups known as quorums is as follows: twelve deacons, twenty-four teachers, forty-eight priests, and ninety-six elders. The high priests' quorum has no fixed number. The quorums of seventy when complete have a self-evident number, and there may be seven quorums.

Other functions of high priests properly chosen for specific work include that of the bishopric and the evangelists. Because both of these officers hold the basic office of high priest their groupings are not known as quorums but orders, and their numbers are governed by the needs of the work of the church. The twelve apostles are referred to as the Quorum of Twelve or the Council of Twelve. The First Presidency form a quorum of three high priests. All quorums in the church except high priests have a fixed number. The orders do not. Thus the "Order of Bishops."

315. High Priests to Apostles

QUESTION

Since an apostle is an elder (Doctrine and Covenants 17:8), does he have to be a high priest first?

ANSWER

All ministers of the Melchisedec priesthood are described by the title "elder." The statement that an apostle is an elder simply explains that he is in this priesthood. When a man is ordained to be a member of the Quorum of Twelve Apostles, if he has not previously held the office of high priest this is attended to at the time. The apostles are high priests; therefore a call to this council assumes the ordination involves high priesthood. An apostle is first a high priest, and his high priesthood is extended in his call to apostleship. When his tenure of office in the council ends he is still a high priest.

316. Joseph Smith an Apostle

QUESTION

Was Joseph Smith an apostle?

Yes. The literal meaning of the word apostle is "one sent." Doctrine and Covenants 17:1 refers to both Joseph Smith and Oliver Cowdery as apostles.

However, at this time there had been no Council of Twelve chosen. This was not done until 1835, but these two men were called apostles.

Doctrine and Covenants 139:1 b states concerning the two new members of the First Presidency, J. F. Garver and F. H. Edwards of the Twelve, "Their apostleship is extended in presidency."

317. More than Twelve Apostles

QUESTION

Is there any evidence that there were more than twelve apostles in the early Christian church? Were there more than twelve at one time, and how long was the office maintained?

ANSWER

There were more than twelve apostles.

Paul in his letters describes himself as an apostle and argues his authority. He also includes James (the Lord's brother) and Barnabas in his recognition as apostles. There is the case of Matthias (Acts 1:26) who was chosen to succeed Judas. Claim is made by some students that they can identify about a score of apostles in the New Testament; others dispute a number of these. The fact remains, however, that there were more than twelve. Allowing for the fact that the word apostle often has a general usage describing "one sent," it is certain that this was so.

As to whether there were more than twelve persons actually holding office at one time it appears that Paul, Barnabas, and James were in addition to the original eleven and Matthias at one time. The records are obscure so it is doubtful that this can be proved, but some have seen the possibility of fifteen at one time indicating First Presidency of three other than the twelve. This practice was instituted in the Restoration, and the presidential responsibilities have been referred to as extensions of apostleship.

The office of apostle does not appear to have persisted under that name after the first century. At least there is no record. Gradually the monarchial episcopate—that is, government by bishops—came to be accepted, these claiming succession by apostolic authority.

321

318. Extended Apostleship

QUESTION

*In Doctrine and Covenants 145:3 it is stated that a member of the
Council of Twelve was called to be a counselor to the president and
as a member of the quorum of First Presidency. It is also stated that
his apostleship is extended in presidency. How can an apostleship
be extended in this way? Does this give us fifteen apostles?*

ANSWER

The answer to this depends upon the definition of the word
"apostle." If one sees it as referring only to members of the Council
of Twelve then there is a problem. If, however, the word is defined
in a broader sense as "one sent," it constitutes no real problem because
under this definition to extend one's apostleship means to enlarge
one's mission.

Three quorums have special apostolic missions to fulfill. Members
of the First Presidency are apostles especially appointed to preside
over the whole church. Joseph Smith was called to be an apostle, but
he was not one of the Twelve (Doctrine and Covenants 19:1). There
are occasions when members of the Seventy are regarded in the apostolic
sense. This is clearly stated in Doctrine and Covenants 120:2 d. Here
is found the definition, "those sent."

Members of the First Presidency are not normally referred to with the
title "apostle" but as "president," thus being distinguished from the
Quorum of Twelve Apostles who are described in Doctrine and
Covenants 122:9 as the "second presidency." To have one's apostleship extended is to have one's mission enlarged, and in the case in
question it means being called from among the brethren in the second
presidency into the first presiding quorum of the church.

In the broad sense there are more than twelve apostles, but in the
quorum known as the apostles there are only twelve.

319. High Priesthood and First Presidency

QUESTION

*Should the members of the First Presidency be chosen from among
the high priests?*

ANSWER

Any man may be called to the quorum of the First Presidency, and
if the person were not at that time of the high priesthood this latter

calling would be presumed. However, it has been our observation that those who have been called into the first quorum of the church have been those who have functioned in the Melchisedec priesthood previously and therefore have had, in varying degree, preparatory experience. Often one of the Twelve has been chosen for membership in the First Presidency, but this is by no means obligatory. Floyd McDowell was a high priest when so called, and L. F. P. Curry was Presiding Bishop when he was chosen.

In the early church, and particularly in the organizational period, God chose for senior responsibilities men without previous opportunity for wide experience or functioning in lesser offices. There is no provision in the law which says one must move through progressive stages of ministry and that summit responsibilities are limited to the call of priesthood of certain grades. Although in actual practice men may naturally move to greater responsibility through successive stages, it is not in itself a requirement.

Should a call to an office requiring high priesthood be to one not already ordained, this would be attended to in order that he could move into his quorum responsibility. Your question is largely theoretical, but I have answered on basic principle.

320. RLDS and Utah Section Change

QUESTION

The RLDS edition of the Book of Doctrine and Covenants gives Section 83:6 i as "And all those who come not to this priesthood." The Utah church edition renders it "Woe unto all those who come not to this priesthood." Which is correct?

ANSWER

Reference to a copy of the 1835 (first) edition of the Doctrine and Covenants indicates that a change was made in the Utah edition. The Reorganized text is identical to the original Doctrine and Covenants.

The basis for the alteration is not indicated in the Utah commentaries available in my office. However, the variation does bring the rendering into harmony with some peculiar and unscriptural doctrines expounded in Utah by various leaders since departing from the original body. With these teachings we, of course, cannot agree.

One of the new doctrines taught in Utah is that exaltation in the celestial glory cannot be received without priesthood. Therefore, the rendering "Woe unto all those who come not to this priesthood" would be a supporting text to that error.

323

In a publication, *Doctrines of Salvation,* Volume II, 1955, compiled by Bruce R. McConkie from the works of Joseph Fielding Smith of Salt Lake City, I quote, first from page 37. A caption of a section reads "Priesthood Essential to Salvation."

Again on page 44: "No man can obtain that exaltation without receiving the covenants that belong to priesthood."

Then concerning woman's place, he adds: "No woman can obtain this great honor and glory without receiving the blessings of faith . . . and obedience to the covenants that are promised to her and her husband in the temple of the Lord."

If this were true, it would certainly be woe to one not attaining the priesthood. Admittedly, the passage as contained in the original is somewhat obscure, but I see no justification for adding the word "woe."

321. High Council

QUESTION

Doctrine and Covenants 17:17 states: "Every president of the high priesthood (or presiding elder), bishop, high councilor, and high priest, is to be ordained by the direction of a high council, or General Conference." Specifically, what is meant by a high council in this case? Is this referring only to the Standing High Council of the church?

ANSWER

The reference indicates that "a high council" may approve an ordination to the office of high priest. This is not necessarily the Standing High Council. The fact that paragraph 17 was inserted in Section 17 in 1835 after the organization of the first high council in 1834 at Kirtland, Ohio, and that the broad description is used rather than the more specific "the" indicates the envisioning of other high councils. Later councils were organized in Missouri and Illinois.

The basis for high council organization is found in Doctrine and Covenants 99. A study of paragraph 11 c, d will show reference to "the high council of the seat of the presidency of the church." This indicates the final council of appeal and of highest action on the matters properly coming before it.

Other matters of a particular nature come before the high councils in the respective stakes, and the ordination of high priests within the stake are approved by these councils.

Ordination of others are dealt with by the high council at the seat of the presidency or by the World Conference.

322. Common Council

QUESTION

What is meant by the statement in Doctrine and Covenants 104:37 a where it is provided that if the president of the high priesthood transgress he should be "had in remembrance before the common council of the church"? In answering please explain the term "common council."

ANSWER

Provision is made in the law for a council of twelve high priests, known as the Standing High Council of the church. This was established to deal with "the most important business of the church, and the most difficult cases of the church" which could not be satisfactorily settled at lower levels of judgment. In the regular constitution of this high council, twelve high priests presided over by the presidency of the high priesthood were empowered to make final decisions upon controversies in spiritual matters (Doctrine and Covenants, sections 99 and 104:35).

It is further stated in principle that "There is not any person belonging to the church, who is exempt from this council of the church." Because normally the duty of the presidency of the high priesthood is to administer the law after taking counsel as aforestated, the law also provides that should the president of the high priesthood be personally involved as a transgressor, he would not be in a position to be either a judge of himself or an administrator in such a personal matter. Thus it is provided that "he shall be had in remembrance before the common council of the church, who shall be assisted by twelve counselors of the high priesthood."

I know of no other use of the word "common" in this connection except one which occurs in Doctrine and Covenants 104:33 a, which speaks of the work of a bishop as "a common judge among the inhabitants of Zion." I would think the word would be used in the same way as it is used in describing certain secular courts, *viz*, "court of common pleas," as applying to certain ordinary matters.

Though it is not specifically stated it would be expected that "the bishop of the church" would be the presiding bishop and the common council would be a bishop's court. F. Henry Edwards in *Commentary on the Doctrine and Covenants* (page 345) states succinctly, "This means before the bishop's court." This procedure was not established to facilitate trivial action against the chief minister of the church and could be envisioned as operable only in matters of grave personal charges. It would not apply in matters of administrative objections, since there is ample provision through normal procedures for the settling of these matters. Nor would I imagine that the procedure was instituted to facilitate the pursuance of negative actions by litigious individuals.

323. Family Limitation?

QUESTION

Please explain Doctrine and Covenants 87:6 f, "Let your families be small." Does this apply only to Joseph Smith, Sr., as to his taking in of others other than his family? Does it have further implications of family limitation?

ANSWER

A full reading of Section 87:6 will show that there is a specific problem of housing under consideration. Provision is suggested for housing for several families—those of F. G. Williams and Sidney Rigdon, counselors to Joseph, and also for Joseph Smith, Sr., patriarch of the church.

Because of the social doctrine of the church and its particular background in Kirtland where this revelation was given, many misconceptions were held by members of the church as to their privileges in connection with the "all things common" ideal. Thus people imposed on church families, especially officials who felt unduly obligated to Christian hospitality. Many needed to be counseled as to industry, and the Lord spoke against idlers, etc.

This imposition placed an undue burden on certain families and required means and time being expended for guests' board, etc., which would have more properly been spent in fulfilling the mission of the gospel. Apparently Joseph, Sr., was overly conscientious in taking in all those who might ask or appear to have need. He was especially mentioned because of this. The principle of wisdom in entertainment applies to our ministerial and missionary families of today as well.

As a boy I remember a member arriving at my father's home from a neighboring state; having been lodged for the time, he stayed on. When approached by one of the bishopric as to his obligations to the missionary family, he replied that he had paid his tithing and thought his sustenance was accounted for. The bishop acquainted him with the true purpose of family allowances, etc. One can imagine where this misconception would lead.

No. I am sure it has no implication in the realm of what is modernly termed "family limitation."

324. Hebrews Questioned

QUESTION

What is the meaning of Hebrews 7:12, Inspired Version, "For the priesthood being changed, there is made of necessity a change also of the law."

ANSWER

The whole chapter must be read to get the context. The writer of Hebrews is explaining to these people that prior to the coming of Christ they have been living under a law of "carnal commandments," that is, living by rules and penalties of an outward nature. The old Mosaic Law was a schoolmaster to bring them to Christ (Galatians 3:24). Now Christ, the great High Priest, has brought them a liberating concept, freeing them from mere obedience for preservation's sake alone and giving them a "law of liberty" which has an inward result rather than an outward form.

Thus the law of love fulfills all that is gained by keeping rules, plus the spiritual advantage of quality of soul. The gospel having been demonstrated in the person of Jesus Christ, there is of necessity a new approach. The new approach is a law of love rather than compulsion. This is what is meant by a change in the law. Carnal commandments involving sacrifices, etc., are no longer needed by those who walk in love. Galatians 3 is an excellent exposition of this.

325. Offices of Presbyter

QUESTION

Alfred Yale's book, "Life and Letters of Paul" (page 52) contains the statement: "Distinguish between 'presbyter' or 'elder' and 'bishop.'" Why do we not have the office called "presbyter"?

ANSWER

There is no distinction between presbyter and elder. The Greek word "presbyter" means "elder." An older form is "presbys" meaning "an old man." The office of elder is ancient, and has come through the Hebrews to the Christian church. Among the Hebrews it first referred to seniority, mainly of age, but gradually it came to have the connotation of a spiritual office. The elders were the leaders of the Hebrew congregation as in the Christian church. The elders as a group in the early Christian congregations are referred to as the presbytery, and the individual members of the presbytery are therefore "presbyters" (I Timothy 4:14; II Timothy 1:6). We think it not correct to insist that to be an elder one would have to be part of an organized council such as the presbytery to be called a presbyter. We do have presbyters in the church in the sense that we have elders, but we do not use the older term.

The term "bishop" specifically means an "overseer." Elders are admonished as "overseers" (Acts 20:17, 28), but the title "bishop" came in time to mean a special "overseer," and according to the revelation to the church in these days the bishop has the temporal responsibilities of the church under his care. He is chosen from the high priesthood, all members of which come under the general classification of elder. It should be noted that the bishop has spiritual oversight, too, but particularly in relation to temporal stewardships as an expression of spiritual principle.

326. Terms in News Reporting

QUESTION

How should the presiding officer of a branch be described in a news report? Should he be referred to as pastor, elder, or reverend?

ANSWER

All members of the Melchisedec priesthood are described by the title elder and may be so designated in any statement. However, there are times when the particular function of a minister needs to be made clear. The word pastor is understood by the general reader to denote the minister supervising a congregation or group of church members. The term is scriptural. The pastoral function in the RLDS church is wider than in Protestant denominations and extends in some ways beyond the work of the presiding minister, but use of the term "pastor" is often justified to make the ministerial relationship clear.

There is no ruling of which I am aware that either endorses or prohibits the use of the title "reverend" to describe a minister of our church. We do not use the word as descriptive of our pastors or other ministers. It is a term used by most Christian denominations to indicate an ordained minister of the gospel but not to describe those they would classify as lay ministers.

This title is not offensive to us when used by a newsman and, in my opinion, there seems to be no reason to make an issue or explain if our men are so described. Documents originating from our church sources do not use the title but use a description in keeping with the function of the priesthood officer concerned. In connection with your particular question a presiding officer of a branch could be described thus: "Elder Brown, pastor of the Greenville congregation of the RLDS Church."

Church Organization and Procedures

327. RLDS and Protestant

QUESTION

In "Restoration: a Study in Prophecy" by E. A. Smith, it is stated that our church is not Protestant. Please explain.

ANSWER

This statement is based upon the reasoning that the so-called Protestant denominations owe their existence to the fact that they stem from the Roman Catholic organization. Their early leaders are known as reformers and had obtained their initial ministerial authority from the parent church. Luther was a priest of the Roman Church and protested vigorously against certain doctrines and practices. The dominant church did not tolerate this, and the result is a matter of history. Luther's followers were truly protestant. On the other hand the Church of England had its rise in other difficulties having to do with the papal disciplines applied to King Henry VIII. The refusal to accept the rulings of the Pope resulted in the established church in England. Many Anglicans thus reject the term Protestant, considering their church to be a part of the Catholic body. Certainly because they proceeded upon lines centered in the English monarchial leadership as separated from Rome, reforms have taken place in teaching and practice, but this has also occurred within the Roman Catholic Church.

Other churches stemmed from the initial reformers and depend for their authority upon their original priestly connections. John Wesley made attempts to revitalize the English church but his work was unacceptable within that body and his follows eventually became

Wesleyans. Wesley depended on the channel of priestly autho. handed down originally from the Pope by the Archbishop of Canterbury.

With all this in the background we see Joseph Smith's announcement of a restoration of priesthood authority which, according to Latter Day Saints, was made necessary by the apostasy of the Roman Church. The fact of an apostasy is attested not only by the very existence of the reforming churches which are generally described as Protestant but also by the counterreformation which took place within the Catholic Church itself.

Because our church depends upon its claim of a new and specific dispensation of authority to Joseph Smith and Oliver Cowdery, it is not strictly correct to class the church as Protestant unless, of course, it be reasoned that the movement protested the errors of all bodies both Roman and reformed. The difference is between reformation and restoration.

328. Present-Day Gentiles

QUESTION

Are the people of the present-day church Gentiles?

ANSWER

A Gentile is one not of Hebrew blood. The concept that those born into the church by baptism became "Israel by adoption" led to an early practice of calling others not of the church Gentiles. This is purely an older usage.

Paul pointed out that all those who claimed the blessings of Israel because of birth were not necessarily truly of the chosen group, *viz:* "They are not all Israel which are of Israel" (Romans 9:6).

Racially one is a Gentile if not of the Hebrew blood, but in the spiritual family all are of Israel who are spiritually members of the household of God. Paul also said that in Christ all are one, whether Jew or Gentile, bond or free (see I Corinthians 12:13).

329. RLDS Church and World Council of Churches

QUESTION

Does the RLDS Church belong to the World Council of Churches?

ANSWER

No. Though our relationships with and membership in various

331

local and area committees of interdenominational councils are good in in most places, no formal affiliation has been made with the national or world council.

In Independence, Missouri, our headquarters, our ministers belong to the Ministerial Alliance, and at times one of our ministers has held the chairmanship. This is true in other areas and countries but does not carry with it affiliation with the councils with which your question is concerned.

Previous to these times when ecumenical feeling was not as advanced as it is today affiliation would have required a more narrow and rigid definition of faith than a movement such as ours would feel justified in subscribing to.

As far as I know there is no official movement either by this church or the World Council to change the situation. Certainly relationships are friendly, and at times our officials enjoy attending conferences and such activities as observers.

This is a matter of policy which must be officially determined, and there is no Conference action on the matter.

330. Use of Pulpit

QUESTION

Can a member of the church not holding priesthood use the pulpit when speaking or offering prayer? Can he assist an elder in this way?

ANSWER

There is no rule that I know of, either scriptural or by General Conference resolution, that would prohibit any person from speaking from a pulpit.

The pulpit is not an altar in the sacramental sense. We do not have provision for altars in the sense that there is a sacred spot that is desecrated by the trespass of those other than ordained men. The Communion table may be said to become an altar when the Saints present themselves before the emblems and members of the priesthood officiate in their office. But this is because of the nature of the sacrament being performed, the right to actual administration and prayers of blessing being reserved for priesthood only. There is no "holy of holies" in the truly Christian church building. This was a "type" under the old law and for a purpose now fulfilled.

This question constantly arises, possibly because of a confusion arising from a carry-over from the Mosaic Law. True followers of Christ in the Restoration have never instituted "holy places" which are restricted from use by any of the members. I am sure the day will never come when "no admittance" signs will be found on any of our places of worship or parts thereof.

Of course no one other than one called and ordained may function in the administration of the ordinances involved in priesthood. This does not refer to functions such as prayer, speaking, singing praise, and so on. These are not exclusively priesthood functions. Others than members of the church are often invited to speak to us in our meetings, and if they speak from the pulpit there is nothing amiss. It is generally recognized that the elders are to take the lead of meetings and may invite others to participate. Balanced judgment is necessary, and men of the priesthood should always be used to assist in harmony with their specific callings. But this does not exclude others in the matters under question here.

I quote a paragraph from *Saints' Herald,* Volume 104, page 371 (April 22, 1957), given by Elder Wayne Updike in answer to a similar question:

"One other than the priesthood may offer public prayer at any time or in any position at the invitation of one in charge of the meeting. This applies in all situations other than in offering those prayers which have a specific part in the ordinances, such as the prayers at baptisms, Communion services, ordinations, confirmations, and blessings. Although the pulpit is a place for dignity and respect, it does not in itself constitute an altar. Altars are found in the Restoration at the time when priesthood and membership are in proper relationship within the performance of one of the ordinances. We are counseled to be careful not to change the ordinances, but in other situations all members may participate freely as long as they are amenable to the leadership of the presiding officer so that order and reverence are preserved."

331. Name Confusion

QUESTION

Why was the name Latter-day Saints allowed to be kept by the Utah church and the name Reorganized Latter Day Saints given to the original church? This confuses people and seems to indicate to them that the Utah body is the original.

I, like others, have had to contend with this misunderstanding all my life. Others did likewise for forty years before the turn of the century after the word "Reorganized" became part of our church name.

As a matter of fact, when the dispersed members and branches found opportunity to weld the scattered fragments, they referred to their assembled body as "The Church of Jesus Christ of Latter Day Saints." The first minutes of this reassembled church are captioned: "Minutes of a Conference of the Church of Jesus Christ of Latter Day Saints held June 12th A.D. 1852 at Newark Branch, Rock County, Wisconsin." It is interesting to note in passing that as well as the church name the word "branch" is used to designate the locale.

At the same meeting resolutions were passed which rejected the "pretensions of Brigham Young, James J. Strang, James Colin Brewster, William McLellin, William Smith and Joseph Woods joint claim to the leadership of the Church of Jesus Christ of Latter Day Saints as an assumption of power in violation of the Law of God."

It was also resolved:

"That we believe that the Church of Christ organized on the 6th of April A.D. 1830 exists as on that day wherever six or more saints are organized according to the pattern in the Book of Doctrine and Covenants. . . ."

It is difficult to decide when the word "Reorganized" actually became the final designation, but although this can be pinpointed sufficiently for legal purposes at an early date, it is evident that those concerned with the earliest moves to place the church upon an effective operational basis were faced with using a distinguishing term. And so, first in our publications and then in our documents, the prefix became general usage. One of the major concerns of the Saints was to rid themselves of the odium of Utah polygamy and other apostate doctrines.

Several moves have been made to change this traditional title, but after considerable airing of the pros and cons, both in councils and on the Conference floor, the church has not been prepared to make this change. I think this must be explained to inquiring friends and left to their intelligent reaction. Since so much time has passed, I doubt that it would be practicable to challenge the use of the original name by any group present or past.

332. Is Government Hierarchical?

QUESTION

Is the government of the Reorganized church hierarchical?

First, we must define the word "hierarchy." Its root meaning is found in two Greek words, *hieros* (sacred) and *archos* (a ruler). According to standard encyclopedias, a hierarchy is the organization and orders of the Christian clergy in successive grades. This is further classified in two phases:

1. The hierarchy of orders with powers exercised in worship and administration of the sacraments.
2. The hierarchy of jurisdiction with power over the members of the church.

The description of an ecclesiastical government as hierarchical therefore conveys a concept not in complete harmony with the Restoration church. The church of Rome is an example of a movement described correctly as hierarchical in both senses of the definition given. The direct opposite of hierarchical government is the democratic form of church government where the people are the authority.

There is a definite principle of priestly authority in our church, but it is necessary to distinguish our priesthood concept from the usual connotation of hierarchy. In a true hierarchy there is little democratic expression of authority, and in matters of discipline there is none. Government is dispensed. In a democracy, government is in the hands of the people who make (often through representatives) all the laws and create the authority through which laws are carried out.

Our church form has been described as a theocratic-democracy. In this organization there is in a sense a dual authority fused in a way which envisages no schism in its application. Divine authority is exercised through priesthood but is not expressed in the legal sense without the free and intelligent consideration and consent of the body in general. On the world level this is expressed at a General Conference of ex officio delegates and delegates elected by the membership in the various administrative areas of the church. By the exercise of the principle of common consent, the administrative and sacramental prerogatives of ministry have been defined, as in accepted scriptures and in General Conference resolutions.

Men of the priesthood do not attempt to exert controlling power over members but are vehicles of Christ's ministry as his representative servants. Such standards of discipline, which of necessity apply to membership, are not coercively administered. Therefore it should be stated that there is no lawful hierarchical domination by priesthood. Agency is basic in our belief.

333. Supreme Directional Control

QUESTION

I would like to know whether supreme directional control is a legal tenet of the RLDS church. Does it nullify all things being done by voice and common consent of the local churches and districts? Does the ministerial line extend down from the president through the departments of the church, having precedence over all other church rule?

ANSWER

Your question illustrates the problems created by the use of terms without clear definition or understanding. What you mean by "supreme directional control" may be different from another's definition. Your question is one which cannot be answered at all points by an unqualified yes or no, the classic example of which is "Have you quit beating your wife?" An innocent husband cannot explain his position with either yes or no.

If by "supreme directional control" you mean the unassailable right of any one individual irrespective of any other member, officer, or quorum to dictate action or policy, then I would answer that there is no legal basis for such.

But if you mean that along the administrative line there is legal right and responsibility of decision and implementation of procedure, it must be definitely said that there is invested in duly appointed and/or elected officers the burden and responsibility of such decision and implementation. This is true of the highest executive. These relationships are being more and more understood and defined as our history lengthens. There is ample provision in the law for the correction of misuse or abuse of office. However, in matters of unresolved conflict concerning administration, a decision must rest at some level where the law validates the function of an office. Any other philosophy leads away from common consent and makes for anarchy.

The expression "ample provision in the law" takes into consideration both administrative and judicial institutions which must be respected by all with no exceptions of either those administering or those administered. For instance, the law gives certain officers administrative jurisdiction over branches and districts, and these officers may "set in order" or even rule "out of order" some actions of the lesser conferences you mention. There is always the right of appeal both administratively and judicially (see Doctrine and Covenants, Section 120, paragraphs 4 to 6).

Final responsibility must rest administratively or judicially somewhere, and to argue otherwise is not realistic. In administrative function the highest authority must, therefore, focus in the First Presidency. This is indicated by the word "first." If you substitute for the words "having precedence over all other church rule" used in your question, the words "in harmony with the provisions of the law," I could answer this particular part in the affirmative.

In all this I am assuming that your question refers to no specific existing situation. This column does not trespass upon administrative areas, and only answers involving general principles are considered. You will find a study of the official text, *Rules and Resolutions,* pages 9-15, especially helpful. One may even argue theoretically as to what may or may not be dealt with on a General Conference floor, but the principle that all officers function by the consent of the body and because the right of recall is invested in that body ultimately preserves the inherent rights of the body's self-determination. In this they must abide the consequences, but herein is agency. However, it was not intended that conferences administer.

Because of an emotional tone often associated with the term "supreme directional control," I would prefer to use one such as "final administrative responsibility." Even the word "authority," though completely defensible, has overtones for some, because of a period of tension which now should be viewed in the light which historic perspective brings. I hope I have helped.

334. General Conference Representation

QUESTION

Please explain what the instructions were that were given to Joseph Smith III as mentioned in Doctrine and Covenants 125:7. These were on the rules of representation of General Conferences.

ANSWER

If this information were available it would be most helpful. The details of the recommendations were not placed on record. Presumably they were made orally, and as no verbatim reports of speeches were kept this appears to have been the case. Had they been accepted there would have been record made in the minutes.

The passage is the only reference we have to the fact that these recommendations were made and rejected. The statement reads:

"My servant was directed to present to the church rules of representation, and he so stated to the body at different times tha' he was so led; but the conferences of my people saw proper to change these articles and rules of representation, and propositions are pending that they be still further changed.

"The direction of the Spirit is that they be left as they now are until such time as the increased numbers of the members of the church shall require either an enlargement of the number entitled to delegate, or that there may be a closer line drawn as to the number of delegates which the church shall require to meet."—Doctrine and Covenants 125:7 a, b.

335. Appointing Delegates

QUESTION

When delegates to the World Conference are elected and later some find they will be unable to attend, is there any other authority to appoint others in their place when there are not sufficient alternates at the district conference to fill these places?

ANSWER

There is no authority for the election of delegates to the World Conference other than by vote of the district or stake conference or of the branch in unorganized territory. No officer can be authorized to fill vacancies other than from alternates endorsed by the said business meetings.

General Conference Resolution No. 936 states:

"That the principle of having all delegates selected by vote of the members in the several stakes and district conferences, should be maintained against any action which violates this principle by providing that district officers be empowered to appoint part of the delegates."

336. Right to Vote

QUESTION

The statement is made that ordinations to the priesthood and appointment of the one to preside over the mission should be approved by the branch rather than by the mission. Does this deprive the members of the mission of all right to vote?

This procedure does not deprive the mission members of the right to vote. I am presuming you have the correct definition of a mission in mind, that is, a group of members meeting together as a subsidiary of the main branch.

The basic unit of legislative authority is a branch. Members of any subsection of the branch have their right of vote in the branch business meetings. The appointment of an officer to take charge of any subsidiary grouping of members is a pastoral responsibility; therefore, if there is approval to be given it is at the branch level first. Should a pastor present a name to a mission as pastor, any approval of that group would be purely permissive as an expression of confidence.

All ordinations definitely should be approved by the branch and not the mission. In this vote the mission members share.

Missions usually move somewhat gradually to branch status and assume responsibilities progressively, but until full branch organization is achieved under proper administrative oversight, the branch or district to which the mission is attached is the legislative body in which governing decisions are made.

337. Voting of Baptized Children

QUESTION

Should a child who has been baptized be privileged to vote in business meetings when vital matters such as a budget involving thousands of dollars are under consideration?

ANSWER

The legal right of a baptized child to cast a vote in the business meetings of the church cannot be rightly questioned. Undoubtedly all baptized members have the privilege of casting a vote on all motions brought before assemblies properly constituted to conduct business. This naturally is qualified by the fact that in delegate assemblies only accredited delegates vote. The only qualification ever placed upon the exercise of membership privilege has been that of "membership in good standing" (Doctrine and Covenants 125:9).

Petition was made to the General Conference of 1919 to consider the advisability of some qualifications being added to control the age at which minors should vote. Action was deferred at that time, and a search of the Conference resolutions fails to reveal any subsequent qualifying action.

On the question of the advisability of children exercising a vote where important matters are involved, I would suggest that it is impossible to draw a line as to who would have sufficient comprehension on all matters to make a fully informed decision, whether he be a child or adult. Age alone is not sufficient guarantee. Matters should be presented and studied in such a way that the vote of all members will be intelligently exercised.

338. Method of Voting

QUESTION

Has a branch the right to choose the method by which members vote in a business meeting, that is, by ballot or otherwise?

ANSWER

According to parliamentary procedures based on *Robert's Rules of Order,* a vote may be taken in several ways. Usually a legislative group such as a branch looks to the chairman to arrange proceedings in an orderly way and so suggest the method of voting. However, should the assembly wish to follow a certain method, this may be expressed by a motion properly presented. It may be decided that a vote be taken by "aye" and "no," that is, by voice, by signifying by hand, by standing, by division of the assembly, or by ballot.

A helpful manual, *Parliamentary Procedure in the Church,* by F. L. Young has recently been published by Herald House; in it the accepted procedure for the conduct of these matters is outlined. The rules are explained simply in this manual and I suggest you read it carefully.

339. Secret Ballot in Church Assemblies

QUESTION

Under what circumstances is a secret ballot in legislative assemblies of our church justified?

ANSWER

A secret ballot is permissible if specially provided for by the body. It has been called for on occasions. However, it is undesirable for provision to be made for this to be a standing rule. The reason for this is that the very nature of a secret vote is foreign to the spirit in which our common consent decisions are made. The spirit of unfettered brotherhood should rule so that one may vote openly without offense or being misinterpreted by another in a personal way.

The chairman is normally given the right of deciding how a vote shall be taken, and he may ask for a ballot if voting by preference is necessary where a large number of candidates are nominated. In General Conference the method has usually been to vote by a show of hands on all issues, a procedure which has presented no great difficulty in the highest of our legislative assemblies.

The secret ballot when used for political or partisan reasons is out of harmony with our purposes and attitudes as a people, and paper voting seems hardly necessary in normal-sized gatherings. Of course, as in the case of the Center Stake of Zion—where more than a hundred delegates are to be selected out of a nomination list of perhaps more than two hundred names—there is no alternative but to mark the names of those one desires to vote for on a printed list of the candidates.

In a simple decision on a motion there is usually no reason why a voter should want to avoid indicating his vote. One should have the courage of his convictions. If common consent is interpreted as seeking the will of God together, then one can vote openly in complete confidence.

340. Order of Voting

QUESTION

In a business meeting when a vote is required to elect an officer is it correct to vote on all candidates in the same order in which they are nominated, or should the last nominated be first and so on in reverse?

ANSWER

When election is on nomination and the vote taken by show of hands, the names should be presented in the order they were proposed. This is clearly set out in paragraph 110 of the *Rules of Order,* edited by Frederick M. Smith and endorsed by the church. On page 81 of the more recent reference work, *Parliamentary Procedure in the Church* by F. L. Young, this is clarified as follows:

"Naming candidates by nomination instead of by motion provides greater freedom of action in making choices. Nominations are voted on in the order nominated."

341. Absentee Vote

QUESTION

May a church member absent from his home branch participate in the election of officers by means of an absentee vote?

ANSWER

There is no provision in church law for voting by any other procedure than being present at the duly announced business meeting and casting a vote in person. This is usually done by sign and a counting of those for or against. Even where secret balloting is the procedure, there is no means provided for this to be shared in by other than members attending the announced meeting.

This is a wise custom and in my opinion prevents may abuses of a political nature. That only members present vote assures that all participating have an opportunity of hearing viewpoints presented from various angles and therefore are in a position to make better judgment. I have at times changed my mind after hearing a full discussion of a point at issue. Had I voted as an absentee I would have made a decision based on less information than I received by being present at the formal discussion on the floor.

342. Nonmember Vote

QUESTION

Should a nonmember vote in women's meetings if she is active, pays dues, and contributes to activities?

ANSWER

A person who has not sensed the importance of this church sufficiently to become a member would not normally expect to have a decisive say in the conduct of its activities. One could hardly expect to guide a movement of which one is not a responsible member. No unbaptized person has legislative rights, and in matters of the legislative gatherings of the church under no circumstances can cast a vote.

There is some qualification to be made, however, in respect to departmental participation. The basic legislative function of the church is at the branch level and therefore action initiated by sections of the branch are "permissive." It is difficult to draw an arbitrary line, but it is obvious that sections must make some decisions in keeping with their function.

342

We grow in our understanding of the gospel and the church as we work in it, and many fine members have joined as a result of being drawn into the movement by being included in the activities of the departments.

The responsibility of the branch and its departments is to work toward having these participants become full-fledged members.

An understanding friend and worker in the department would not seek to dominate a program nor should one be allowed to decide the policies and direction of the church. The usual matters discussed at the "business" meeting of these groups would not involve this fundamental. I see no reason why a friend of the church sharing in activities mentioned could not have a share in the minor decisions incident upon usual activities of such a department. The holding of leadership responsibility is another matter. One cannot lead unless one is ahead, and if one is not a baptized member, the first steps have not been taken.

This answer applies only in individual cases, because it must be evident that if there were a number of such participants it would hardly be a church organization.

343. Members Campaigning for Church Offices

QUESTION

Should members campaign for the election to church office of those they favor or for the removal of someone they consider unfit for any reason? Is canvassing of members privately ethical?

ANSWER

It is not in the interest of the church to have campaigns for office prior to the business meeting for election. And canvassing for the election of a particular person often leads to many abuses of the privilege of common consent.

As a rule the place to decide the suitability of a person for office is at the business meeting. However, if there are moral reasons why any person is not fit for office, one should bring the matter to the attention of the presiding authorities responsible before the business meeting so that valid objections may be considered and, if necessary, ministry performed to help the person and protect the church. Christian ethics forbid whispering of tales detrimental to another's standing among the Saints.

I know of no rule that would prevent persons from openly discussing the work of the church and the capability of those who may possibly

343

be chosen to serve. But the thing to keep in mind is that at no time should statements be made in a situation where the accused or criticized one does not have the opportunity to defend his actions or good name.

The scriptures counsel that all things in the church should be done by common consent and by much prayer and faith. Then when the Saints come together in business meeting capacity they should look for divine guidance in their deliberations and choices.

344. Term "Pastoral"

QUESTION

Is the term "pastoral" rightly used to describe a prayer or sermon given by other than the pastor?

ANSWER

Any member of the priesthood could preach, teach, or pray pastorally. A sermon is pastoral in nature when it feeds the flock. In the Communion service the prayer specifically directed to the needs of the people is often listed as the "pastoral prayer." I see no objection to the use of the term. People know who their pastor is and are not likely to misunderstand when the term pastoral is applied to part of the service.

345. Distinction between Branch President and Pastor

QUESTION

Is the branch president also the pastor? If not, what distinguishes the two offices? Is it correct to call all elders "pastors"?

ANSWER

The branch president is the pastor or presiding elder. There is no difference. All standing ministers, however, are pastoral in their calling. All elders may be called pastors in the general sense, such as "pastors of the flock," but this would not denote presidency. If "pastor" is used as a title, it usually indicates the presiding officer. If other than an elder is the branch president, he would be the pastor.

346. When Elder Becomes Presiding Elder

QUESTION

What factors determine when an elder becomes a presiding elder?

ANSWER

The law of the church provides that the presiding elder of the branch be elected by common consent. This is the only determining factor. He may be nominated by an administrative officer or by a member of the branch. The process is the same. It is assumed that the person holding the office of elder is in good standing as such when nominated.

347. When Branch President Is Priest

QUESTION

If the pastor (or branch president) of a branch is a priest, and there is an elder in the branch as well, does the authority of the elder still take precedence over that of the priest in matters pertaining to the business of operating the branch?

ANSWER

There is something wrong in the setup of a branch where it is necessary to elect a priest instead of a member of the Melchisedec priesthood. Of course there may be other factors, such as health, which would make it wise that an elder not be elected. However, where conditions are such that a priest is elected as the president of the branch, he holds responsibility as the president, administratively. This does not include functions of the Melchisedec priesthood in the ordinances which authority he does not possess as an Aaronic priest. That is why I say it is a difficult situation and many of the ministries would be denied to the people. His authority as branch president, however, is unquestioned.

348. Elect Assistant Pastor

QUESTION

Is it correct to elect an assistant pastor, or should the pastor have counselors?

ANSWER

The one administrative officer in a branch provided for in the Doctrine and Covenants is the branch president or pastor (see Section 120:2 a). All other elective officers are permissive and are provided for under the administration of the pastor. The number of officers depends largely upon the size of the branch and the various departments to be administered. Thus a pastor may desire to have an assistant, or he may desire to have counselors. When counselors are chosen they are the choice of the pastor and are sustained as such by the branch.

Each of these officers works only under the direction of the pastor—that is, he uses them to assist or to counsel him when he feels there is need. The terms "assistant" and "counselor" mean precisely what the titles imply—to assist, and/or to counsel.

349. Administrative Training

QUESTION

Would it not be wise procedure to require administrative training and/or experience in the ordained man before he would be eligible for election to a pastoral post?

ANSWER

The election of the pastors (branch presidents) is governed by the law as found in Doctrine and Covenants 120:2:

"A branch may be presided over by a high priest, an elder, priest, teacher, or deacon, chosen and sustained by the vote of the branch."

This is in harmony with the principle of common consent. General Conference Resolution 834 states:

"Resolved, That this Conference affirm the right of the membership to nominate in filling all elective offices in church, stake, district, and branch organizations in the various conferences and business meetings, general and local; and be it further

"Resolved, That this action shall in no way be interpreted as denying the right of presiding officers to present to the appropriate conferences or business meetings concurrent nominations for the filling of such elective offices."

The approval of calls is also a prerogative of the electing body of members, and therefore the undoubted right of members to express approval and acceptance of those who are to be their ministers is conserved.

The solution to the problem which you raise no doubt lies in encouraging and stimulating those designated and chosen to ministerial office to qualify by study and training to be entrusted with the important presiding responsibility. In the pastoral function this is vital. When an elder is so qualified, the membership senses his ability to serve and generally shows considerable wisdom in electing the most suitable elder to the responsibility.

All priesthood members should take advantage of the various schools offering training. Where they do, congregations and administrators are quick to discern the qualified leader and place confidence in him.

350. Parliamentary Rules Adopted

QUESTION

Is there any set of parliamentary rules that have been adopted by the World Conference for the use of the church?

ANSWER

The last approval of parliamentary procedure was in 1922 with minor amendments in 1956 (see General Conference Resolutions, 1956 edition, No. 989).

At the 1876 Conference the first rules to govern the church and its deliberative assemblies were adopted. These were published as *Rules of Order and Debate*. This book had some revision and reprinting until the 1904 edition. It was composed of seventeen chapters. Chapters two to twelve dealt with administrative, court, and representation rules, while chapters one and thirteen to seventeen were rules for parliamentary procedure.

The rules of these last named chapters were revised and adopted by action of the Conference of 1916, appearing in book form in 1922 as *Rules of Order for Deliberative Assemblies*. This is the last action on parliamentary rules other than the minor considerations of 1956.

The other chapters of the 1904 book were not dealt with at the time, but in 1952 the present publication, *Rules and Resolutions,* was endorsed by the Conference; it provides for procedures other than parliamentary. This is added to as Conference action provides resolutions from time to time.

The 1922 work varies in some details from the standard of *Robert's Rules of Order* as, for instance, in majorities required for the passing of certain motions. A presiding officer therefore should be aware of the 1922 procedures as *Robert's Rules* were not adopted as such by the church. *Parliamentary Procedure* by F. L. Young is a text published by Herald House, and is aimed at simplification for easier understanding. It follows the 1922 adopted procedures and, as the preface states, was prepared in close collaboration with church officials. It is based on *Robert's Rules* with the exceptions I have here noted.

351. Ministerial Relationships

QUESTION

Please outline RLDS organization with reference to ministerial relationships, grades, and so forth?

ANSWER

The various duties of the specific priesthood officers in the church could not be covered here, so we must be content with a broad outline. Priesthood functions under two main classifications: Melchisedec and Aaronic. The Melchisedec priesthood includes those ordained to the office of high priest and all those holding the office of elder. This priesthood is also referred to as the "Order of the Son of God." Though the elder is included in this Melchisedec priesthood, Doctrine and Covenants 83:5 states that the elder is an appendage to the high priesthood. From the office of high priest certain specific callings arise, and men are further ordained or set apart, as the case may be, to administer these particular responsibilities. First, a high priest is chosen by revelation to be prophet, seer, and revelator to the church; and with him two others to share the burden of presidency. This is the First Presidency. Twelve others are chosen, similarly, as apostles, constituting the Traveling High Council. There is also the Standing High Council, twelve high priests at the seat of the presidency, constituted to deal with such matters as may be brought before it.

Other high priests are called to be bishops, who constitute an order. One of these is chosen as the Presiding Bishop; he with two others constitute the Presiding Bishopric. Another order of high priests is that of evangelists or patriarchal ministers.

The elders are standing ministers to the church. From the elders, seven quorums of seventies may be chosen. These have a special responsibility as missionaries and may represent the apostles when sent in special capacity. There are seven presidents of the seventy, one of whom is the senior president.

The second, or Aaronic priesthood, of which order the bishop is president, includes the offices of priest, teacher, and deacon. The duties of these ministers are defined in Doctrine and Covenants 17. These serve as standing ministers to the local branch.

The various areas of administration under the general direction of the First Presidency are cared for in apostolic missions, and in turn various subsidiary areas and districts are administered by high priests or elders.

The principle of common consent is expressed at various levels, the administrative ministry holding responsibility by vote of the membership concerned, either in conferences or in branch business meeting, as the respective relationships of officer and jurisdictions may require.

I suggest you read Doctrine and Covenants, Section 104, for a general statement of priesthood responsibility and gradation.

352. Book Steward and Church School

QUESTION

Who is responsible for the selection of the study books, etc., in the church school? What is the relation of the book steward in regard to their selection?

ANSWER

The church school director is primarily responsible for the choice of study materials in his department. He follows as closely as possible the curriculum suggested by the General Department of Religious Education, with due consideration of the interests and needs of his particular church school. He consults with the teachers concerned and often the pastor so that there is harmony. Neither a teacher nor a class would have a successful study if the decision were arbitrary or out of the field of interest of those most intimately concerned. Adult classes often appreciate a choice where this is practicable.

A book steward is appointed by the pastor in consultation with the official church publishing organization, Herald House. It is the duty of the book steward to promote the sale and use of church books among the membership and to handle such business as is placed through him. Normally in a well related corps of branch workers, the church school and other departments' ordering of books would be handled through the book steward. Where there is an efficient officer, those ordering would be glad to have his assistance. However, individuals may naturally order directly if they so desire, but the branch receives the advantage of a commission on all sales placed through the steward. The steward has no responsibility whatsoever to decide studies; he acts simply as an agent for Herald House.

353. Historians

QUESTION

How are stake, district, and branch historians appointed?

349

All historians are appointed by the General Church Historian. This procedure is based on General Conference Resolution No. 498:

"Whereas, The Church Historian recommended the appointment of district historians in districts to assist him, therefore be it

"Resolved, That he be empowered to appoint such persons and in such places as he may deem proper, according to his direction."

It is usual to request the presiding officer of the stake, district, or branch to suggest a name of a person qualified to so function. After consideration and consultation, the appointment is made by the Church Historian and is usually placed before the body for endorsement. This is, however, an appointment and not an elective office as is the secretary and other officers.

354. Woman Church School Director

QUESTION

I have heard discussion as to whether a woman may hold the office of church school director in a branch. Is it permissible for a woman to hold this office?

ANSWER

Yes, a woman may hold the office of church school director. A woman may hold any branch or departmental position not involving ordination to the priesthood. Obviously this is qualified by the availability of ordained men for positions of major responsibility. Where priesthood is not involved by right of ordination, the common consent of the body is the deciding factor.

355. Relationship of District Women's Leader

QUESTION

What is the relationship of the district women's leader to the local branch department?

ANSWER

The relationship is that of a connecting link between the General Department of Women and the branch women's department. The district leader should be aware of the goals and general objectives of the church to be achieved through the women's department and be in a position to interpret these for local departments with special relation to the local needs and their contribution to the general goals.

The district leader functions only in an advisory capacity, assisting by her counsel the growth and development of unified endeavor of the departments in her area. She should be helpful in lifting the sights of the women to a district and also general church level. She does not take executive action in a branch, but beyond giving help in ways just mentioned she should work with the pastor should she feel that executive action is required. All administrative acts in branch departments are the responsibility of the pastor, and he should so function in the light of this basic administrative principle.

It is assumed that the pastor has a balanced and sympathetic understanding of the value and importance of the women's department and has made himself aware of the principles set out by the *Handbook for the Department of Women* prepared by the General Council of Women. A study of this manual by all concerned will bring a clearer understanding of the relationships involved and further the total work of the church.

356. Popular Songs for Worship Services

QUESTION

Are popular songs such as "Somebody Up There Likes Me" and "He" appropriate for worship services?

ANSWER

These are not appropriate in my opinion. Of course you have used extreme examples. I am conscious of the fact that there are differences of opinion as to where to draw a line, but the examples you have given are, in my opinion, irreverent rather than worshipful and are sure to bring association of the type of voice and singer which obviously does not enhance the feelings of devotion. I am sure this is so, at least in Western culture, but my comments do not apply to other cultural backgrounds. It is difficult enough to lift the standard of musical appreciation when we have such a travesty of so-called music injected into our homes on the common vehicles of entertainment, but to bring it to the sanctuary is almost unforgivable.

I cannot see the "Beatles" performing in church, even though some may admire their unorthodoxy in the secular field. I would say leave such items to other situations.

351

357. Visiting in Church Building

QUESTION

Is it considered wrong to visit in the church building provided the conduct is not boisterous and the visiting is a matter of friendly concern for each other?

ANSWER

Most questions of this type require a qualified answer rather than a simple "yes" or "no." My reaction to the problem you raise is that it depends on the facilities available for social contact. Some churches (most of recent construction) are planned to provide for the opportunity of fellowship following worship. Where this is done a quiet exit is a logical procedure, and visiting may take place in the narthex. Unless this facility is available, it would militate against the fellowship, for instance, to have the congregation ushered out into the inclemency of weather, either hot or cold.

I have observed that a moderate fellowship after (not before) services at Stone Church is the custom. Quiet greetings are exchanged as the worshipers move to the exits. I have been in churches where exit ushering is made very formal, and—where the facilities for visiting have been lacking—this has militated against development of the congregational family atmosphere in my opinion. We are a fellowship of believers; this implies fairly close association more than espousing a common belief.

My reaction should not be taken as a suggestion for free and uncontrolled chatter in the sanctuary. If a place is especially intended for worship, that purpose should be treated with respect. Fellowship of a proper nature comes before mere formality. We should not resent the efforts of the congregational leadership to bring dignity and order to the worship of the church. Our buildings should facilitate proper emphasis on fellowship and dignity at the right time and in the right place.

358. Pictures of Christ in Worship Centers

QUESTION

Should pictures of Christ be used as centers of worship?

ANSWER

There is no authentic portrait of Jesus in existence, nor do we have

352

any evidence that there ever was one. This presents the first difficulty in endeavoring to bring a literal image of Christ before a congregation at worship.

Theoretically an adult worshiper should see the picture as a thought-centering aid, but repetition and constant familiarity tends to foreshorten the spiritual sight, and the object becomes the substitute for that which it represents.

To me there is little difference between a picture and an image or model. Both are mediums used to portray a personality. For this reason I see little difference between images in a Catholic church and a picture hung in one of our own. I have not the same objection to a picture in our church that I have to an image in another probably because in the latter case the passage of time has shortened the spiritual perspective until in practice the image has become a substitute. In our churches the picture certainly has not had this effect. However, when Rome first fused pagan objects with Christian thought no one saw the real end to these innovations.

Therefore, upon mature consideration of the question, I must now lean to the more conservative reaction. This is somewhat of a modification of my former views.

The same difficulty, of course, is found in the use of all physical symbols such as the cross, candles, and so forth, but the difficulty is at a more sensitive point where a picture of our Lord is a literal and direct portrayal. Historically the decline and apostasy of the Christian church parallels the introduction of mechanical aids such as extravagant vestments, altars, pictures, and images.

The Hebrews were very clearly instructed as to this danger because of the ease with which heathen cults tended to be absorbed into their culture. The Old Testament is most specific in this. (See Exodus 20:4, 5; Deuteronomy 4:15, 16, 19; 27:15; II Kings 23:24; Isaiah 17:18; Jeremiah 8:19; Ezekiel 6:4-6; 7:20.) The New Testament contains similar counsel. (See Acts 17:29; Romans 1:20-25.)

What I have said applies to your specific question and not to moderate and artistic use of theme centers wherein the central thought of the service is further focused or to the dramatizing of a truth. Nevertheless, one does not anticipate our services becoming a series of dramatic presentations either by tableau or picture. This, however, is another question which would need individual treatment. For a helpful discussion of worship centers I suggest you read an article by Pauline Arnson in the *Priesthood and Leaders Journal* (December, 1961), Vol. 1, page 392.

359. IHS

QUESTION

What is the meaning of the letters "IHS" in the monogram which is used in religious symbolism? Are they legitimate Christian signs or of significance to us?

ANSWER

The three letters "IHS" have been used in connection with the Christian faith and tradition. They have appeared on altar furniture and vessels, etc. Sometimes the letter "J" is used instead of "I." Sometimes "C" has replaced the "S."

There has been some confusion as to their origin, although it appears fairly certain that they are an abbreviation of the Greek word "Iseous" for Jesus. Jesus is a Latin word. Both the Greek and Roman forms spring from the Hebrew name Yeshua meaning "Jahweh is Salvation." The Aramaic is similarly "Yeshu." The Greek symbols cannot be printed here but it is clear that "IHS" is the abbreviation referred to.

It has been suggested they are the initial letters in the three Latin words "Jesus Huminum Salvator" which means "Jesus, Savior of Men." This is not considered the real explanation of the origin of the words. Others have attributed English words also in error.

The monogram which they form is of as much symbolic worth as its origin implies and which the respectful use of the divine name requires. This should never be used carelessly or casually, which of course applies to any Christian symbol; used thus it would not be in good form. I do not know of any general practice of using this in connection with our worship or literature. I see no reason to use it in any particular way.

360. Foot-washing in Reorganized Church

QUESTION

Is the washing of feet practiced in the Reorganized Church? What is the historical connection of the restored church with this practice? Is it likely to be instituted?

What is the church's answer to the direct commandment given the apostles by Jesus? (John 13:14).

ANSWER

This ordinance is mentioned in Doctrine and Covenants 85:44-46.

This reference relates to the establishment of the School of the Prophets in the house of the Lord in Kirtland, Ohio, in 1836.

This was performed at the dedication of the Temple in March, 1836. It is recorded that on Tuesday, March 29, at a meeting of some of the leaders, this ordinance was attended to and that on the next day about three hundred officials of the church engaged in this procedure. Reference to this event can be found in *Church History*, Volume 2, page 46.

I am not aware of this practice being continued in the Reorganized Church. It does not appear to be an ordinance involved in the salvation of souls. The concept has its roots in antiquity and is an Oriental custom, somewhat associated with arid conditions of Palestine. Foot-washing was an action of hospitality and also became somewhat of a ritualistic procedure. When performed it symbolized humility, especially when performed by one of "superior" status for one of lower social or religious standing. The towel and the basin were symbols of this relationship.

I cannot say with any confidence that this will ever be reinstituted in the church. There is certainly no present commandment in this direction.

As to the last question, I doubt if it is a correct interpretation to say that John 13:14 is a direct commandment in the sense that Jesus was instituting an ordinance of universal application as in commanding baptism. What happened according to the narrative was that Jesus followed the ritualistic custom in setting an example of humility. Rather than placing the emphasis on the foot washing, he was demonstrating a relationship which involved serving one another, using the Hebrew cultural setting to teach his lesson.

361. Removal of Name from Church Records

QUESTION

Is it possible to have one's name removed from the church records? If so, what are the conditions and procedures?

ANSWER

Yes. A person may lose membership in the church through commission of a sin which leads to action being taken by the church through church courts. The details of this are too numerous to include here, but it is termed "court action." A person may also request withdrawal from the church for other reasons which do not involve an attempt to avoid court action.

A person desiring to withdraw should make application to local administrative officers, who are under obligation to labor with the person in an endeavor to help the person resolve difficulties that have motivated the request. Should these be unresolved and the person persist in his desire to withdraw, the administrative officers should present the request to the First Presidency with a full report and/or recommendation. The Presidency may then take action as seems proper in the case. Permission to withdraw is not granted when court action for some cause is indicated.

If the person is granted withdrawal he may apply for reinstatement and, on going through administrative procedures again involving consideration by the First Presidency, be granted readmission without rebaptism. This readmission without rebaptism is possible only where the life of the person has continued to be Christian. A person joining another church in the intervening period obviously must sever connection from that church before asking that he be reinstated.

362. Lent in Our Church

QUESTION

I was shocked to notice a program in our church with the cover featuring Lent. It was my understanding that this was a Catholic custom. Why should we observe it in our church?

ANSWER

The word "Lent" originally meant "spring," and as the preparation of the early Christian church for the remembrance of the sacrifice of the Savior was at this period of the year in the Northern Hemisphere the term became identified more with the religious event than with the season.

The custom of using a period prior to Easter as one of preparation through contemplation of the divine sacrifice began very early in the Christian church. There is definite evidence of this custom as early as the first period of the second century.

It was natural that the Jewish custom of preparation for the Passover should carry over to the celebration of the death and resurrection of Jesus in view of the fact that these events occurred about the time of the Passover. Paul implies this in I Corinthians 5:7, 8. He counsels the celebration of the feast with Christian significance. Paul speaks of our "Pascha which hath been sacrificed."

A dispute concerning the time of this celebration arose in the second century between Polycrates, Bishop of Ephesus, and Irenaeus, Bishop of Lyon, and it is in their correspondence that we get the first intimation of a period of preparation being observed in the Asian churches, dating back to A.D. 155. According to Eusebius, an early Christian historian, the Western Lenten custom is traced back by Irenaeus to A.D. 120. Thus it appears that the saints from the early days of the church recognized the appropriateness of some definite time being spent in contemplation of this greatest of all events in history. The form of the observance and the length of time devoted to it have varied through the years and in different communions.

The Lenten period of forty days is mentioned in the fifth canon of the Council of Nicaea, A.D. 325, and seems by then to have been a well-recognized custom. The Roman Catholic and some Protestant churches have adopted procedures and observances which have little significance to us. Our church prescribes no rule which enjoins upon its members the observance of Lent. That our people should spend time in fasting through meditation and the exclusion of those things which tend to detract from devotion is obviously a wise procedure in connection with any religious focus in our church life. Our emphasis is upon continual preparation for fellowship rather than upon periodic disciplines.

363. Relationship of Church to Sanitarium

QUESTION

Can you tell me the relationship of the church to the Independence Sanitarium and what relation the city has to this institution?

ANSWER

The Independence Sanitarium and Hospital was established on instructions given to the church April 14, 1906. It opened its doors in October, 1909, and has been in continuous operation since.

The hospital is owned and operated by the Reorganized Church of Jesus Christ of Latter Day Saints. The management is entrusted to a Board of Trustees consisting of nine members. These nine members are designated in the articles of incorporation to be the members of the First Presidency of the church, the members of the Presiding Bishopric, the chairman of the Medical Council of the church, the elected judge of Eastern Jackson County, and the mayor of the city of Independence. The board is the policy-setting body of the hospital.

In association with the hospital are efficient training schools designed to contribute qualified personnel to the related fields of service. The School of Nursing was established in 1910, the School for Medical

Technologists in 1951, the Training School for Technicians in 1944, and the Training School for Medical Technicians in 1961. All are accredited.

The hospital is essentially a church-sponsored institution serving on a wide community basis. It is nonsectarian and nonsegregated. The hospital serves more than three times as many patients not of the sponsoring church as it does Latter Day Saints. There have been a number of fund-raising campaigns for improvement and expansion over the years, and in all these the community has donated generously both in time and money and shares in the pride members have in this institution.

364. Publishing Liberal Theology Articles

QUESTION

Is it right to publish articles on liberal theology in our church magazines?

ANSWER

If the church or its publications were to limit the right of individual members to express points of view at variance with more traditional concepts, it would be taking a step in the direction of the dogmatic ecclesiastical pronouncements of past centuries. As a result of that tendency to give dogmatic rulings, belief became a matter of obedience rather than faith. Thus agency was minimized and an atmosphere developed which often stifled the discovery and statement of truth.

In most magazines considerable latitude is given to responsible editors in exercising discretion as to the propriety of publishing varying points of view. The question to be decided is whether the publication of an article is in harmony with the goals of the institution or movement the magazine represents. This of course involves the long view and not only immediate reaction of readers.

There is always the responsibility of the church to see that the members are as broadly informed as practicable so that intelligent faith may be held with full knowledge of other points of view.

My observation has been that our editors have endeavored to allow a wide expression of serious thought while properly publishing material only of positive and constructive nature.

Before I leave this question, I think it is important that something more be said. Labeling people or their concepts by names which tend to be narrowly definitive is unsound. In these days of intensity of political and religious conviction, this practice can be harmful. Emotionally charged words such as "liberal" and "fundamental" are used with a disregard for their real meaning and are made to do service in the heat of debate to the consequent clouding of real issues. I suggest that often these words are used in an unchristian way and can bring about prejudices equally disastrous with those classifications of race, color, and religion which have left us a legacy of intolerance and bigotry, the evidence of which is seen in most parts of the world today.

Having said this I do not think any article which tended to depreciate the divinity of Jesus Christ would find place in any Christian periodical. If someone holds a different point of view on some aspect of that divinity, I do not feel it improper for him to express it. Only by so sharing do we find more truth.

The Temporal Law

365. Latter Day Saints and Stewardship

QUESTION

Are Latter Day Saints right in stressing the laws of stewardship as the means of establishing the kingdom of God when Jesus said, "My kingdom is not of this world"?

ANSWER

A correct understanding of this depends on one's definition of stewardship. If stewardship is defined as merely the rules which govern the procedures for handling temporal things the understanding is inadequate.

Actually stewardship is a principle rather than a procedure, and the basis of this is a spiritual one. Christ approached the political and economic problems of his day upon a spiritual basis. This is primary. When we say primary we do not mean that secondary and tertiary matters are unimportant and therefore to be neglected.

Christ said that his mission was to the souls of men. He preached the rebirth as the basis of his kingdom. Reborn men have accepted their stewardship under God and therefore of their own volition are obedient to the laws which enable an effective execution of the principle.

One who says he accepts Christ and then fails to attempt to understand and keep his law is not really converted.

The statement made by Jesus that his kingdom was not of this world should be seen in the setting in which it was made. Jesus was replying to Pilate who cross-examined him to find out if he had revolutionary intentions, and the Master was emphasizing that the ways of the world were not the methods by which he planned to achieve his kingdom. It was rather to be by spiritual motivation. He said, "Except a man be born again he cannot see the kingdom of God."

To emphasize material rearrangements alone will not bring the kingdom on earth, but on the other hand one cannot achieve this for which Jesus told his disciples to pray without committing oneself to obey the laws of stewardship. Christ's kingdom involves a material universe with men motivated by spiritual power consequent to conversion.

366. Solicitor and Inventory

QUESTION

Should a bishop's solicitor come to the home and proceed to have the inventory filed as a matter of regular annual procedure?

ANSWER

This is not the province of the solicitor. The filing of an inventory, though a definite responsibility of each member, is a matter of voluntary personal response. The value to the Saint is in the fact of freely given obedience.

Members of the Bishopric and their representatives teach the law and may come to your home to do so. If you invite or request their help in filing an inventory they will gladly help.

These officers do not attempt to take charge of your personal affairs. The inventory is yours to offer as a demonstration of your stewardship. Many congregations make a feature of inventory day, arranging a service where you may lay your accounting before the bishop or his representative. It is conveyed promptly to the Bishopric, the details of which are not the concern of the solicitor. He is, as his title implies, an agent to receive tithes and help in any way he can to enable you to fulfill the financial law.

367. Diverting Funds

QUESTION

If an offering is taken for a specific purpose should those administering the finances of the branch use it for other purposes if the quota set is exceeded? For instance, could amounts exceeding an Auditorium offering be used for local purposes?

When a person gives an offering for a specific purpose that is his considered desire and it should be so used. Moneys given for General Church purposes are the stewardship of the Presiding Bishopric. No one should deflect those to local purposes. Those handling moneys of this kind at the local level are merely channels of conveyance and have no discretion as to what is done with them.

368. Auditorium Built with Tithing

QUESTION

Was tithing used in building the Auditorium? If so, how much?

ANSWER

This has not been calculated as a special item, various appropriations having been made in the 1950's. Prior to that the work was mainly carried forward by offerings so designated. All expenditures from general funds which would include tithing were made by General Conference appropriation. A perusal of the relevant Conference reports would give the details.

369. Branch Obligations or Tithing

QUESTION

If an individual found it impossible, to his way of thinking, to keep up his branch obligations and at the same time to pay his tithing, which should be given preference?

ANSWER

This question is answered in the *Handbook on Financial Law* published under the direction of the Presiding Bishopric, page 38, question 62, which I reproduce in full.

"The law on the matter is quite clear, so it is our suggestion that such a person proceed on the following basis:

a. File his tithing statement to determine the amount of tithing due, setting this up as an obligation to the General Church.

b. Try, insofar as possible, to keep current tithing paid and make such payments on accumulated tithing as may be possible.

c. Make such contributions in the way of offerings as may be within the range and ability of the individual to maintain and carry on the branch work. There should be no arbitrary decisions regarding the procedure in this connection.

d. It should also be noted that the fact that he has an increase is evidence that there is left nine tenths of the increase out of which he can make offerings to the local church."

Reference to paragraphs a and b in particular will emphasize where one's primary obligations lie, but paragraph c brings to attention the necessity of the exercise of individual stewardship. The individual alone is aware of all the circumstances involving local needs, and so forth. Therefore, the handbook counsels that an arbitrary decision would be unwise.

370. Publicize Financial Figures

QUESTION

Is it proper to print the tithing and other General Church financial figures for the branch in the report for the year?

ANSWER

It is customary to do this in many stakes and branches, and is often found helpful in making contributors and those not responding to the church law aware of their obligations and their degree or lack of compliance.

An informed membership is likely to bring intelligent participation. I see no reason why a branch should not have the statistics of its giving. Of course no private personal information should be included in the published report; this is confidential, and no responsible officer or employee of the church would consider giving this information to unauthorized persons.

371. Money out of the Branch

QUESTION

We pay tithes, contribute to missionaries, and to the district budget in addition to trying to develop our local building. How can we do this local work when so much goes out of the branch?

ANSWER

Admittedly the task of adequately financing the total program of the church requires generous and even sacrificial giving on the part of

363

the Saints. The temporal law provides for the payment of tithing as one tenth of increase for the carrying on of the general work of the church. This is a primary obligation of the church member, but it is only the beginning of financial stewardship which includes also surplus, freewill offerings, and consecrations which are contributed from the remaining nine tenths of increase (Doctrine and Covenants 129:8). The tithing can be readily computed by making the stewardship accounting.

Beyond this the individual is under stewardship obligation to contribute offerings for branch operating and building needs, to support a district program, to help in meeting the elder's expenses, to assist the poor through the oblation offering, and to help as he is able in special offerings for Auditorium construction, institutions, and so forth. These voluntary offerings should be made according to the interests of the contributor and his desire to share temporal blessings in promoting the work of God.

The temporal law provides a freedom of choice for the individual in his giving which is not possible in churches which teach tithing as one tenth of income. Studies of the giving of our membership show that our per capita giving appears to be low in comparison with the general level of church giving in the United States and Canada, and after the tithing is paid there should be resources available for rather generous giving as offerings. This is evidenced by the fact that many branches and districts which contribute most generously in tithing are also financing extensive missionary and building programs.

It should be noted that recent cost studies of the World Church budget show that the tithing received from a number of domestic districts and nearly all missions abroad is insufficient to meet even the direct costs of ministry provided by the World Church in these areas. When a proportionate share of general costs are added (office expenses, family allowances of departmental and General Church officers, Graceland College budgetary assistance, subsidy to operating expenses of missions abroad), a substantial number of districts in the domestic field fall short of meeting these costs with their tithing contributions and must be subsidized by tithing received from stronger districts and stakes.

Leaders in districts and branches have a responsibility of determining local needs and setting reasonable goals of achievement in the light of the total church program. Each member should participate in proportion to the temporal blessings God has bestowed upon him, by paying his tithing, contributing offerings, giving surplus, or making consecration if he is in a position to do so. The temporal law is designed to bless members spiritually and to make them effective participants in the work of the kingdom. It is important, therefore, that members give in good spirit as they are able to do so and with thankfulness to God for the opportunities of service afforded through compliance with the financial law.

372. Tithing for Local Missionary Work

QUESTION

Our branch is asked to pay $35.00 a week expenses for the mission-ary when he is doing even a limited amount of work in our area. Should not the tithing be used for this? If not, then what is it for?

ANSWER

Tithing should not normally be used for this expense in organized areas. The tithe is for the general work of the church, and from this tithe allowances for appointee family needs are met.

The missionary's personal and official needs, traveling and medical costs are not included in family allowances, and it is proper for the Saints where he labors to meet those needs. He uses a car (supplied by the Bishop from tithing) which requires gas, tires, and mechanical maintenance, and he also needs funds for meals, tracts, visual aids, postage, telephone. When the local people share in supplying these needs, they free many dollars of tithing to take the gospel to places where there is little likelihood of church income.

Bishop Walter Johnson, when announcing the offering at a Stone Church service, said, "We now have an opportunity of making an offer-ing from the *increase* with which the Lord has blessed us." If one considers the question with this realization of his blessings, in the spirit of stewardship, he is drawn to enlarge rather than restrict his giving. I know that the form in which the invitation was made caused me to react to the love of God extended to me in so many ways, and which the Psalmist described as a cup running over. This "running over" portion is so often used for less important purposes.

373. Difference between RLDS and Communism

QUESTION

What is the difference between the social principles of the RLDS church and Soviet Communism? Is it simply a matter of freedom?

ANSWER

The difference between our movement's ideals and Soviet Commu-nism is in our concept of stewardship. Our belief is in the stewardship of the individual, and Soviet Communism holds that the state is the steward. In Communism the individual exists for the state; Christian stewardship holds that the state and all organized society is for the benefit of mankind, individually and collectively, and recognizes responsibility to God.

Freedom is a relative term. True freedom does not mean license, and even under the Christian order of society individuals have to conform in behavior at certain points for the common good, and because others have rights, too.

The evil of being enslaved is not that one must obey laws but that agency is removed, and where there is no agency, personal quality of soul has no room for growth. The children of Israel in Egypt exemplified this.

The constructive value of personal Christian stewardship is inestimable. The purpose of Zion is to create an environment in which souls can be developed to a condition where they will be fit for the presence of God. Zion is a society under the "law of liberty"; our obedience is voluntary so that we are free to grow in grace and the beauty of holiness.

374. How to Draw Up Branch Budget

QUESTION

How should a branch budget be drawn up, and who should share in this?

ANSWER

The officer responsible for the preparation of the branch program is primarily the pastor. His first consideration is the task to be done, which he formulates after detailed study of the goals of the church in general and of the specific area and branch with which he is immediately concerned. To do this he must be in sympathetic contact with general officers and other administrators and also with the departments and sections of his own branch.

The pastor then seeks to relate the program to the budgetary considerations necessary to achieve it. He will thus seek the knowledge, advice, and experience of his department leaders and others responsible for activities in his branch. This may be done as wisdom directs, and usually a grouping of certain leaders will allow him to grasp the necessary detail to formulate a budget based on the total program. Any conclusions of such a committee are not binding on the pastor but will most likely be fairly representative of the congregational mind. The pastor is the one responsible for the budget as presented to the branch business meeting and therefore should not delegate his administrative responsibility to a committee.

375. Advance Notice of Budget Consideration

QUESTION

Should advance notice be given of a branch business meeting at which the budget is to be considered?

ANSWER

For action of a deliberative assembly to be legal, and therefore its decision binding, due notice of the meeting should be given together with at least the general nature of the business to be dealt with. It should be assumed that all active church members would be aware of the nature of business to be transacted at regular business meetings. They should be properly announced, and reasonable opportunity to be present should be given. A special meeting to consider budget approval undoubtedly should be announced in advance.

The members of the branch in business session are responsible for approving, with or without amendment, the budget thus presented.

Help is given in the *Pastor's Handbook* concerning matters which should normally receive consideration in the preparation of the budget. The treasurer is responsible for the custody and disbursement of all moneys, naturally in association with the pastor. Provision normally is made by the branch for the safe handling of finances.

376. Minister's Salary

QUESTION

I am often asked by nonmember friends whether our ministers receive a salary. Would you clarify this?

ANSWER

Those ministers who are not serving under Conference appointment earn their living in the usual secular occupations and perform their ministerial functions during many hours generously offered to the Saints and to those not of our faith. Some of these serve as pastors of their branches or congregations (a heavy responsibility apart from earning a living) while others serve as district presidents, bishops, and patriarchs. Other high priests, elders, priests, teachers, and deacons serve in similar devotion to the needs of people.

The relatively few men under appointment give their full time to the work of the church in the capacity to which they are appointed. These men and their families are largely sustained by the finances of the church. This financial allowance is based upon the stewardship principle. Each year on January 1 each family presents an estimated

367

budget of needs for the ensuing twelve months. These submissions are reviewed under the supervision of the Presiding Bishopric and a determination of the allowance necessary and practicable is made.

Wherever the appointment of such ministers is to an area where the Saints can do so, it is expected that their personal needs such as board, clothing, and traveling expenses will be met by those among whom they labor. Where this is possible no provision is made from the general funds in the hands of the Bishopric. All appointees, in addition to filing inventory statements annually, make a monthly report on all moneys received for personal elder's expenses from whatever source and account for the expenditure of these funds.

377. Money for Funerals, Weddings

QUESTION

Should RLDS ministers receive money for funerals, weddings, or any other function, especially involving others besides members? What should be done with the money if received? Does it make any difference whether members or nonmembers are concerned?

ANSWER

No minister of the church receives money for the performance of rites in the sense of payment for particular services rendered. However, there are expenses frequently involved in the serving of persons, both members and nonmembers. Those ministered to are usually sensitive to this and offerings are made to compensate. It is a matter of judgment between the minister serving and those involved. The minister should be careful that he does not place himself under obligation by the personal receipt of gratuities.

Where an appointee is involved the matter is quite simple. Every minister under appointment by the General Church is under obligation to report to the Presiding Bishopric monthly all moneys received as a result of his service in his field. Should he therefore receive more than a specific duty incurs, the balance naturally goes toward the more general needs of his ministry. Local ministers, though not required to report in this way to the Bishopric, have the moral responsibility to avoid even the appearance of mercenary attitudes toward ministry. On the relatively few occasions when offerings are made over and above out-of-pocket expenses, the local minister should accept the responsibility of seeing that the surplus is channeled to church funds.

Self-sustaining ministers sometimes have to leave work with consequent loss of pay to offer ministry, and most people are sensitive to this loss and other out-of-pocket expenditure.

Kingdom of God—Zion

378. Gathering

QUESTION

Is the gathering a definite principle of the church? If so, when and where and who are involved? What is its time in relation to the millennium?

ANSWER

The gathering is a general principle of our church and is taking place and shape now. Independence has been designated as the "center place," and the people involved are those willing to become stewards by obedience to divine law in all aspects of life. No man knows when the millennium will come. There are a number of things that prophetic scriptures indicate must precede such a condition, but first and foremost is the quality of our personal stewardship. It is not good to lay undue emphasis upon the time factor (millennium means a thousand years) but rather to give priority to the work of the perfecting of God's people. The parable of the wise and foolish virgins is apropos (Matthew 25:1-3).

379. Raise Up a People to Build

QUESTION

What foundation is there for the statement that if we do not build Zion God will raise up a people who will?

369

In a letter to W. W. Phelps written from Kirtland, January 11, 1833, Joseph Smith, Jr., said:

". . . for the Lord will have a place from whence his word will go forth in these last days, in purity; for if Zion will not purify herself so as to be approved of in all things in his sight, he will seek another people: for his work will go on until Israel is gathered, and they who will not hear his voice, must expect to feel his wrath."—*Church History,* Vol. I, pages 267, 268.

Presiding Evangelist Elbert A. Smith in a message given at a Communion service in Lamoni, Iowa, November 4, 1917, is recorded as saying under inspiration:

"Again, at this time, you are admonished that you be not unduly concerned because you are few in number as compared with the world. That is not your concern, but be concerned only that your righteousness shall be very great. For a few righteous men can accomplish very much, and a little leaveneth a great lump.

"I have many forces at work in the world, saith the Lord. I have many spiritual forces at work that you know not of. You see but the smaller part of my work, and the world perceives it not at all.

"Therefore be not concerned because you are few in number, but let each one look to himself, and to the condition of his own heart and life."—*Saints' Herald,* Volume 64, page 1081.

Presiding Bishop Albert Carmichael preached a sermon in the Stone Church, June 6, 1928, in which he said:

"If we think that the men whom God has chosen to do this task will not do it, then there remains for us another task, and that is to find another group of men who will do it, for somehow the *work must be done.* This people must have a chance to comply with the will of God, that Zion might be. . . .

"Zion, the final, ultimate, complete work, the finished product of the eternal God, can never be redeemed except by a group of men and women who will work as God works, humbly, spiritually, intelligently, earnestly, with their whole souls wrapped up in the service of humanity, the redemption of the world. And God is calling, and he will continue to call until out from the creations

370

of the infinite a human race will come, a race consecrated to the great task of saving their fellow men by losing themselves; for it has been written across the wide expanse of eternity, 'Zion *must be*.' "—*Saints' Herald*, Volume 75, pages 673, 675.

F. A. Smith, while serving as presiding evangelist, said in a sermon at Independence, Missouri, January 26, 1919:

"I remember President Smith making a statement once in talking to the people of this place. Some of these older ones will remember this undoubtedly; he made the declaration that if they came in here and lived honest, pure, clean lives, consecrated to the service of God, they would be blessed; they would be content; they would be happy, and they would remain; but if they came in here, became discontented and dissatisfied, and did not live the clean, pure life that God asked them to live, they would have to leave. They would not be permitted to stay, and they would go away tinctured with the spirit of evil.

"You think for a few moments about it, and you will see where we stand. He did not make any mistake. We have seen them come. We have seen them go. We have discovered that his statement was true. Individuals have manifested and demonstrated the truthfulness of the declaration beyond the shadow of a doubt, and it will be done again and again, until God has accomplished his work, and raised up a people who will serve him in the spirit of truth and willingness and obedience, as he has asked them to do."—*Saints' Herald*, Vol. 66, page 486.

These sentiments have their foundation in scripture and sound reasoning. God's work cannot be frustrated (Doctrine and Covenants 2:1); therefore, if one group of people does not fulfill the task, another must. This does not mean another church. No generation has yet accomplished it, but as a succeeding generation we have the responsibility to try. It will be done by this people and should be furthered considerably if not completed by this generation. I know of no other movement with the true concept of Zion.

Index